Jude

THE CROSSWAY CLASSIC COMMENTARIES

Jude

by

Thomas Manton

Series Editors

Alister McGrath and J. I. Packer

CROSSWAY BOOKS

A DIVISION OF GOOD NEWS PUBLISHERS

WHEATON, ILLINOIS • NOTTINGHAM, ENGLAND

Jude

Copyright © 1999 by Watermark

Published by Crossway Books
    A division of Good News Publishers
    1300 Crescent Street
    Wheaton, Illinois 60187

First printing, 1999

Printed in the United States of America

Library of Congress Cataloging-in-Publication Data
Manton, Thomas, 1620–1677.
    Jude / by Thomas Manton.
        p.   cm. — (The Crossway classic commentaries)
    ISBN 1-58134-120-2 (alk. paper)
    1. Bible. N.T. Jude—Commentaries Early works to 1800.
I. Title.   II. Series.
BS2815.3.M36 1999
227'.97077—dc21   99-29575
                                                          CIP

15	14	13	12	11	10	09	08	07	06	05	04	03	02	01	00	99
15	14	13	12	11	10	9	8	7	6	5	4	3	2	1		

First British edition 1999

Production and Printing in the United States of America for
CROSSWAY BOOKS
Norton Street, Nottingham, England HG7 3HR

ISBN 1-85684-194-4

Contents

Series Preface

The purpose of the Crossway Classic Commentaries is to make some of the most valuable commentaries on the books of the Bible, by some of the greatest Bible teachers and theologians in the last 500 years, available to a new generation. These books will help today's readers learn truth, wisdom, and devotion from such authors as J. C. Ryle, Martin Luther, John Calvin, J. B. Lightfoot, John Owen, Charles Spurgeon, Charles Hodge, and Matthew Henry.

We do not apologize for the age of some of the items chosen. In the realm of practical exposition promoting godliness, the old is often better than the new. Spiritual vision and authority, based on an accurate handling of the biblical text, are the qualities that have been primarily sought in deciding what to include.

So far as is possible, everything is tailored to the needs and enrichment of thoughtful readers—lay Christians, students, and those in the ministry. The originals, some of which were written at a high technical level, have been abridged as needed, simplified stylistically, and unburdened of foreign words. However, the intention of this series is never to change any thoughts of the original authors, but to faithfully convey them in an understandable fashion.

The publishers are grateful to Dr. Alister McGrath of Wycliffe Hall, Oxford, Dr. J. I. Packer of Regent College, Vancouver, and Watermark of Norfolk, England, for the work of selecting and editing that now brings this project to fruition.

THE PUBLISHERS
Crossway Books
Wheaton, Illinois

Introduction

When Christians are asked to name their favorite book of the Bible, or even their favorite group of books, the letter of Jude rarely, if ever, receives a mention. This is understandable. Being brief and embattled and mostly concerned with spiritual perversity and the horrific realities of final judgment, and containing problem statements about Michael the archangel and Enoch the seventh from Adam, it does not appeal in the way that some biblical books do. Yet Jude, like James, was Mary's son and Jesus' half-brother (I do not say "brother," as the New Testament does, lest I be thought to have forgotten the virginal conception of our Lord). His letter, though brief, is weighty and has in it some magnificent utterances on standing firm for Jesus Christ in the face of apostasy and immorality within the churches; and Peter thought it so good that he echoed much of it in his own second epistle. It is not a letter to overlook.

But does a twenty-five-verse letter merit an entire volume in this Crossway Classic Commentaries series? That question is best answered by describing the commentary itself. It is a homiletical exposition—a series, that is, of written-up sermons—by Thomas Manton, the Commonwealth Puritan whom C. H. Spurgeon and J. C. Ryle hailed as the supreme Puritan expositor. Of his printed sermons Spurgeon declared, "For solid, sensible instruction, forcefully delivered, they cannot be surpassed." And Ryle wrote: "I find it easier to read fifty pages of Manton's than ten of some of his brethren's; and after reading, I feel that I carry more away." The Jude sermons run to over half the length of what Manton published on James, an epistle that is about four times as long as Jude; but this is an index both of Manton's thoroughness in drawing out the doctrinal and ethical implications of Jude's statements, and of his sense that it all had unusual contemporary relevance.

Writing in the 1650s, in the original edition, Manton described those against whom Jude wrote to give warning as a "fanatical and libertine party" and went on to speak of them as "a creeping party . . . a kind of mean and loose sort of people, that vented monstrous and gross conceits, chiefly out of envy, against those that excelled in gifts and place; and if our modern Ranters, Familists, Quakers, be not here described in their lively colors (as if the apostle had lived to hear their blasphemous expressions and that contempt which they cast upon the officers of the church), I confess that I understand nothing of the whole epistle." It is not impossible that some who read this commentary may feel that the closing of the twentieth century is being marked by similar outbreaks in certain quarters. At all events, Manton felt that Jude was a very direct word for his times and so spread himself (very fruitfully, be it said) in his exposition. But he is not repetitious, nor does he waste words. Readers will, I think, feel that the length justifies itself.

"Anyone who means business with God will find that Manton grabs, searches, humbles, and builds up in a quite breath-taking way." So I wrote in my introduction to Manton on James, and I repeat my words as I introduce Manton on Jude. Why? Because they apply as much to the one work as to the other, as readers will quickly find out.

J. I. PACKER

Dedication

To the religious and honorable lady, Letitia Popham, wife of Colonel Alexander Popham.

Madam, It is lovely when goodness and greatness meet each other. People of wealth in the world have more temptations and hindrances than others, but greater obligations toward God. The great landlord of the world expects a rent from every country cottage, but a large revenue from great houses. It would not please you if I shouted from the housetops what God has done for you or enabled you to do for him. But you must go on being faithful. There are few people I know who have more reason to honor God than you have.

That I have inscribed this commentary with your name will not seem strange to those who know my great indebtedness to you and your husband, and your interest in Stoke Newington and the people among whom I have had so many enjoyable days, and, I hope, the glorifying of God. I would never have moved from there but for those weighty considerations that took me away.

If any should be so foolish to object that it is unsuitable to dedicate this book to a woman, as it seems that Jerome did, I will not plead that two books in the Bible, Ruth and Esther, are named after women, but will simply state that this commentary is of interest to all Christians, both men and women. Persevere with your instructing others about the knowledge of the true God and in due time you will reap a reward if you do not give up. The good Lord comfort you with the graces of his Spirit more abundantly in your heart, which is the unquestionable wish of him who is, madam, your most respectful servant.

THOMAS MANTON, 1657

Commentary

Verse 1

Commentary on Verse 1

Jude, a servant of Jesus Christ and a brother of James, To those who have been called, who are loved by God the Father and kept by Jesus Christ.

This letter, like others, begins with the usual Christian greetings. They are found in the first two verses, where you find:

The person sending the greeting, the author of the letter—**Jude.**

The people who are greeted, the believers of that time—**those who have been called.**

The form of greeting, verse 2—**Mercy, peace and love be yours in abundance.**

This first verse tells us about who sent the greeting and to whom the greeting was sent. The person sending the greeting is called **Jude**; his office is **a servant of Jesus Christ**; and his relative is James—**a brother of James.** Those who are greeted are described by their condition—**called**—and by the results of this calling; first, they **are loved by God the Father;** second, they are **kept by Jesus Christ.**

The person sending the greeting, **Jude,** is "Judas" in Greek.

His office is **a servant of Jesus Christ.** This is the normal way apostles speak of themselves (see Romans 1:1; Philippians 1:1). This phrase, "a servant of God or Christ," is used in several ways in Scripture. It may refer to anyone who is humbly carrying out God's will. Even wicked people are called God's servants, insofar as they carry out God's purposes. Thus Cyrus was called God's servant, as was Nebuchadnezzar (see Jeremiah 27:6).

This term also denotes a godly wish to carry out God's revealed will. So anyone who is called in the Lord, whether he is slave or free, is said to be Christ's servant (see 1 Corinthians 7:22).

This term also refers to any public office that is held for God's glory. Prominent people who serve God in some special office are called God's servants (see Romans 13:4). This is particularly true of ministers and servants who hold public office in the church (see 2 Timothy 2:24). In the Old Testament priests were called the Lord's servants (see Psalm 134:1).

The author of this letter refers to one of his relatives—**a brother of James.** Judas is called this partly to distinguish him from Judas Iscariot.

Now we come to those who are greeted. These people are described as **those who have been called.** This results in two things, their sanctification and their preservation.

1. They were **called.** There is an outward calling; as Christ said, many are called or "invited, but few are chosen" (Matthew 20:16). They are outwardly called in the invitations of the Word, and this includes all wicked people who live within the hearing of the Gospel. But it seems that they are only called when they live among the elect, those who are "called according to his [God's] purpose" (Romans 8:28). But there is an inner and effectual calling, through the work of the Spirit or through the "voice of the Son of God" (John 5:25) who brings life. The apostle is speaking here about those who are "called according to his purpose."

2. We now see how they are **called.** God has called us by his Word and by his Gospel (see 2 Thessalonians 2:14). Few Christians hear audible voices, and those who claim to are often deluded. God's normal way of calling us is by his Word, which usually means the preached Word. But I have to agree that this Word is not always effective at the moment it is heard. Peter, for example, was convicted a long while after he heard Christ's words. "Then Peter remembered the word Jesus had spoken: 'Before the cock crows, you will disown me three times'" (Matthew 26:75). In this way God often brings to mind old truths and makes them effective a long time after they have been spoken. So the Word is effective either when we hear it or as we recall it and meditate on it. Can you remember such an experience when God called you through his Word and spoke words of comfort to your heart? Oh, I will never forget one particular sermon in which the Lord spoke directly to my heart. God's Word leaves an abiding impression that cannot be eradicated.

3. Next we consider how we respond to God's call, for the idea of vocation implies not only God's action, but ours as well as we respond to his call. We know that Christ's sheep hear his voice. When Christ said, "Mary," she responded, "Rabboni," or "My Lord" (John 20:16). God's call is the offer of grace; our answer is accepting this grace. There must be receiving as well as offering. Vocation is not effective unless it ends in union. The Scriptures frequently imply and signify that God's creatures must answer his call. God says, "Seek my face!" And the soul, like an echo, responds, "Your face, LORD, I will seek" (Psalm 27:8). Similarly we read in Jeremiah, "Return, faithless people; I will cure your backsliding." And we respond, "Yes, we will come to you, for you are the LORD our God" (3:22). The soul is enabled to do what it is exhorted to do. God says, "Come to Christ," and the soul replies, "Lord, I come." So then, have you obeyed the call? Have you received Christ as your Lord and Saviour? The

correct answer to the call is to take Christ wholeheartedly. Offering is the call, and receiving is the answer. Christ will be with you with all his graces and benefits if you will be for him in all your desires.

4. You may know your calling by the concomitant dispositions of your soul when you give a positive response to Christ's call.

a. You will experience godly sorrow. "They will come with weeping; they will pray as I bring them back" (Jeremiah 31:9). This refers to the conversion of the Jews. When God comes to lead them, they will bewail their hard hearts and their unbelief. This is how every returning sinner responds.

b. You will also experience holy wonder. This stems from comparing our own wretchedness with God's rich mercy in Christ. So the apostle Peter writes that God "called you out of darkness into his wonderful light" (1 Peter 2:9). Here Peter implies that God's grace is amazingly wonderful when we are converted, just as light is to a prisoner who has been kept in a dark cell. Thick darkness is turned into marvelous light. Everything is wonderful about this change, both the sweetness of that grace and the power of that grace. The grace was sweet when God came to offer Abraham the grace of the covenant, and he fell on his face in humble adoration and reverence (see Genesis 17:3). The grace was powerful when Peter was amazed at his deliverance by an angel from a prison. We have even greater reason to be amazed as the yoke of sin is broken and we are set free by Christ. The sweet effect of this grace puts us in awe that we have the peace of God that transcends all understanding.

c. You will also experience freedom and confidence to obey God's will, no matter what adverse difficulties are against you. This was true in Abraham's case. "By faith Abraham, when called to go to a place he would later receive as his inheritance, obeyed and went, even though he did not know where he was going" (Hebrews 11:8). Where faith is sensitive to one of God's commands, it does not argue but carries out God's will. The Spirit speaks to the soul as the disciples did to the blind man: "Cheer up! On your feet! He's [Christ is] calling you" (Mark 10:49).

5. You should have evidence concerning your call—namely, the fruits you bear. For this call infers a change from your previous life, both in heart and behavior.

a. There will be a change in your whole heart. The activity of the new nature is first seen in mind and judgment: "made new in the attitude of your minds" (Ephesians 4:23). Also, our will and emotions will always incline toward pleasing God. "You are my portion, O LORD; I have promised to obey your words" (Psalm 119:57). The soul, finding comfort in God, sets all its strength toward him. God cannot abide sin, and a sanctified heart cannot abide it either. The new life has an antipathy toward everything that is contrary to it.

b. There will be a change in your behavior. Redeemed people walk in a way that is worthy of their new calling and do not bring disgrace on it with any ungodly deeds. "I urge you to live a life worthy of the calling you have received" (Ephesians 4:1). When David was a shepherd, he thought about nothing but looking after his father's sheep. But when God called him to look after people, he changed his way of living accordingly. A new calling requires a new way of living. "Live lives worthy of God, who calls you into his kingdom and glory" (1 Thessalonians 2:12). The divine calling gives you an honor; it is not fit for princes to embrace refuse or for eagles to catch flies. You are not to be worldly, as other people are. You are called into fellowship with saints and angels. If you saw a man working in a ditch, with his clothes covered in mud, would you think he was the heir apparent to a crown and was called to inherit a kingdom? Who will believe your calling when you remain in the mud of pleasures and are carried along by secular interests? The apostle Paul reproved the Corinthians for living "worldly" lives (1 Corinthians 3:1). When Antigonus was about to enter a prostitute's home, someone reminded him, "You are a king's son." Remember to walk in a way that is worthy of your high calling. Remember that the one who called you is holy, so you must also be holy (see 1 Peter 1:15-16).

We now move on to consider the effects of this calling. The first result of this calling is sanctification—"sanctified by God the Father" (KJV). We see two things here. First, the state, **sanctified**, and second, the author of sanctification, **by God the Father.**

1. The state of sanctification: *hegiasmenois*, "to those who are sanctified"; instead of the reading in some manuscripts, *egapemenois*, **loved by God the Father** (NIV). Let us keep to the former reading, as the other is a mistake and is found in only a few Greek manuscripts.

2. The author of sanctification is **God the Father**. But why is it attributed to the Father? Is not Christ our sanctification (see 1 Corinthians 1:2)? Is it not also called "the sanctifying work of the Spirit" (2 Thessalonians 2:13)?

a. It is true that the whole Trinity, one way or another, brings about our holiness. The Father sanctifies, the Son sanctifies, and the Holy Spirit sanctifies. The same may be said about our calling and our persevering in our calling.

b. Although each person of the Trinity works with the others, they each play a distinctive part in our sanctification. The love of the Father combines with the glory of the Son, and the glory of the Son combines with the power of the Spirit. You can see how the Scripture indicates this. You will find, first, that no one comes to the Son unless the Father calls him (see John 6:37). Christ also said, "No one can come to me unless the Father has enabled him" (John 6:65). Nobody comes to the Father from the grip of sin and Satan except through the Son, through his redemption and mediation. "Jesus answered, 'I am the way and the truth and the life'" (John 14:6). It is also clear that nobody is united to the Son except through the Holy Spirit, who works in those whom the Father has chosen and the Son redeems. So the sanctification of the Spirit is as necessary as the blood of Jesus (see 1 Peter 1:2). So each person of the Trinity has a distinctive role in our sanctification. Sanctification is *from* the Father, *in* the Son, and *through* the Spirit.

c. Because the initial work of sanctification comes from the Father, the Scripture sometimes says that the whole work of sanctification is his. The Father is "the one who justifies the man who has faith in Jesus" (Romans 3:26). Christ does not work in a person who has not been given to him by the Father. We are **sanctified by God the Father**.

Kept by Jesus Christ. This is the second and last manifestation of their effective calling. We are not only sanctified for the present through God the Father's abundant love but will always be **kept** in that state by Jesus Christ.

Notes on Verse 1

Note 1. **Jude.**

1. Christian names should signify something, so that people are reminded about their duty.

2. We are allowed to reveal or conceal our names when we write, depending on which will give the greater glory to God. Jude mentioned his name, but the writer of the letter to the Hebrews did not.

3. Godly and wicked people may bear the same name. So we have Judas the apostle and Judas the apostate. We have Enoch, Cain's son (see Genesis 4:17) and Enoch, Seth's son, who walked with God (see Genesis 5:22).

Note 2. **A servant of Jesus Christ.**

1. Concerning his role Jude uses **servant** as one of his titles. He might have mentioned other things to show off to the world, but he does not do such a thing. It is sufficient for him to write, **Jude, a servant . . .** As Jude, the Lord's brother, calls himself a **servant**, so does Mary, the Lord's mother, call herself "the Lord's servant" (Luke 1:38). Even Christ himself did not think it dishonorable to be called God's servant. To be a groom in God's service is better than being a lord anywhere else. As you have a glorious Master, remember whom you are servants with—the glorified saints (see Ephesians 3:18). When we realize that we have fellowship with such fellow servants, we should never mind that we are engaged in lowly work. Remember that Moses refused to be called the son of Pharaoh's daughter when he grew up (see Hebrews 11:24-25). Galeacius Carraciolus left his noble position as a marquis for an obscure life, working for the Gospel in Geneva. Paul never thought of his imprisonments as being disgraceful but as a mark of honor (see Philemon 1; Acts 28:20).

2. Note also how Jude describes himself in relation to Christ. He acts as a **servant** in this matter. He says he is James's **brother** but Christ's **servant**. If we are to be Christ's, it must be in the form of a servant.

a. Whoever is Christ's servant must give himself up wholly to Christ's will. Your tongues are not your own to speak whatever you please (see Psalm 12:3-4). Your hearts are not your own to think as you please. Your hands are not your own to do as you please. By virtue of your creation you belong to each other and are bound to live for one another, according to God's will and for his glory.

b. Having given yourself up to God's service, you must walk as Christ's servants. The angels are God's servants, carrying out his will (see Psalm 103:21). A servant does not have any will of his own but has given up his freedom in order to carry out somebody else's wishes. A faithful servant would not knowingly offend his master, and so would seek to do his will. Doing the Master's will is sufficient motive for us (see 1 Thessalonians 4:3; 1 Peter 2:15).

3. Note that this phrase, **a servant of Jesus Christ,** is applied to those who come before the Lord in some special office or work, such as the apostles did; and so, as a consequence, do ministers of the Gospel. Note that ministers of the Gospel are servants of Jesus Christ. Paul was a servant, and Jude was a servant.

a. This word hints at the duties ministers are to carry out. It teaches us to be diligent in our Lord's work, for we are servants and must give an account (see Hebrews 13:17) of how we spend our time. We are entrusted with talents that must be employed for the glory of God and the benefit of other people. We are servants employed in our Master's service (see Galatians 1:10).

b. This word *servant* tells us about the duty people have toward ministers. They should view ministers as God's servants and give them the honor they deserve. Listen to their teaching with meekness and patience, for they are but servants. If their message does not please you, remember that they are passing on a message from their Master. You must look on them as servants and must not idolize them. "What, after all, is Apollos? And what is Paul? Only servants, through whom you believe—as the Lord has assigned to each his task" (1 Corinthians 3:5).

Note 3. **A brother of James.** We should try to avoid being the cause of creating scandal. I say this because the Scripture says, "Then Judas (not Judas Iscariot) said, 'But, Lord, why do you intend to show yourself to us and not to the world?'" (John 14:22). The Scripture wants you to know that it is not Judas Iscariot who is asking this question. People drink less freely from fountains of which they are suspicious. Because Jude was held in high honor, his letter would be welcomed. James had a good reputation, and Paul thought he was among the "pillars" of the church (Galatians 2:9).

1. It is right to make use of someone's good reputation for the sake of the Gospel. Paul sometimes quoted from secular writers and poets when he spoke to a non-Jewish audience, as he knew they would be respected. It is sometimes a good idea to bait the naked hook of truth with someone's respected reputation.

2. We should live so that we bring honor to our families. One of Jude's titles is **a brother of James**. He treated it as an honor to be related to such an eminent apostle. Worthy people enhance the reputation of their families. Live in such a way that you do not bring shame on your family.

Note 4. God's people are a **called** people. This is how they are often described (see Romans 1:6; 1 Corinthians 1:2; Hebrews 3:1). The saints are a called people because everything they have and enjoy is from God's calling. A Christian is nothing and has nothing except for what God has seen fit to work in him through his creative word. "God gives life to the dead and calls things that are not as though they were" (Romans 4:17). God's outward call must be understood by men as the voice of God. Samuel was not initially convinced that God was calling him but thought it was Eli.

God's people are rightly said to be a **called** people, and they are called in many different ways.

1. They are called from self to Christ. Christ said, "Come to me, all you who are weary and burdened" (Matthew 11:28). The main purpose of a call is to bring Christ and the soul together. All of God's dispensations have a voice. God speaks to us through conscience and through his deeds, but chiefly through his Word, which, when it is applied by the Spirit, is a call that rouses us from sleep. But the main call of God is by the voice of the Gospel, where the offers of grace are found. Come, poor, weary soul, come to Christ, and you will find rest and comfort.

2. God's people are also called from sin to holiness. "For God did not call us to be impure, but to live a holy life" (1 Thessalonians 4:7). While the end result of divine calling is faith, the middle stage is holiness, just as the final end is glory. Thus we are called out of Babylon into Zion, from the tents of Kedar into the tents of Shem, from nature to grace, and from the power of Satan into the kingdom of God. In short, this call is a separation from uncleanness and all common and vile practices.

3. They are also called from misery to happiness and glory, from being aliens to being friends, from darkness to light (see 1 Peter 2:9), from being enemies to being reconciled, from being objects of wrath to being heirs of glory. All these kinds of calling are sometimes referred to as a heavenly calling. "God has called me heavenward" (Philippians 3:14); we "share in the heavenly calling" (Hebrews 3:1), a holy calling—"[God] has . . . called us to a holy life" (2 Timothy 1:9). It is no small matter to be God's children (see John 1:12), joint-heirs with Christ (see Romans 8:17), and "a kingdom and priests" (Revelation 1:6). Many people are promoted and are called to high

office in the world because they have served faithfully. A Christian's calling is better, for he is called to be holy, a spiritual king, and a holy priest to God. It is a "holy" calling because of its effects and its purpose. A human calling may be dignified and bring great honor for us, but it cannot infuse grace; it may change our condition, but it cannot change our hearts. It is a "heavenly" calling because God by his Spirit is its author, and because of its aim, which is heaven (see 2 Thessalonians 2:14; 2 Peter 1:11). We are first called to grace and then to heaven. First the wonderful voice says, "Come to me," and then the great voice says, "Come up higher." We are called from self, sin, and the world so that we may enjoy God in Christ forever.

Application 1. This helps us listen for God's call. Many people miss God's call because of vain, worldly pleasures or out of fear. The first type of people who neglect God's call should read Proverbs 1:25-26: "Since you have ignored all my advice and would not accept my rebuke, I in turn will laugh at your disaster; I will mock when calamity overtakes you." God's wrath is never worse than when it is aroused because we ignore him. There are two things that men cannot stand being ignored—their anger and their kindness. When David thought his kindness was being ignored, he threatened to kill Nabal. The Lord will certainly respond with just anger when his constant messages of love are neglected.

The other type of people are those who refuse God's call because they are frightened. They complain that while it is true there is mercy in Christ for sinners, Christ does not call them. My brethren, what are you looking for—an audible voice to speak to you, saying, "You, John" or "You, Thomas"? You are included with everyone else, so why do you exclude yourselves? If God says *sinners*, you should say, "I am the chief." John 10:3 says that Christ "calls his own sheep by name," and "the sheep listen to his voice." How does Christ call them by name? By speaking expressly to their condition, as if he tapped them on the shoulder, saying, "Here is comfort for you." It is like a great feast at which there is set out a massive dish of food for all the guests to help themselves freely. But when we take some food, we say, "Here is a dish for me." So you should apply and take to yourselves your own portion. You should say, "This was a dish provided for my hungry conscience and intended for me." But some will reply, "Surely there is no mercy for me—I am so unworthy." I answer that the invitation takes no notice of worth but only of thirst. "Whoever is thirsty, let him come; and whoever wishes, let him take the free gift of the water of life" (Revelation 22:17). You are not worthy, but are you thirsty?

Application 2. We are again told to "be all the more eager to make your calling and election sure" (2 Peter 1:10). This means that we are to show evidence of our election by our calling. For calling is but election put into practice. Election is nothing but God's love and intention to bestow saving grace on people. Calling is nothing but the actual manifestation of God's love, the application of saving grace. "And those he predestined, he also called" (Romans 8:30). Calling is the first and immediate fruit of election, by which it springs out and is exercised in mercy. "From the beginning God chose you to be saved through the sanctifying work of the Spirit and through belief in the truth. He called you to this through our gospel, that you might share in the glory of our Lord Jesus Christ" (2 Thessalonians 2:13-14). Here is the complete view of salvation. The first spring of mercy was at election, which flows out through effectual calling and flows down in the channels of faith and holiness until it loses itself in the ocean of everlasting glory. By calling, God works out in time what he had decreed before all time. The person who is called may look back on the eternal purposes of grace and forward to the eternal possession of glory. "But," people ask, "if a calling gives a definite experience of God's grace, why do so few of God's children have assurance or any sense of their conversion?" I will give five answers to this question.

1. It is possible for God's power to be in us, and yet we are not aware of it. There is a difference between our inner and our outer senses. We may lose our spiritual feeling. There was a great power working in the Ephesians, but they were not sufficiently aware of it (see Ephesians 1:18-19).

2. It is the fault of God's children when they are not aware of the power that is at work in them. Sometimes it is their carelessness, sometimes it is their peevishness. Their carelessness lies in not observing God's approaches and how he works and breaks in on their hearts through the Word of God. Sometimes it is peevishness and perverseness of judgment. A sense of sin and of many weaknesses, like a thick cloud, hinder their clear discerning. God has called them, but they will not own and acknowledge it, and so they undervalue their spiritual condition.

3. God does not call everyone in the same way. Some people's conversion is gentle and silent, while Christ comes to others like a strong man who snatches them out of the fire. Some are drawn in such a way that they are hardly aware of it, and God's love overcomes them slowly. For others the Spirit comes like a mighty rushing wind, and they are carried to Christ, as it were, through the gates of hell. In natural birth some children are born more easily and with less pain than some other children, whose birth is an agonizing experience. In the same way, the new birth in some is without trouble and comes immediately.

4. This different dispensation God uses according to his own pleasure; no certain rules can be given. Some people are acutely aware of sin and of God's judgment, while other people are hardly upset at all as they enter God's kingdom. Those who experienced a turbulent conversion are fully aware of that omnipotent pull by which their hearts were divorced from their corruptions and can tell you the time, the means, the manner, and all the circumstances of their calling in great detail. But not everyone is able to

give a formal account of their conversion or tell you the exact method and successive works of grace in their lives.

5. While there may be different dispensations used in calling, there is still enough evidence to distinguish the uncalled from the called. Conversion is evident if not in feeling, then by fruit. We may not know exactly how we were converted or the precise moment, but still we were born. No soul ever came to Christ without a load on his back, though everyone is not ready, like the jailer, to kill himself because of his anguish.

With these considerations, work hard to have your calling supported. With them you may rebuke your doubts and fears. When conscience asks, "What have you to do with these comforts, to see yourselves as objects of God's election and heirs of glory?" you may reply, "I did not take this honor on myself—I was called by God."

"But," you may ask, "what are the infallible marks of effective calling?" My answer is as follows. You may know your effective calling partly by the preparations made for it. Though the work itself is done in an instant, and often when we are least expecting it, God does, however, usually make preparations for his mighty work. Redemption needed no preparation, but conversion does. As Moses brought the people of Israel to the borders, but Joshua led them into the land of Canaan, so usually the law is at work, although we are called by the Gospel. The law drives us out of ourselves, but the Gospel pulls our heart to Christ. It is God's way to speak about terror before he speaks about comfort. Christ showed this method at work when he said, "[The Spirit] will convict the world of guilt in regard to sin" (John 16:8). So the Spirit convicts and makes a person yield and say, "Certainly I am a sinner, an unbeliever, a wretch who does not deserve Christ." The soul says, "Surely I am stark naked and in a lost condition." So if you have always entertained good thoughts about yourself, and only a slight or general understanding that we are all sinners, you are not prepared. This is not enough. There must be a particular and humbling sense of sin. A sense of our own unworthiness is the first thing that brings us to Christ.

Note 5. **Sanctified by God the Father** (KJV). God's people, whom he has called out of the world to himself, are a sanctified people. I will show you, first, what it is to be sanctified and, second, why God's people must be sanctified.

1. First, what it is to be **sanctified**. There are many definitions of this term. The two most well-known are to set apart or to cleanse. These two ideas will be enough for our purpose.

a. To sanctify is to set apart and dedicate. God's people are set apart by God (see Psalm 4:3), and they dedicate themselves to his service. They become "an instrument for noble purposes, made holy, useful to the Master" (2 Timothy 2:21). They are set apart by God both in time and before time. Before all time they were set apart by God's decree to be a holy seed to himself in and through Christ, separated from the perishing world. But then in time they are regenerated and actually set apart. Sanctification is an actual election by which we are set apart from the perishing world to act for God and to seek the things that bring him glory. So we are said to be a holy priesthood (see 1 Peter 2:9), as priests are men set apart to minister in God's presence.

b. To sanctify is to cleanse, which with its positive actions renews and adorns us with grace.

I will speak, first, about the cleansing work of sanctification. People who are sanctified must not only be separated for holy service but must also be cleansed. We all come into the world polluted with the stain of sin, which is purged by degrees now and at death completely, but never before. The work of grace for the present consists in rubbing away the old filth and weakening original corruption more and more, as well as washing off the new defilement that we contract every day through contact with the world. See John 13:10, where our Saviour alludes to a man who has been bathing himself but after his return from walking outside has got his feet dirty again and needs another wash, of his feet at least. This cleansing work is like washing off stains and purging away diseases.

I move on now, second, to the positive work of sanctification—to the soul being adorned with grace. As the priests under the law, when they came to minister before the Lord, were not only washed in the great laver but were clothed with wonderful apparel, so to be sanctified is more than to be purified. In addition to the removal of sin, there is the infusion of grace. We now have new hearts and new spirits (see Ezekiel 36:25-27). There is a new heart of conformity to God's nature and a new life of conformity to God's will. The pattern of that sanctification that takes place in the heart is God's nature or image (see Ephesians 4:24; 2 Peter 1:4). The pattern of that sanctification that takes place in our lives is God's law or revealed will (see 1 Thessalonians 4:3).

2. I now move on, second, to show why God's people must be sanctified.

a. For the honor of God, of every person of the Trinity—Father, Son, and Spirit. For the honor of the Father, that his choice may not be disparaged (see Ephesians 1:4; 2 Thessalonians 2:14). It would be unthinkable that God should set his affections on a people who were completely different from him. We are afflicted so that we may share his holiness (see Hebrews 12:10-11).

Our sanctification is also for the honor of God the Son, of whose body we are members. Head and members must be all of a piece, like one another. It is unthinkable that Christ should have a body like the one Nebuchadnezzar saw in his dream, where the head was of pure gold, the thighs of bronze, the feet of iron, etc. For as long as you continue to sin,

25

you disparage your Redeemer and put him to shame. Christ's aim is to make us holy. For this purpose he redeemed us, that he might sanctify us and make us a glorious church, without stain or wrinkle (see Ephesians 5:26-27). Celsus opposed Christianity on the grounds that it was a sanctuary for villains and for people who led an immoral life. Origen answered him that it was not a sanctuary to nourish them in their evil practices, but a hospital to cure them. Under the law, all the cities of refuge were cities of Levites and schools of instruction; similarly, Christ has made the church a school where we learn how to be holy.

Our sanctification is also for the honor of God the Spirit, and his called people should be holy because they are in his charge, under the instruction of the Holy Spirit, with the goal of being sanctified. Sanctification is the personal work of the Holy Spirit (see 2 Thessalonians 2:13; 1 Peter 1:2). He is to shape all the vessels of glory, to clothe the bride of Christ with the jewels of the covenant. It is the great benefit in the dispensation of grace that we have God to plan it, God to purchase it, and God to bring it about. The Father, Son, and Spirit together sanctify the believer and make him holy.

b. Another reason why we must be sanctified is on account of the hopes to which we are called and the happiness that we expect. Now we cannot have this unless we are holy (see Hebrews 12:14). We are told in that verse to pursue peace, but most of all to pursue holiness. If our hearts are set on seeing Christ as he is, we will desire to be like him, and this means that we must be holy. "Everyone who has this hope in him purifies himself, just as he is pure" (1 John 3:3). Because we expect that our bodies will be like Christ's glorious body, we do not use our bodies as a channel for lust. So because of our hope we must be sanctified. The foundation and seed of glory is laid in grace, and that life we must live forever has begun.

Application 1. Sanctification convicts us. If God's people are a sanctified people, then here is sad news for two kinds of persons.

1. The profane, who do not care about holiness. See what John says about people who wallow in their filthiness: "He who does what is sinful is of the devil, because the devil has been sinning from the beginning" (1 John 3:8). The devil trades in sin and makes it his work and business.

2. Sanctification convicts people who scoff at holiness. When you deride men for their holiness, you deride them for the exact image of the glorious God, and so deride God himself. You hate God more than you do the saints if you hate them for their holiness, which shines in them with a faint luster but that originates in God. Scoffing Ishmaels who mock are sure to be cast out by God (see Genesis 21:9-10), for they do not belong to God. Remember that holiness is the badge worn by those who are the Lord's called people, and it should be a matter for reverence, not reproach.

Application 2. Sanctification serves as a caution to us and prevents us from making mistakes. Be warned that many things look like sanctification but are not. I will now mention four of these—civility, formality, restraining grace, and temporary grace.

1. *Civility*. This is nothing more than a fair demeanor in the world or, in the apostle's expression, "those who want to make a good impression outwardly" (Galatians 6:12). Such people usually live in ignorance and have little knowledge about Christian institutions. They live well, are not drunks, nor blasphemers, but know little of God and have little insight into religious matters. Like Nicodemus, a strict Pharisee, they are grossly ignorant (see John 3:10). There is little of Christ in such souls. Those who are satisfied with their own righteousness do not seek Christ's righteousness. Their thoughts are constantly focused on themselves. They have no hungering and thirsting after Christ. Such people do not see their need for his grace and the help of his Spirit. Often these people excel in one particular sin. Civility is only another form of slavery. One way or another Satan holds them as his prisoners, and their outward appearance before the world hides their lust or, one of the most common sins of all, their worldliness. Such people are more concerned about outward behavior than their inner motives and thoughts. Anger, pride, and evil thoughts are swept under the carpet because they can parade about as people who have never murdered anyone. Paul bewailed his lusts and the law of sin within (see Romans 7), which reflected his rebellious nature. So much for civility.

2. *Formality*. This is pretended grace. This may deceive you, and so the apostle speaks of "true . . . holiness" (Ephesians 4:24), as opposed to counterfeit holiness. False grace is always concerned about external considerations. False grace is always in decline until it is completely lost. It is like bad salt, which loses its saltiness and is eventually thrown onto the rubbish pile. But true grace can grow into a tree from a tiny seed. So examine yourself and see if you are increasing or decreasing in your spiritual life. If you are going backwards from zeal to coldness, from strictness to looseness; if you are careless about your duties and are not concerned about this, it is a sign that grace never worked in you properly.

False grace must not be confused with humility. You should be suspicious when the more people profess, the more proud and conceited they become. Genuine grace is always accompanied by spiritual poverty or a sense of our own spiritual need (compare 1 Corinthians 8:2 with Proverbs 30:2-3). The more true faith people have, the more they bewail their unbelief and see their need to increase their faith (see Mark 9:24). It is excellent when the soul is kept hungry so we forget what lies behind and strain toward the goal (see Philippians 3:13-14).

3. The next thing is *restraining grace*, which is nothing other than conscience leading people to avoid sin even when they do not hate it. Love is of little use and force with such people. They are chained by their own fears. The great evangelical theme is mercy: "Therefore, I urge you, broth-

ers, in view of God's mercy, to offer your bodies as living sacrifices, holy and pleasing to God—which is your spiritual worship" (Romans 12:1). It is good to serve God with reverence, but a servile awe has little grace in it. It is indeed true that it is better to have a slavish fear than none at all. Thus David says to those who would be held back with no other restraints, "In your anger do not sin" (Psalm 4:4). You will be able to see that this formality is not genuine sanctification because it does not destroy sin but only prohibits its use. Abimelech's lust was not quenched, yet God stopped him from sinning against Sarah (see Genesis 20:6). The heart is not renewed, although the action is checked. Israel possessed an adulterous heart toward God when her path was "block[ed] . . . with thornbushes" (Hosea 2:6). Again, the trouble with these people is that they are imprisoned by conscience and want to be free and find their own way.

4. The next thing that looks like sanctification but is not is *common grace*. This is a distinct thing from everything else, yet I call it common grace because it may be in those who fall away and depart from God. It is different from civility because it is more Christian and evangelical. It differs from formality because that is only a pretense and a show, whereas this is a real work on the soul. It is different from restraining grace because that is only a duty engaged in out of a servile awe of God. It is a common work, good in itself, that God ordains in some to be a preparation and a beginning of the work of grace. The apostle speaks of this when he refers to "those who have once been enlightened, who have tasted the heavenly gift, who have shared in the Holy Spirit" (Hebrews 6:4). There are three things to note here: first, that the light spoken about does not result in humility; second, the taste is not ravishing, drawing the soul more and more after Christ; and, third, the gifts are not renewing and sanctifying.

a. That light is not humbling. He says they are "enlightened," but he does not say that they are humbled. Foundations totter that have not been laid deeply enough. The more true light people have, the more they will abase themselves. You can never magnify Christ enough, and you can never abase yourself enough, and, Christ is most exalted when you are most abased (see Isaiah 2:19). Dagon must fall on his face if you mean to set up the ark. And if Christ is to be precious to you, you must be vile in your own sight. Nobody is genuinely revived except for the humble (see Isaiah 57:15-16). True humility, far from weakening your comforts, makes them more full and sure. So the main thing that was lacking in the people referred to in Hebrews 6 was humility, and their fault was coming to Christ rashly, in pride.

b. Their taste was not ravishing and did not affect their hearts so that they sought Christ. They had but a loose and slight desire of happiness, glimpses of the glory of heaven and the comforts of the Gospel. These were not serious and holy desires after Christ or after grace and strength to serve him. The saints who do have a taste for spiritual things groan in their longing for fuller communion in God's graces and comforts (see Psalm 119:5; Romans 7:24). The experience they have already had of Christ makes them long for more.

c. Their gifts are not renewing and sanctifying. The gifts that these people receive might possibly make them useful to the Church but do not change the heart. The apostle says they have shared in the Holy Spirit. They may have had a plentiful share of church gifts, so that they were able to carry out duties for the edification and comfort of others. But, alas, how are people better if their hearts are still oppressed with sins and not upright with God? "If I speak in the tongues of men and of angels, but have not love, I am only a resounding gong or a clanging cymbal" (1 Corinthians 13:1). Even if you can speak about the things of God at length and with much feeling and can offer sweet prayers, everything is but a clanging cymbal with God if saving grace is absent. It is clear proof that we are as the apostle says when our feelings do not match what we say about our duty and when our gifts do not fully influence our practice. So much for that point.

Note 6. **God the Father.** Here we note that sanctification is God's work, carried out in us by the Father. No creature can cleanse his own heart, nor can he make himself holy, any more than he can create himself. We are able to defile ourselves, but we cannot cleanse ourselves. A sheep can go astray by itself, but it can never return to the fold without the shepherd's help and care. Evil desires are too hard for us, as are the duties of obedience. God, who gave us his image at first, must again plant it in the soul. Who can repair depraved nature except the author of nature? When a watch needs repairing, we take it to the workman. "We are Christ's workmanship" (Ephesians 2:10). Sanctification is God's work. "I the LORD, who makes you holy . . ." (Leviticus 21:8). Human efforts contribute nothing to the work of salvation, as all we do is resist God and rebel against God, or else why should the same Word preached by the same minister work in some and harden others? Everything depends on God's grace, which acts according to God's pleasure.

Application 1. Let us wait on God until the work is completed. Our wills are obstinate and perverse, but God never made a creature too hard for himself. God is able to do this thing for us, and it comforts us that we have such a God to go to. The ungodly, who groped and felt after God, sought a power to quell their evil desires, but everything is made easy for you in God's power through Christ. Crates advised someone who came to him asking how he could subdue his lust of uncleanness to either starve himself or hang himself. Democritus made himself blind because he was unable to look at women without having evil desires about them. God teaches us to remove the eye of our lust, not of our bodies. Bless God that you know whose work it is and to whom to go for sanctification.

Application 2. Praise the Lord whenever this work is accomplished. It is not self-effort but grace. Sanctification can never be ascribed to our deeds or to any power that comes from us but is due to God's mercy, Christ's merits, and the Spirit's work. Sanctification is from God. "Fine linen, bright and clean, was given her to wear" (Revelation 19:8). God the Father issues orders from heaven, just as Esther was clothed from the king's wardrobe as a result of the king's orders. Then there is merit in Christ. The stream in which we are washed flows out of Christ's own heart. "The blood of Jesus . . . purifies us from every sin" (1 John 1:7). Then there is the Spirit's work. Only his power can overcome a proud heart. It is noteworthy that grace is expressed not only by the idea of creation (see Psalm 51:10; Ephesians 2:10; 2 Corinthians 4:6), which is making things out of nothing, but also through victory (see Luke 11:21-22; 2 Corinthians 10:5; 1 John 4:4) or a great power overcoming opposition. In creation, as there was nothing to help, so there was nothing to resist and hinder; but in man there is, besides a death in sin, a life of resistance against grace. We do not deserve sanctification. It comes from the Father's good pleasure and Christ's merit; we cannot bring it about; it is accomplished by the power of the Holy Spirit.

Note 7. Note that our thoughts in believing must not wait until we ascend and come to God the Father. The Scripture is always mentioning our acts of faith to him: "for us who believe in him who raised Jesus our Lord from the dead" (Romans 4:24). This refers to those who believe in God the Father. Christ said, "When a man believes in me, he does not believe in me only, but in the one who sent me" (John 12:44). That "not" is not negative but corrective. "Not only in me, but his thoughts must ascend to the Father also, who manifests himself in me." "Trust in God; trust also in me" (John 14:1). As well as believing in Christ, we must believe in God the Father as the first fountain and author of grace. I will now mention four reasons why this is true.

1. Because all grace begins with the Father. It is the Father who flows out to us in Christ and in the Spirit. Whatever Christ has and is, he has from God the Father who is the originator of all things. "It is because of him [God] that you are in Christ Jesus, who has become for us . . . our . . . holiness" (1 Corinthians 1:30). The high priest went into the sanctuary before he blessed the people. So Jesus Christ sanctifies you in the Father and from the Father. As Mediator, Christ is to be considered God's servant and agent.

2. Because whatever is done to you by Christ is done with respect to his Father's love. "Father, the time has come. Glorify your Son, that your Son may glorify you. For you granted him authority over all people that he might give eternal life to all those you have given him" (John 17:1-2). Also look at John 17:6: "I have revealed you to those whom you gave me out of

the world. They were yours; you gave them to me and they have obeyed your word." That was the basis of Christ's respect for the Father. Therefore, you must look to the Father's love as well as to Christ's care. The Son loves us because the Father required it, and the Father loves us because the Son asks it. Since Christ is faithful to his Father, we are sure to be loved.

3. Because it is a great support and comfort to faith to consider the Father in the act of believing. Two are better than one; and it is often said to be a privilege to have "the Father and . . . his Son" (1 John 1:3; see also 1 John 2:23-24; 2 John 9). There is the Father's love and the Son's merit. Neither by itself will give us that joy and peace in believing, and therefore it is good to have them both together. There is no access to the Father but in the Son. What will guilt do when faced with justice? What will stubble do when faced with consuming fire? God apart from Christ is terrible rather than comforting. That is why Peter says that through Christ we believe in God (1 Peter 1:21); that is, through Christ, on account of his merit, we come to God the Father. Likewise Christ, apart from the Father, does not give us such firm grounds of confidence. There must be some act of the Father to give us complete security; for in the business of redemption God the Father is seen to be the one who is offended, the wronged party, who is to receive satisfaction. Our consciences are aware of wrong actions, and we must also be alert to God's favor and grace toward us. We should see him in all acts of grace.

4. Because in the Father's love there are many ways in which he engages the soul that are not found in the other members of the Trinity. In the Father's love and in his acts of grace there is an original fullness. Christ's fullness as Mediator is derived from the Father's abundant grace. "For God was pleased to have all his fullness dwell in him [Christ]" (Colossians 1:19). All that Christ dispensed was according to the charge and commandment given him by the Father. "To sit at my right or left is not for me to grant. These places belong to those for whom they have been prepared by my Father" (Matthew 20:23). In the Father's acts we have the purest understanding of love. "For God so loved the world that he gave his one and only Son" (John 3:16).

Application. This urges us to give glory to God the Father. You need to have a correct understanding of the divine persons of the Trinity. It is said that "all may honor the Son just as they honor the Father" (John 5:23). God is most honored when your thoughts are most explicit in this matter. Do not forget the Father. You are his gift as well as the Son's purchase and the Spirit's charge. If God the Father had not loved you before the world was created, Jesus Christ would not have redeemed you. And if Christ had not redeemed you, the Spirit would not have sanctified you. The Spirit does not work unless you look at him as Christ's Spirit: "He [the Spirit of truth] will bring glory to me by taking from what is mine and making it known to you" (John 16:14). Christ came to glorify the Father and to complete his work (see John 17:4). Bless them and praise them all then. If you receive anything, see the Father's bounty in it, his free and everlasting love stamped on what you have. And if you desire anything—holiness, comfort, grace, pardon—do not just reflect on the fullness of Christ's merit, but on the Father's love that he freely gives. You deal with a God of compassion; Father, Son, and Holy Spirit are all yours.

Note 7. **Kept by Jesus Christ.** Observe that God's called and sanctified people are preserved and kept in their state of grace and holiness in and by Jesus Christ. This point asserts two things—that they are kept *by* Christ and *in* Christ; that is, not only for his sake, but by virtue of union with him. Jesus Christ is the cabinet in which God's jewels are kept. If we want to stand, we must get out of ourselves and get into Christ, in whom alone there is safety. Union with Christ is the basis for our safety and preservation. Here is some general teaching about the perseverance of the saints. I will first mention the state of perseverance and how far we may expect to be preserved, and then I will mention the certain grounds and assurance of perseverance.

1. I start with how far we may look for preservation. The doctrine of perseverance is much abused. Let us grant what can be granted, and then the truth will be burdened with less prejudice. It appears that grace may be lost. "Take the talent from him" (Matthew 25:28). "Even what he thinks he has will be taken from him" (Luke 8:18). Comets and meteors soon burn up and fall from heaven like lightning, while stars keep revolving in their orbit. A building founded on sand will totter, and hypocrites are unmasked in front of the congregation (see Proverbs 26:26). Again, initial grace may fail, as is spoken about in Hebrews 6:4-6. Examples of initial faith are illumination, outward reformation of behavior, temporary faith, and devout moods. Abundant blossom does not always produce a good crop of fruit. Some die as they are born, and others are stillborn.

Even genuine grace may suffer from decay, but it will not be utterly lost. The leaves may fade, but the root lives on. God's children are severely shaken by temptations. Their heel may be bruised, as Christ's was, but their head is not crushed. Peter denied Christ but did not fall from grace. Chrysostom's comments on Christ's prayer for Peter ("But I have prayed for you, Simon, that your faith may not fail," Luke 22:32) are worth noting. Chrysostom writes, "Note that Christ does not say, 'I have prayed for you that you should not deny me,' but 'I have prayed that your faith should not altogether vanish and be abolished.'" Again, the graces we have in Christ, such as joy, peace, and cheerfulness, may be taken away. A man remains a human being even when he has lost his well-being; a man remains a man even when he is bankrupt, poor, ill, or suffering from a disease. And it is possible for a person to be a Christian although he may not be living a full spiritual life.

The work of grace may also face great obstacles for a long time. A bout of fainting is not the same as the state of death. There may be few signs of visible life, yet the seed remains. And this condition may last for a long time. David lay in a spiritual swoon for nine months and was not aroused from this until Nathan came to him. Left to ourselves the grace we have would soon disappear. But grace is a jewel entrusted only to safe hands. Perseverance is God's gift, not man's act. Christ has been given the work of keeping the saints safe (see John 6:37-40). "I give them eternal life, and they shall never perish; no one can snatch them out of my hand. My Father, who has given them to me, is greater than all; no one can snatch them out of my Father's hand" (John 10:28-29). They neither *will* nor *can*. God and Christ are engaged in keeping them. Christ by God's command is the Mediator, and God keeps them safe because of Christ's merit. So anybody who wants to separate us from God must fight against Jesus Christ himself!

We do not suggest any wild assurance and certainty of perseverance. We do not say that those who neglect the means of grace or grieve the Spirit will definitely not have a spiritual miscarriage. But when God makes people persevere, he makes them persevere in using the means he has given. Hezekiah was assured by God that he would live for fifteen more years, but he still applied a fig poultice to his boils (see Isaiah 38:5, 21). Even clearer is the example of Paul trusting in God and yet using all the means at his disposal to escape drowning, as is recorded in the Acts of the Apostles. Paul said to the sailors and soldiers, "not one of you will be lost," but he also said, "Unless these men stay with the ship, you cannot be saved" (Acts 27:22, 31). We will live for as long as God has any service for us to engage in, but we are still responsible for our clothes and food and to use all means to preserve life. Satan's argument against God's protection of Christ was in effect, "You are sure not to fall; therefore throw yourself into danger" (see Matthew 4:5-6). It is a teaching learned from the devil that you can do whatever you like because you are sure to be safe. That is the devil's deception. And it is against the nature of this assurance. Anyone who has tasted God's love in God's way cannot reason like this. A child of God does not neglect God's means of grace. God's grace is nourished by godly exercises. You may as well say that a fire should make people freeze with cold as say that the certainty of perseverance in grace should make us do anything contrary to grace.

Again, we do not say that a believer is so sure of his state of grace that he does not need to keep on being alert and watchful. "So, if you think you are standing firm, be careful that you don't fall!" (1 Corinthians 10:12). People who trust God most are also the people who trust themselves the least, in case they fall into corrupt ways. Christ had prayed that Peter's faith might not fail, but he still told him, with the other apostles, to watch (see Luke 22:40-46). The fear of God is a preserving grace and is part of God's covenant. "I will make an everlasting covenant with them: I will never stop doing good to them, and I will inspire them to fear me, so that they will never turn away from me" (Jeremiah 32:40). This is a fear that stands shoulder to shoulder with faith and certainty. It is a fruit of the same Spirit and does not hinder assurance but guards it. It is a fear that makes us watchful so that we do not sin or become spiritually slack but rather desire to never offend God. The man who has an inheritance given to him by his friend in court takes care not to offend him.

Again, this certainty of our standing in grace does not exclude prayer. "Get up and pray so that you will not fall into temptation" (Luke 22:46). Perseverance is God's gift, and it must be looked for in God's way— through Christ's prayers, to preserve God's majesty, and by our prayers, that we may constantly profess our dependence on God and renew our acquaintance with him. In addition to this, by asking blessings in prayer we are made more aware of our duty. Prayer is a means to keep us gracious and holy. Those who often talk with kings need to be decently dressed; similarly, the person who often speaks to God is bound to be more holy, so that he may be more acceptable to him.

Again, it is not a discontinued but a constant perseverance we are praying for. It is not as if an elect person could be driven out of the state of grace, for he will be saved at the end. He cannot fall from grace and godliness unless his whole person consents to this. He may sin badly but will not fall away completely, nor finally. There is something that remains, a seed, an anointing, a root in a dry ground that will bud and flower again. In short, true grace will never be completely lost, even if it is considerably weakened; as the means of grace are used, a person is preserved to eternal life.

God not only requires us to stand or to continue to use the means of grace, but there is also no doubt at all that he gives us his grace of perseverance. The precepts of the covenant of grace are also promises. "This is the covenant I will make with the house of Israel after that time, declares the Lord. I will put my laws in their minds and write them on their hearts. I will be their God, and they will be my people" (Hebrews 8:10). These statements about the covenant are set out in the form of promises. God always continues to give faith and love and fear and all his other graces so that the soul will persevere.

2. Now I move on to consider the grounds for assurance, by which it may appear that we will be preserved in that state of grace to which we are called in Jesus Christ. The grounds are many. If you put them all together, you would have the recipe for the perseverance of the saints.

a. There are some grounds for assurance given to us by God the Father.

There is his everlasting love and all-sufficient power. Take his everlasting love. God does not love us for one moment only but forever. "But from everlasting to everlasting the LORD's love is with those who fear him" (Psalm 103:17). God the Father's love for us precedes the creation of the world and extends beyond the destruction of the world. God's love does not rest on any temporal accident but on his own counsel, in which there can be no change because the same reasons that moved him to choose us at first continue to apply forever. God never changes his mind in time about what he had planned before all time. "For God's gifts and his call are irrevocable" (Romans 11:29). By "gifts" the apostle Paul means those that are right for the elect to possess; and by "call" he means effective calling according to God's eternal purpose. God never changes his mind about these. The other basis for our certainty is God's all-sufficient power. God's almighty nature is engaged in the preservation of grace by his eternal love and will. "I give them eternal life, and they shall never perish; no one can snatch them out of my hand. My Father, who has given them to me, is greater than all; no one can snatch them out of my Father's hand" (John 10:28-29). Can they pluck Christ from the throne? Are they stronger than Christ's Father?

b. There are grounds for assurance given to us by Christ. Consider his everlasting merit, and the close union between him and us, and his constant prayers for us. We read about his merit in the letter to the Hebrews. "He entered the Most Holy Place once for all by his own blood, having obtained eternal redemption" (9:12). Legal expiations did not last from year to year, but Christ's merit lasts forever and ever. His redemption is eternal, not only as it is of use in all ages of the church, but for every individual saint as well. Those who are redeemed by Christ are not redeemed for a certain length of time, until they fall away. This would mean that the virtue of Christ's blood was exhausted and could uphold them no longer. But Christ keeps them saved forever. "Because by one sacrifice he has made perfect forever those who are being made holy" (Hebrews 10:14). Christ has not only bought the possibility of salvation but everything we need for complete salvation. Our salvation is not for a limited length of time but for eternity.

Then there is the close union between Christ and us. This is the idea of the phrase "preserved in Christ." Just as it is impossible to separate the yeast from the dough once they have been mixed and kneaded together, so Christ and a believer, once they are united, will never be parted. Can Christ's mystical body be wounded or lose a member?

Then there are Christ's constant prayers for us. This is a further ground of the certainty of our perseverance. Christ prays, "Holy Father, protect them by the power of your name—the name you gave me" (John 17:11). "Therefore he is able to save completely those who come to God through him, because he always lives to intercede for them" (Hebrews 7:25). Christ is interceding with God, that the merit of his death may be applied to us. This is salvation "to the uttermost" (KJV) or "to the end." The heirs of salvation need not worry about miscarriages. Jesus Christ, through his will, has made over the inheritance to them, and he is also the executor, and he lives forever and ever to see his own will carried out. He died once to *make* the covenant, and he lives forever to see it *made good*. Whenever we are in danger, he is entreating his Father for help from his grace.

c. There is constant assistance from the Spirit to maintain the essence and seed of grace. The Father's love is continued by the merit of Christ, that he may not depart from us. And we are preserved by the Spirit of Christ, that we may not depart from him. Not only does he put faith, fear, love, and other graces in our hearts to start with, but he maintains and keeps them, so that the fire will never go out. Our hearts are his temple, and he does not like to leave his dwelling-place. And in the economy of salvation, it is his office to glorify Christ and to be our comforter. So, for the honor of Christ and for the comfort of believers he preserves the grace that is in our hearts. Christ has received a charge from the Father to "lose none of all that he has given me" (John 6:39)—that is, none of the elect. In order to be true to his trust, Christ sends the Spirit as his deputy or executor, that his merit may be fully applied. It is for the honor of Christ that wherever the work starts, wherever he has been the author, there he will see it through to the end. "Let us fix our eyes on Jesus, the author and perfecter of our faith" (Hebrews 12:2). It was said of a foolish builder that he started to build a house but was not able to complete it. This dishonor can never be laid at Christ's door, because of the power and faithfulness of the Spirit. "He who began a good work in you will carry it on to completion until the day of Christ Jesus" (Philippians 1:6). The Spirit does not leave us in midstream. He is faithful to Christ, just as Christ is faithful to the Father. The Father chooses the vessels, Christ buys them, and the Spirit transforms them so they are fit to be vessels of praise and honor. But that is not all. As our Comforter he preserves and enables us to continue in the state of grace. That is why we "ourselves . . . have the firstfruits of the Spirit" (Romans 8:23), and "his Spirit in our hearts as a deposit" (2 Corinthians 1:22). "Now it is God who has made us for this very purpose and has given us the Spirit as a deposit, guaranteeing what is to come" (2 Corinthians 5:5). This is a foretaste to show us *how good* eternal life is. And it is a pledge to show us *how certain* it is.

I now move on to share with you six applications of this teaching.

Application 1. It encourages us to persevere with more care. This is no unreasonable inference. "As for you, the anointing you received from him remains in you, and you do not need anyone to teach you. But as his anointing teaches you about all things and as that anointing is real, not counterfeit—just as it has taught you, remain in him. And now, dear children, continue in him, so that when he appears we may be confident and unashamed before him at his coming" (1 John 2:27-28). Since we have so much help to ensure that we stand, let us not fall away. Oh, how great will be your sin if you dishonor God and fall away! We are sorry for a child who falls because he is not being looked after properly. But when a restless child deliberately puts itself outside the protection of his family, we are angry with the child. You have greater reason than others to stand, for you have been brought into an unchangeable state of grace. You are held in the arms of Christ, and God will be angry with you if you pull away from his loving hands. Mercy holds you firmly as you seek to slip away from his grip. If you fall, it will be because you disparage the Spirit's custody, Christ's merit, and the Father's mercy. "Therefore, since the promise of entering his rest still stands, let us be careful that none of you be found to have fallen short of it" (Hebrews 4:1). Notice that some people seem to stand who are not really standing, just as some seem to fall away completely but do not do so in reality. A child of God cannot come short, but he can give that impression. When our spiritual progress is interrupted and we give way to sin and folly, it appears that we have fallen short of the mark, and so discredit God's love, as if God's love could change.

Application 2. If you fall because of weakness, do not be utterly dismayed. As the spinster leaves a lock of wool to draw on the next thread, so there is something left. When you have strayed from God, go back to him and say, "Forgive me, please." David pleaded in this way: "I have strayed like a lost sheep. Seek your servant, for I have not forgotten your commandments" (Psalm 119:176). It is as if David said, "Lord, I have sinned through weakness, but I hope there is some grace left in my heart that turns toward you." God would be angry with you if you did not plead for forgiveness. In this way turn your falls to your advantage.

Application 3. When you stand, be overcome with love and thankfulness. Nothing makes God's saints love God more than God's unchanging love. When they see themselves safe in the middle of weakness and Satan's daily attacks, it endears God to their souls. Certainly Daniel was greatly affected when he was preserved in the lions' den, when he saw the lions roaring around him and yet restrained with the chains of providence so they could do no harm. God's children must love the One who preserves them when they think about all the dangers that surround them and how little they can rely on their own strength. So the saints love and praise God not only for the grace that is freely given to them, but because this grace is constant and unchanging. "His love endures forever" is repeated twenty-five times in Psalm 136. "Give thanks to the LORD, for he is good; his love endures forever" (Psalm 106:1). No words are more frequently on the lips of saints. And this is just as well, for if we were left to ourselves, we would damn ourselves every hour. We have "stubborn and rebellious hearts"

(Jeremiah 5:23). We cannot stand by ourselves. We have an enemy who tosses us about like wheat (see Luke 22:31). If it were not for God's everlasting mercy, what would become of us? People who do not love God for their preservation are not aware of their condition in the world. What an evil heart they carry around with them! It is a miracle that grace should ever be preserved in such hearts, where there is so much pride, love of pleasures, preoccupation with the world, and animal desires. It is amazing that a heavenly plant can exist in the middle of so many weeds. How busy the devil is as he constantly takes advantage of them, like a dog wagging his tail (this is Chrysostom's comparison) and expecting some tidbit. Satan's malice is most strongly exercised against those who have the most grace.

Finally, these people do not recall that the world is full of snares and dangerous allurements. If they did, they could not but seek God's blessing on them. One of the fathers imagined the flesh saying, *Ego deficiam* (I will surely fail and miscarry), and the world saying, *Ego decipiam* (I will deceive and entice them), and Satan saying, *Ego eripiam* (I will snatch them and carry them away), and God saying, *Ego custodiam* (I will keep them— I will never fail them nor forsake them). That is where our safety and security lie.

Application 4. This teaching informs us that if we fall often, constantly, frequently, easily, then we have do not have God's grace. "No one who is born of God will continue to sin" (1 John 3:9). He does not keep on sinning deliberately. God's children often slip, but not with the same frequency and constant readiness in the same sin. A meadow may be flooded occasionally, but marsh ground is drowned every day by the tide. Wicked people are carried away with every temptation. I make an exception of those sins that come on you suddenly and stir up your bad temper and your vain thoughts and so distract you from your duty. And yet for these a person should be even more humble and watchful. If you do not battle against these sins and do not mourn when you are caught by them, it is a bad sign.

Application 5. This teaching stops us from being lulled into a false sense of security. Here are three things you should not be content with.

1. You should not be content with outward happiness. An immortal soul must have an eternal good. All things in the world are frail and pass away, and so they are called "uncertain" wealth (1 Timothy 6:17). It is uncertain whether we will obtain them, and uncertain if we will keep them, and uncertain if we will live long enough to enjoy them. Wealth is no good to us in the next world. "What is better" will not be taken away from us (see Luke 10:42), and by seeking that we may have other things with a blessing also. "But seek first his kingdom and his righteousness, and all these things will be given to you as well" (Matthew 6:33).

2. You should not be content with gifts. You must not rely on gifts.

Judas could cast out devils but later was cast out among the devils. "Eagerly desire the greater gifts" (1 Corinthians 12:31). After the apostle Paul had given much teaching about gifts he wrote, "And now I will show you the most excellent way" (1 Corinthians 13:1). And what is that way? Love— grace that endures forever, as he explains in that chapter. Many people who have great abilities, such as praying and preaching, still fall away. They may have great gifts of knowledge, utterance, abilities to comfort, direct, and instruct others, to answer doubts, to reason and argue for God, and yet still fall away. They are like those in Hebrews 6:4 who had "shared in the Holy Spirit"; that is, they had a large share of church gifts. And this is not all. Gifts themselves fade and vanish as human strength wanes. "'All men are like grass, and all their glory is like the flowers of the field'" (1 Peter 1:24). The "glory" of man refers to whatever excellent things we naturally have, such as humor, understanding, and strength, as well as wealth and riches. We are often like the dry stalk that remains long after the flower has gone. Only the gracious work of the Spirit lasts forever.

3. You should not rest content with false faith, which starts in joy but ends in tears. Hymenaeus and Alexander are said to have shipwrecked their faith—false faith (see 1 Timothy 1:19-20). Planting the tree of genuine faith is no easy matter at first, but it leads to true comfort. Otherwise we may view the Gospel as some kind of delicacy for a while and are like thorns that only last for a few moments as they blaze under the pot because they cannot keep the fire burning. So do not rest in having "tasted the goodness of the word of God" (Hebrews 6:5) as if you were trusting in some passing comfort.

In addition to this there is the formal profession of faith. This may begin in the Spirit and end in the flesh (see Galatians 3:3). A person may appear to himself and to the church of God to have true grace and yet may still fall away. God delights to unmask hypocrites by letting them fall into some scandalous sin or by changing the circumstances of their lives. Paint is quickly washed off. So do not trust in these outward and superficial changes, but in solid and substantial grace working in you.

Application 6. Genuine assurance about our salvation is comfort for God's children. Grace is secure, as are its privileges. Grace itself remains sure even if your folly stays with you for most of your life. It is the advantage of spiritual comforts that they not only satisfy our desires but help us in our fears. The redeemed of the Lord have "everlasting joy" (Isaiah 35:10). Once you are in Christ, you are forever preserved in him. Grace would be little better than temporal things if it only gave you temporary refreshment. I will now apply this truth to five different circumstances that we often have to face.

1. During great troubles God may seem to hide his face. Oh, how comforting it is to hear God say, "I will not leave you until I have done what I

have promised you" (Genesis 28:15). This will encourage your heart. In times of distress we are prone to think that God has left us and will never again look after us, even though we had previously genuinely experienced his grace. What foolish creatures we are, to weaken our assurance when we should come to use it. We should make use of all our hope and experiences in times of trouble, which is the best time to make use of them.

2. In the hour of temptation and hard conflicts with doubts and corruptions. When we are alive to the power of sin and how difficult it is to eradicate from our hearts, we are apt to say, as David did after all his experiences, "One of these days I will be destroyed by the hand of Saul" (1 Samuel 27:1). That is the moment when you must recall that you are preserved in Christ and that nothing can separate you from him. Sarcerius went to Camerarius' wife after she had suffered a long and tedious conflict and read to her the second half of Romans 8. Camerarius then said triumphantly, using Paul's words, "In all these things we are more than conquerors through him who loved us" (Romans 8:37). Dear Christians, neither sin nor the devil nor this world can separate you from Christ, for Christ did not only "crush Satan," but he did so "under your feet" (Romans 16:20).

3. In times of great danger and defection, either through error or through persecution. This especially affects us when other people fall through fear, particularly if it happens to Christians we looked up to and respected. People who were just about to be martyred were upset to hear that some great Christian scholars had fallen away. When Hymenaeus and Philetus, two eminent Christians, fell, many people were shaken in their faith. "Nevertheless, God's solid foundation stands firm" (2 Timothy 2:19; see also 2 Timothy 2:17-18). This is the comfort the apostle always prescribed in such cases.

4. In times when you are disheartened, when the means of grace seem to be a burden. To bring your Christian walk alive again, think about God's unchanging love. All graces rise in proportion to the amount of faith. A feeble hope weakens us. "Therefore I do not run like a man running aimlessly" (1 Corinthians 9:26). So you are to continue, confident that God will bless you and keep you for his everlasting kingdom.

5. In the hour of death. When everything else fails you, God will not fail you. Olevian comforted himself with these words: "Though the mountains be shaken and the hills removed, yet my unfailing love for you will not be shaken" (Isaiah 54:10). As he lay dying in pain, he said, "Sight is gone, speech and hearing is departing, feeling is almost gone, but the loving-kindness of God will never depart." May the Lord give us such a confidence when we face death, that we may die trusting our Redeemer to preserve us.

Verse 2

Commentary on Verse 2

Mercy, peace and love be yours in abundance.

We now come to the third thing in this greeting that was so often included in apostolic salutations in the form of a prayer. Here we observe, first, the theme of the prayer, or the blessings prayed for, which are three— **mercy, peace and love**; and, second, how these are to be appropriated, **in abundance**.

I start with the theme of this prayer or the blessings prayed for. It is helpful to note the different words used in this greeting. In the Old Testament *peace* was usually mentioned without the accompanying word *grace*. "For the sake of my brothers and friends, I will say, 'Peace be within you'" (Psalm 122:8). But in the age of the Gospel, when grace was more fully given, it was also included in the greeting. But even in the time of the Gospel a variety of greetings were given. Sometimes you have little more than a formal greeting: "To the twelve tribes scattered among the nations" (James 1:1). "To the Gentile believers in Antioch, Syria and Cilicia" (Acts 15:23). This was the normal greeting given by non-Christians. The greeting "grace and peace" is the most common one (see Romans 1:7), and in other places the greeting is "grace, mercy and peace," as in 2 John 3 and 1 Timothy 1:2. Jude's greeting is slightly different from all others: **mercy, peace and love**. Causaubon has observed that when the Greek fathers wrote to non-Christians, they would wish them grace but not peace; but when they wrote to a godly person, they wished him grace and peace as well.

Mercy. Mercy is the basis of all the good we receive from God. The Lord would give his blessings in such a way as to defeat despair and human confidence. Man stands in need of mercy but does not deserve to receive any. Despair would keep us from God, and human confidence robs God of his glory. Mercy solves both problems. We do not need to run away from God. "But with you there is forgiveness; therefore you are feared" (Psalm 130:4). False worship is accompanied by fear, but God captures our hearts with his love and mercy. And we have no reason to ascribe any virtues to ourselves since mercy, and not justice, gives us standing in the court of heaven. It is part of God's supremacy that all his blessings should come as gifts to us. Merit detracts from God's royalty and supreme majesty.

Peace. What is peace? It is tranquillity of mind arising from the sense of a definite relationship with God. Two things spring to mind about this peace. First, it is based on friendship with God. In Scripture this is called "peace with God" (Romans 5:1). It is the immediate effect and fruit of actual justification. And, second, there is an experience of this peace with God, which is sometimes called "peace of mind" or "peace of conscience." It is a special privilege for those who are in Christ's spiritual kingdom. In Romans 14:17 Paul links "peace" to "joy in the Holy Spirit."

I now come to the third thing prayed for, and that is **love**, which here is not God's love to us but our love toward God. It may be defined in this way: a gracious and holy affection that the soul, once it experiences God's love in Christ, gives back to God through his grace.

In abundance. We should not only seek grace from God's hands—we should continue to seek it more and more.

Notes on Verse 2

Note 1. I will make five general observations on this verse.

1. Spiritual blessings are the best blessings we can desire for ourselves and for other people. The apostles in their greetings do not want temporary happiness but spiritual grace. God's people pray for one another as they are in communion with the Spirit. So they do not seek wealth and honor for themselves or for one another, but they seek more of God's favor. Our first and main request must be for **mercy, peace and love,** and then we may add other things. The way to be heard in other things is first to beg for grace. Solomon sought wisdom, and along with wisdom he was given riches and honor in abundance. So then, when you pray for yourself, make a wise choice—beg for spiritual blessings. Also, when you pray for other people, start by praying that they may receive more of God's grace.

2. Notice also how apt these requests are for the people Jude prayed for. Those who have been **called** (verse 1) are still in need of **mercy, peace and love.** We need **mercy** because we deserve nothing from God, either before we received grace or after we received it. Our glory in heaven is a fruit of mercy, not of merit. Our obligation to free grace never ends. We also need more **peace.** There are degrees of assurance as well as degrees of faith. And then **love,** which is a grace in us, always needs to grow and grow. Only in heaven will it be complete. This means our love for God. In heaven we will cling to God without distraction and without becoming tired. It may also mean love for the saints. This also will only be complete in heaven, where

there is no pride—where Luther and Zuinglius, Hooper and Ridley join in perfect love.

3. Notice how relevant these requests are for the times when they were prayed, when religion was being brought into ill repute by worldly Christians, and man-made teaching was invading the church. In times when the truth is being attacked, there is a great need for **mercy, peace and love.** We need **mercy** in order to be kept from the traps of Satan. We need **peace** and inner comfort so we can live through troubled times. And we need **love** so that we may be of one mind and stand together to defend the truth.

4. Note also how appropriate these blessings are for the people Jude is praying for. Here are three blessings that match up with the three persons of the Trinity. Elsewhere the apostle Paul makes this clear: "Grace and peace to you from God our Father and from the Lord Jesus Christ" (Romans 1:7). Paul says we receive grace from the Father and peace from Christ. And here **mercy** is from God the Father, who is called the Father of mercies and "the God of all comfort" (2 Corinthians 1:3); **peace** is from the Son, for he is our peace (see Ephesians 2:14); and **love** is from the Spirit: "God has poured out his love into our hearts by the Holy Spirit, whom he has given us" (Romans 5:5). So you see that each member of the Trinity contributes to our spiritual well-being.

5. Notice, also, how well these blessings live in harmony with each other. First **mercy**, then **peace**, and then **love. Mercy** is not very different from what is called grace in Paul's letters, except that grace applies more to God's generosity, and **mercy** applies more to our need of grace. So **mercy** means the favor and goodwill of God to miserable creatures. **Peace** signifies all interior and exterior blessings as the fruits of that goodwill, and in particular a calm and serene conscience. Sometimes **love** refers to God's love for us, but here I think it means our love for God and love for fellow Christians for God's sake. So **mercy** is the source of everything, **peace** is the fruit, and **love** is what is given back to God.

Note 2. **Mercy.** Now I move on to consider each grace on its own. The first is **mercy**, which is the basis of all the good we have from God. Man stands in need of mercy, but does not deserve mercy. I will make ten observations about mercy.

1. All of Scripture shows us that God is merciful. It is true that God is totally just as well as completely merciful. Moses asked God to show him his glory, and God told him his name. "And he [the Lord] passed in front of Moses, proclaiming, 'The LORD, the LORD, the compassionate and gracious God, slow to anger, abounding in love and faithfulness, maintaining love to thousands, and forgiving wickedness, rebellion and sin'" (Exodus 34:6-7). This description says more about mercy than justice. He is called "the Father of compassion [KJV, "mercies"] and the God of all comfort" (2 Corinthians 1:3). He is a just God, but he is not called the Father of justice.

43

Mercy is natural to him. He counts it as the proper fruit and product of the divine essence.

2. Mercy is represented as God's delight and pleasure. Micah says that God "delight[s] to show mercy" (Micah 7:18). God loves to bless and protect. He is not disposed to destroy things and only does so when he is forced to. If God is compelled to strike and justice must be exercised, the Scriptures show that the compassionate God is reluctant to do this. "For he [the Lord] does not willingly bring affliction or grief to the children of men" (Lamentations 3:33). God is like a father with a rod in his hand but tears in his eyes.

3. The Scriptures depict God as exercising mercy even if it was sometimes to the disadvantage of his glory. Showing mercy to Nineveh, for example, would not bring credit on his message. Jonah proclaimed, "Forty more days and Nineveh will be destroyed" (Jonah 3:4). Yet God spared Nineveh, and so the petulant Jonah protested, "I knew that you are a gracious and compassionate God, slow to anger and abounding in love, a God who relents from sending calamity" (Jonah 4:2). It is as if Jonah said, "I knew that you would do this, that the prophets of Israel would be disgraced in front of the people of Nineveh. I proclaimed the message, but free grace will make me a liar." God could easily destroy sinners with much honor to himself; but he is long-suffering, even when his patience seems to go against his just nature.

4. The Scriptures speak a great deal about God's readiness to receive returning sinners. Although they have done infinite wrong to his holiness, yet when they repent, and as soon as they start to submit, mercy embraces them and hugs them, as if they had never been separated. "I will . . . go back to my father" (Luke 15:18). "But while he was still a long way off, his father saw him and was filled with compassion for him; he ran to his son, threw his arms around him and kissed him" (Luke 15:20).

5. God not only welcomes sinners back but himself goes out to invite the reluctant to come in. The Scriptures are full of God's loving invitations. He draws us with cords of love, cords that are woven and spun out of Christ's compassionate heart.

6. People who constantly refuse the offers of God's grace are borne with for a long time. "God . . . bore with great patience the objects of his wrath" (Romans 9:22). Everyone should bless God for his patience. They owe a great debt to divine justice, but it is a long time before God asserts his just demands. God bears with them year after year, and after a thousand affronts he is still patient with them, from cradle to grave.

7. God is depicted as being merciful, not only in the Word, but in providence and in all God's dispensations. The whole Word is a great volume, written with characters and lines speaking of God's mercy. "The LORD is

good to all; he has compassion on all he has made" (Psalm 145:9). Every creature bears the marks and prints of divine goodness and bounty.

8. Consider the numerous ways in which mercy is presented to us. God's mercy has many names. It helps us in our faith to consider the different aspects of grace. "The LORD is compassionate and gracious, slow to anger, abounding in love" (Psalm 103:8). See also Nehemiah 9:17, Psalm 145:8, Joel 2:13, and especially Exodus 34:6-7 where you will find God's description of himself. God's Spirit has revealed God's mercy to us in various ways so that we may benefit from meditating on them.

a. The first notion is mercy itself, an attribute through which God succors those who are in misery. This is an attribute that only involves others. God knows himself and loves himself, but he is not merciful to himself. Mercy is given to creatures who are in misery. Mercy alone can relieve our misery.

b. The next notion is grace, which is the free generosity of God. Grace does everything "freely" (Romans 3:24), where there is no hope of recompense. God's external motive is our misery; his internal motive is his own grace and elective love. Am I in need? There is mercy. Am I unworthy? There is grace. The angels who never sinned are saved merely out of grace, but men who were once miserable are saved not only out of grace but also out of mercy.

c. The next notion is long-suffering or slowness to anger. The Lord is not easily overcome by the wrongs or sins of the creature, but easily overcomes them by his own goodness and patience. He does not only have pity on our misery (that is mercy); he not only does us good expecting nothing in return (that is grace); but he bears with our infirmities for a long time.

d. Kindness or bounty, "plenteous in goodness," *berab chesid*, is the next notion. God communicates his grace to us in a variety of wonderful ways. You may say, "God is merciful, gracious, patient, but will he be like that to me?" Yes, he will. It is God's nature to communicate his goodness to us. "You are good, and what you do is good" (Psalm 119:68). So David went to the Lord for grace.

9. Consider your own experiences. We have not only heard that God is merciful, but we have known it. All people can speak about patience and common mercy and outward deliverances, but few use them in a spiritual way.

a. Consider God's patience. How long did he wait for you to be converted? He who spared you can save you. You should think, "Surely God would not have spared me all this time if he did not intend to save me." Such thinking as this encourages us to give ourselves to God. "Do you show contempt for the riches of his [God's] kindness, tolerance and patience, not realizing that God's kindness leads you toward repentance?" (Romans 2:4).

b. Consider God's goodness in giving you food, clothes, dignity, and a joyful heart, all without your deserving any of these things. I see the sun rise every day with a fresh brilliance as it shines on the just and the unjust. This shows how gracious God is. The sun is a type of the Sun of Righteousness, who is willing to display his beams and wings over a poor, languishing soul. Common mercies are the tastes of God's love while you are a sinner, and the common fruits of Christ's death, that you may be invited to come for more. God's children use these gifts to reach higher dispensations. They know that God, like the good householder, brings out his best gifts last of all. So they seek something higher and beyond all these things.

c. Consider deliverances from imminent danger. You thought you were about to die, and God snatched you out of the fire. Every deliverance is a temporary pardon. If you had died, you would have died in your sins and so have been eternally miserable. Forever blessed be the mercy that rescued you.

10. Consider God's invitations. Mercy invites you to come and be saved. How many means has God used to call you to himself! Every spiritual urge is a call, every preacher a messenger sent from heaven to invite you to Christ, every sermon a new summons. Now it is time to stop meditating on God's mercy and to move on to how God's mercy should be applied to us in our lives.

Application 1. God's mercy tells us that people who want to know God must make mercy their only plea. Returning sinners must have these words in their mouths: "Forgive all our sins and receive us graciously" (Hosea 14:2). Lord, we desire your mercy. So David professed that he had no other claim: "I trust in your unfailing love" (Psalm 13:5). Chrysostom helpfully comments: "If any others have anything to allege, let them plead it; Lord, I have but one thing to say, one thing to plead, one thing in which I place all my hope, and that is your mercy." So you must come to the throne of grace saying: "Lord, my plea is mercy, all the comfort I expect to receive is from mercy." The best claim God's dearest servants can claim is mercy. Possidius, in *The Life of Augustine*, recounts the words of Ambrose as he was about to die: "Though I have not lived so that I should be ashamed to live among you, yet I am not afraid to die; not that I have lived well, but because I have a good and gracious Master." This forever remains the basis of the saints' confidence.

Application 2. God's mercy exhorts us to use this encouragement to bring our souls into God's presence. Think about the mercies of God. The vile abuse of this teaching has made it suspect in some people's thinking. But children must not refuse bread because dogs try to destroy it. When Ben-Hadad was dejected and in danger not only of losing his kingdom but his life, his servants comforted him with these words: "Look, we have heard that the kings of the house of Israel are merciful" (1 Kings 20:31).

You have heard how the God of Israel delighted to be merciful. He has sent Christ to you as a pledge of his goodwill and mercy. Why do you not go to him? He who had enough love to give us Christ, has enough compassion to pardon us, and enough bounty to give us heaven and whatever we are in need of. Do not stand in fear of his justice; justice and mercy have made friends with each other (see Romans 3:25-26; 1 John 1:9). God desires to exercise mercy as much as you desire to feel it.

Application 3. This teaches us in all our activities to acknowledge mercy. The saints did this (see Ephesians 2:4; Philippians 2:27; 1 Timothy 1:13; cf. Genesis 32:10). It is good to refer everything to its source. Everything we enjoy is the fruit of mercy, especially saving grace. It is a sure sign that a person has received no benefit through grace if his heart is not stirred up to praise God for it. We have more reason than angels to praise God for his mercy. I mean not only the bad angels, with whom God entered not into a treaty; he dealt with them in justice and not in mercy. But in some respects we have more cause to bless God than even the good angels. Justice awards a similar punishment to all who are found to be guilty. Only God's infinite and eternal mercy makes the difference.

Application 4. There is reason for caution. Do not wrong grace and mercy, the cause for all the good that we enjoy. This would cut off the fountain and make mercy our enemy. And if mercy is our enemy, who would plead for us? But how do we wrong grace? I answer, partly by neglecting what it offers, when we make God speak in vain (see 2 Corinthians 6:1). We offend God greatly when we despise him when he speaks to us with a still, small voice. We wrong grace by slighting it after we have tasted it. When we first come to Christ we accept grace, and God usually gives us a spiritual appetite to look for more grace (see Hebrews 6:4-6; 1 Peter 2:2-3). But if instead of seeking more grace you return to your sinful ways, you proclaim to the world, as it were, that you have found worldly comforts and pleasures more satisfying than fellowship with God. This is the only way your apostasy can be interpreted. The whole purpose of the Word is to make you keep on enjoying God's grace. If you have once tasted it and became bored with it, you effectively are telling the world there is no sweetness in grace at all. This is a great wrong to grace and mercy.

Note 3. **Peace.**

1. Man by nature is at enmity with God. When we lost God's image, we lost his favor. This enmity is mutual. Man is God's enemy, and God is man's enemy. On God's part there is wrath, and on man's part there is hatred. We hate God because we love sin (see Colossians 1:21). God's enmity is suspended in the day of his patience. But the next world is a time of vengeance and recompense. During our life on earth God invites us to lay down our defiant weapons and accept his terms of peace.

47

2. As well as man being at enmity with God, all of God's creatures are at enmity with man. Angels, fire, air, and water are all at God's beck and call and are ready to destroy man whenever the Lord tells them to. The angels listen to God's voice. The fire says, "Let me burn the house he lives in." The water says, "Let me drown his ships; let me swallow him up, as I did to Korah and his accomplices." Certainly the Lord does not lack instruments to carry out his vengeance.

Man, as God's creature, is his own enemy. God does not need to use outside forces, as there are enough within man to destroy him. There are the humors of the body and the passions of the mind, which are all prepared to serve God to punish us. So if God decided to use our thoughts and affections against us, we would be quickly overwhelmed.

3. We, being in this state, can only be reconciled by Jesus Christ. He obtains this by his merit and confers it by his power. For his merit see Colossians 1:20 and Isaiah 53:5. As for his power, he initially works in us and then continues to keep the peace between us and God. He works in us at first as he opens the Gospel to us, in which God is revealed as pacified in Christ. This is the only teaching that can calm the conscience and establish the soul in peace and hope. There is a double enmity in the human heart—the guilt and power of sin. Christ wipes guilt out of the conscience with the application of his own blood and progressively weakens the power of sin.

4. Once we are reconciled with God in Christ, everything else is at peace with us. Angels are at peace with us. Instead of being instruments of vengeance, they become "ministering spirits" (Hebrews 1:14). A Christian has an invisible guard that Satan is aware of, even if we are not. Further, other creatures serve us as if they were in league and covenant with us. This includes the stars, winds, seas, and beasts. "For you will have a covenant with the stones of the field, and the wild animals will be at peace with you" (Job 5:23). As for men, their hearts are in God's hands. God can either destroy people or restrain their anger or turn them to serve you. "When a man's ways are pleasing to the LORD, he makes even his enemies live at peace with him" (Proverbs 16:7). As for peace among the saints, God breaks down the partition wall (see Ephesians 2:14-18) and by his Spirit makes their hearts united to each other. Christ's blood is the best bond of friendship. Christ has called us into a body, so that there might be peace in the church (see Colossians 3:15). We need God's peace not only in our consciences but to rule in our hearts (Colossians 3:16).

5. Although all things are at peace with us, some troubles still remain; but they do not hurt or destroy us. God's peace is a riddle, for it "transcends all understanding" (Philippians 4:7). In the eyes of the world, who can be more wretched than God's children who are hated, reviled, persecuted, and afflicted? How can they be said to be at peace with God and

with all of God's creatures? I answer that the privileges of Christ's kingdom are spiritual. Whoever troubles saints cannot harm them (see 1 Peter 3:13).

6. In heaven there is perfect peace; in the new Jerusalem all is quiet. "He [God] will pay back trouble to those who trouble you and give relief to you who are troubled" (2 Thessalonians 1:6-7). "There remains, then, a Sabbath-rest for the people of God" (Hebrews 4:9). There we rest both from our sorrows and from our labors. There is no more trouble or affliction.

Application 1. If peace is such an excellent blessing and a great privilege of the Gospel, then we must make use of it. Are we at peace with God through Christ? If so, then:

a. Enmity with God is set aside. God's enemies will be your enemies, and your enemies will be God's enemies. There is war with Satan if we are at peace with God. Spiritual conflict is one of the best demonstrations that we have unity with God.

b. Delight in communion with God. "Submit to God and be at peace with him" (Job 22:21). A person who is at peace with God will often be in his company. When peace is made between nations who have been at war with each other, trade is resumed between them. This is how it will be between you and God.

Application 2. It behooves us to make peace with God through Christ. I will mention two types of people—the careless and the distressed.

a. To the careless: Consider that you are born enemies to God. You must make peace with God, for you cannot maintain war against him. Peace must be found now, or else it can never be found hereafter. The day of God's patience will not last forever; therefore let us go into the ark before the flood comes. Our aim should be to be "at peace with him [God]" (2 Peter 3:14).

b. I will now speak to distressed consciences. Lift up your heads. God offers you peace. He sent angels from heaven to proclaim this (see Luke 2:14). The basis of the offer is goodwill, and the purpose of the offer is God's own glory. God is content that we should have peace on these terms, and this peace is assured us by God's covenant. We should not doubt anything that is acceptable to God. God is more pleased with a cheerful confidence than with a servile spirit that is full of bondage and fear.

Application 3. There is reason for caution. If peace is a privilege of the Gospel, let us take care that we settle on a true peace, in case we mistake a judgment for a blessing. It is the greatest possible judgment to be handed over to your own presumptions and to be lulled to sleep with a false peace. There are three grounds for this false peace.

a. Ignorance of our condition. Many go hoodwinked to hell. You must realize that it is very bad with people when they "will not come into the light" (John 3:20). Their confidence is supported by mere ignorance.

b. Sensuality. Some people's lives are nothing but a diversion from one pleasure to another. There is bondage in their conscience, and they will not take any notice of it. This quenches the Spirit. Cain's heart troubled him, so he preoccupied himself with building cities. Saul, to cure his evil spirit, ran to his music. People usually choke their conscience either with business or pleasure.

c. From formality and slightness in the spiritual life. First, they do not take seriously their duties that would make them see what carnal, unsavory, sapless spirits they have. The person who never stirs does not feel the lameness of his joints. Formal duties make people more and more secure. The Pharisee thought he was secure (see Luke 18:11-12), but spiritual duties are like new wine in old bottles. Second, they do not seriously resist sin. When a person yields to Satan, it is little wonder that Satan leaves him alone. Satan rages most when his kingdom is tottering (see Revelation 12:12). Please the worst natures, and they will not trouble you. If you leave Satan alone, he will leave you alone. There is a peace that ends in trouble.

Note 4. **Love.**

1. The basis of love.

a. Love arises from the sense and apprehensions of God's love in Christ. "We love because he first loved us" (1 John 4:19). Love is like an echo—it gives back what it receives. We do not love God until we are filled with a sense of his love. And as the sun's rays in their reflection are more faint and cold, so our love toward God is much weaker than God's love toward us. Valdesso said, "God loves the lowest saint more than the highest angel loves God."

b. The next cause of love is God's grace. There is not only an apprehension of love, but the force of the spirit that goes along with it. Our thoughts, our discourses on the love of God toward us in Christ, and even our sense of feeling this is not enough to have this grace born in us. Love is a pure flame that must be kindled from above. "God is love" (1 John 4:8). Base creatures neglect God and pollute themselves and one another. There is no help for them until the heart is overpowered by grace.

2. The object of love. God is the supreme object of love, and other things are loved for God's sake. God's Word, which is a reflection of his holiness, has his image engraved on it. And God's saints, who bear his living image, are like children resembling their father. In God's creatures we also enjoy God and give thanks to him for his bounty. In short, this makes the soul to be completely content in thinking about God and speaking about God. This is a feast to the soul. Such souls cannot have a greater solace than to think about what a God they have in Christ.

3. Reasons for loving God.

a. God has commanded it. The sum of the law is love. When the expert in the law came to Christ, he asked, "Teacher, which is the greatest commandment in the law?" Jesus replied, "Love the Lord your God with all your heart and with all your soul and with all your mind" (Matthew 22:36-37). Note that "the greatest commandment in the law" is to love God. This is not a sour commandment but is sweet and profitable. This is a duty to be carried out by poor and rich, educated and uneducated. Whatever their position in the world may be, they may all love God.

b. God deserves love. Let us think about God's love for us. He begins and loves us so that we may love him again (see 1 John 4:19). If God hated us, we would still be bound to love him since we, as creatures, are under this obligation. How much more should we love God who has bestowed so many benefits on us?

4. The properties of God's love.

a. God's love is ancient. "But from everlasting to everlasting the LORD's love is with those who fear him" (Psalm 103:17). We can trace God's love from one eternity to another. Before the world was created he loved us, and after the world has ceased to exist God will continue to love us. His love began in the eternal purpose of grace, and it ends in our eternal possession of glory. It is not a thing of yesterday. God is our ancient friend. He loved us not only before we were lovely, but before we were at all. This grace was given to us before we were born. Look on God's love in time. He loved us a long time before we had a thought about him.

b. Consider the freeness of God's love. The value of all benefits arises out of the need of him who receives and the goodwill of him who gives. God did not need us, and our love is no benefit to him; but we wanted him, and we are undone without him. Yet he has more delight in pardoning than we have in salvation, and he is more ready to give than we are to ask. We are not only needy creatures, we are guilty creatures. But God still loves us. This is the miracle of divine love, that a time of loathing is a time of love. And we will wonder at it more if we consider the active and endless hatred of his holiness against sin, and therefore why not against sinners?

c. Reflect on the frequent expressions of his love. It would tire the arm of an angel to write down God's repeated acts of grace. "The judgment followed one sin and brought condemnation, but the gift followed many trespasses and brought justification" (Romans 5:16). On the last day our wonder and amazement will be to see such huge sums canceled with Christ's blood. Our past lives are a constant reminder of our sins and God's forgiveness. We are weary of everything but sin; we are never weary of that because it is natural to us. As a dunghill sends out vapors to obscure the sun that shines on it, so we dishonor the God of our mercies and grieve him each day. How long has God been multiplying pardons, and yet free grace is not tired and has not grown weary!

d. Consider the various ways in which God expresses his love. We have all kinds of mercies. "His divine power has given us everything we need for life and godliness" (2 Peter 1:3). I think this refers to everything that is necessary for natural life, spiritual life, and everything else linked to grace on this earth and our future glory. So the Lord pleads with us, "I have done many things for you; you cannot open your eyes without seeing my love; you cannot go for a walk without hearing and smelling my love."

5. The effects of God's love. I shall only mention three of these: creation, preservation, and redemption.

a. Creation. This deserves love from the creature. All you have, all you can see, all you can touch is God's gift to you and the work of his hands. God made other creatures by the word of command, and man by counsel. It was not, "Let there be . . ." but "Let us make man," to show that the whole Trinity assisted in and joined in this work. He made other creatures for his glory, but not for his love and service. Look at your body and soul, and you will see that we have reason to love God. In the body we find as many mercies as there are limbs. Take note of the frame of your body. David said, "I praise you because I am fearfully and wonderfully made" (Psalm 139:14). The Vulgate translates this as, "painted as with a needle," like a garment made of needlework, with various colors, richly embroidered with nerves and veins. In short, every part of our body is made in such a way that it looks as if God used all his wisdom to create it.

But so far we have only spoken about the casket in which the jewel lies. The soul, that divine spark, is like God himself in every way. What value God has placed on the soul! He made it in his image and redeemed it with Christ's blood. So then, God, who made such a body, such a soul, deserves love. Why should Christ stand at the door and knock (see Revelation 3:20) and ask permission to enter into his own house? He has every right to enter but still waits for us to invite him in.

b. Preservation. We do not appreciate our daily mercies enough. The preservation of the world is a constant miracle. A feather does not stay in the air, and yet what has the world to support it but the air that surrounds it? From the womb to the grave we are looked after by God every hour. How many diseases and dangers might befall us if God did not look after us as a nurse does her child! How many actual dangers have we escaped! "Can a mother forget the baby at her breast and have no compassion on the child she has borne? Though she may forget, I will not forget you! See, I have engraved you on the palms of my hands; your walls are ever before me" (Isaiah 49:15-16). These are different ways to describe God's providential care of his children.

c. Redemption. When we are weighing something, we put more and more weights into the scales until it is balanced; similarly, God gives us more and more mercies to counter our heart. Here is a mercy that is such a heavy weight: "This is love: not that we loved God, but that he loved us and sent his Son as an atoning sacrifice for our sins" (1 John 4:10). Every one of Christ's wounds is an open mouth pleading love. He made himself vile, that he might be more dear and precious to us. Certainly if love brought Christ out of heaven to the cross, to the grave, should it not carry us to heaven, to God, to Christ, who has been so gracious to us? Thus God has deserved our love.

Application 1. Do you love God? Christ put this question to Peter three times in John 21. A deceitful heart is apt to abuse you. Ask again and again, Do I indeed love God? If you do love God, he demands to be loved alone. People who do not give their all to God give him nothing. God will have the whole heart. If there were another God, we might have some excuse for our reservations; but since there is but one God, he must have all. God must have the sole possession of our hearts. The devil, who has no right to anything, desires to have part of our hearts. But the love of God cannot be in the heart where the world rules.

Application 2. This love must be demonstrated in concrete ways.

a. A hatred of sin. "Let those who love the LORD hate evil" (Psalm 97:10). With love for the highest good, there will be hatred of the lowest evil. Friends have common loves and common aversions. The heart must recoil from every worldly thing. "How then could I do such a wicked thing and sin against God?" (Genesis 39:9).

b. By a delight in obedience. "This is love for God: to obey his commands. And his commands are not burdensome" (1 John 5:3). Nothing is difficult or tedious to the person who has any affection for his work. Shechem agreed to be circumcised for Dinah's sake because he loved her, and Jacob endured a further seven years' work because he loved Rachel. Love enables us to obey God cheerfully in things we would not naturally incline toward. Love and work are often linked together in Scripture (see 1 Thessalonians 1:3; Hebrews 6:10). And those who stop doing their first deeds have lost their first love (see Revelation 2:4-5).

c. A delight in God's presence, and grief over his absence. Can a person love God and be content to be without him? If you lose even a ring that you like, you will not stop searching for it until you have found it. Is spiritual love devoid of all feelings? Are there some Christians who are so insensitive that they never notice the presence or absence of God?

One way that helps you love God is to value nothing as if it comes from God unless you can see God's love in it. God gives many gifts to wicked men, but he does not give them his love in salvation. Possessing everything will do us no good unless we have God himself. God's children are not satisfied unless they can see God and enjoy him in every mercy.

Another way that helps you to love God is to give him nothing if it is not motivated by love. "If I . . . surrender my body to the flames, but have not love, I gain nothing" (1 Corinthians 13:3). Love is an act of grace by itself. Other duties are not acts of grace unless they are motivated by love.

Note 5. **In abundance.** I will now mention ten principles that should help you grow in grace.

1. Where there is life, there will be growth; and if grace is genuine, it will definitely increase. A painted flower always stays the same. The artist can give it beauty, but he cannot bestow life on it. So pretense of religion will always keep a person the same. But those who have genuine grace are compared with a living plant that grows in strength and size and beauty. "The righteous will flourish like a palm tree, they will grow like a cedar of Lebanon; planted in the house of the LORD, they will flourish in the courts of God" (Psalm 92:12-13). It is not enough to have peace and love; we must increase in peace and love.

2. If we do not grow, we will go backwards. In Hebrews 6 the apostle talks about "maturity" in verse 1 but of apostasy in verse 4. We cannot keep what we have received if we do not work to make it increase. Those who row against the stream have to use great strength on the oars or they will be carried along by the current. The person who does not make use of his talent loses it. There are no stunted trees in Christ's garden. We should take as much care to increase in grace as we do in not losing grace.

3. It is a bad sign to be content with little grace. The person who does not desire to improve will never get better. Spiritual things do not cloy when they are enjoyed and used. The person who has tasted the sweetness of grace is motivated to seek more and more grace. Hypocrites and apostates are content with tasting the heavenly gift (see Hebrews 6:4).

4. We cannot have too much grace. You cannot have too much love of God or too much fear of God. "Therefore, my brothers," writes the apostle Peter, "be all the more eager to make your calling and election sure" (2 Peter 1:10). Some people are far away from God's kingdom (see Ephesians 2:13). Some are close to God's kingdom but never enter it (see Mark 12:34). Others enter God's kingdom with great difficulty (see 1 Peter 4:18). Others enter with full sails and yet desire more and more of God's grace. It is not possible to have too much of God's grace.

5. God has provided an appropriate reward for those who grow in grace. According to our measures of grace, so will our measures of glory be. Those who have most grace are vessels that have a large capacity; others are filled according to their size. "Remember this: Whoever sows sparingly will also reap sparingly, and whoever sows generously will also reap generously" (2 Corinthians 9:6).

6. This is appropriate for our present state. On earth we are in a state of progress and growth, not of rest and perfection. Grace is not given all at one time but progressively. Christ said, "I have made you known to them, and will continue to make you known" (John 17:26). He also said, "You believe because I told you I saw you under the fig tree. You shall see greater things than that" (John 1:50). There is more grace to come in the

future; so we must not be content to rest on our initial experiences of God's grace. Paul says, "Not that I have already obtained all this, or have already been made perfect, but I press on to take hold of that for which Christ Jesus took hold of me" (Philippians 3:12). When we receive grace, that is not the end. Only a foolish builder would stop building when the house was only half built. He would not be careless about the superstructure just because he has laid solid foundations. The state of saints is expressed by the idea of a growing light. "The path of the righteous is like the first gleam of dawn, shining ever brighter till the full light of day" (Proverbs 4:18). As long as we are not perfect, there should be growth (see 1 Thessalonians 4:1).

7. Seeking to multiply spiritual gifts is best done with the bounty of God. The Father, Son, and Holy Spirit have rich grace for us. God the Father is spoken of as being "rich in mercy" (see Ephesians 2:4; cf. Romans 10:12). We can never exhaust the treasures of grace or impoverish the treasury of heaven. Christ also has a rich and complete merit (see 2 Corinthians 8:9), sufficient to make us rich. God the Son achieved this through all his sufferings, so he could make a large purchase for us and so we might never lack any grace. The Spirit of God too is poured out richly (see Titus 3:6). There is enough mercy in God the Father, enough merit in God the Son, and enough efficacy in God the Spirit. There is nothing lacking in God. If a mighty king opened his treasures and invited people to come with their bags and take away as much as they could carry, do you think anyone would miss such an opportunity? Of course not! They would quickly collect case after case and keep on returning for more treasure. This is how the Lord acts with the covenant of grace. You will lack cases, not treasure.

8. Desiring more and more of God's grace shows our gratitude. We want to have more and more of God's mercy, and so we should take care that peace and love increase in us. If we want God to multiply his blessings toward us, we should add to our graces (see 2 Peter 1:5ff.). When we have food we also desire to have clothes; and when we have clothes we also want a home to live in; and when we have all these things, we want them in more and more abundance. We should seek God's gifts of grace in the same way. When we have understanding, we should seek to have perseverance; and when we have perseverance, we should seek to have faithfulness, etc.

9. We must learn from our Lord Jesus, to whom we should conform in all things: "And Jesus grew in wisdom and stature" (Luke 2:52). This means that his human capacity became bigger as he became older and stronger, for he was like us in every way except that he did not sin. Our understanding should also increase as we become older.

10. We may learn from worldly people "who add house to house and

55

join field to field" (Isaiah 5:8) and are never satisfied. There is a holy covetousness in spiritual things when we add faith to faith (see Romans 1:17) and obedience to obedience. Our happiness is to enjoy the infinite God, and therefore we should not set a limit on our desires.

Application 1. Time is needed before growth is seen. We do not fly to the top of Jacob's ladder but go up step by step. This work takes time. A complete change may take place in an instant, from being a sinner to being a saint. But growth in the Christian life takes time. We can discern if we are not growing, if after a long time we remain the same concerning our doubts, evil desires, and prejudices (see Hebrews 5:12).

Application 2. Different saints make spiritual progress at different rates. All the plants in Christ's garden are not of the same height or stature. Some who are useful in public have five talents, some have two talents, some grow slowly, and some grow quickly. "The love every one of you has for each other is increasing" (2 Thessalonians 1:3). Some people are weak and grow slowly, but they nevertheless bear fruit.

Application 3. Growth in grace is always accompanied by growth in knowledge. "But grow in the grace and knowledge of our Lord and Savior Jesus Christ" (2 Peter 3:18). Plants that grow shaded from sunlight often grow a long stem and produce little if any fruit. Some Christians devote all their energy into growing in love and never think about growing in knowledge. We read that Christ "was filled with wisdom, and the grace of God was upon him" (Luke 2:40).

Application 4. Of all the graces, we need to grow in faith most of all. "Night and day we pray most earnestly that we may see you again and supply what is lacking in your faith" (1 Thessalonians 3:10). All of Satan's temptations tend to weaken our faith, and all other graces depend on our faith growing.

Application 5. Growth in gifts must be distinguished from growth in grace. Many Christians are blessed with many spiritual gifts but do not grow in grace. You can easily spot growth in gifts that is devoid of growth in grace, for it is accompanied by pride. "Knowledge puffs up, but loves builds up" (1 Corinthians 8:1).

Application 6. There are three infallible signs of growth in grace: growing spiritually, becoming more judicious, and growing in humility.

Application 7. Growth is the special fruit of divine grace. God gives the increase (see 1 Corinthians 3:6). Plants thrive better by the dew of heaven than when they are watered by hand. Grace is needed in everything we do.

Application 8. Let us be earnest with God for this increase. You honor God when you ask for more. Desire to have more, for God can give you more. When a person is content with a little, it is a sign of a hardening of the heart.

Verse 3

Commentary on Verse 3

Dear friends, although I was very eager to write to you about the salvation we share, I felt I had to write and urge you to contend for the faith that was once for all entrusted to the saints.

After the apostle has given his greeting, he starts on the body of his letter. This verse is the preface to the whole letter, in which he proposes two things:

First, the occasion of his writing.

Second, the theme of the letter.

The occasion of the writing of this letter divides into his earnestness in desiring their welfare—**Dear friends, although I was very eager to write to you about the salvation we share**—and the urgency of the present necessity—**I felt I had to write and urge you to contend for the faith.**

In assigning his earnestness and zeal for their good, you may note three things, which I will explain in order.

First, notice what he calls these people: **dear friends**. This term was often used in the apostles' writings. The same word was used in 1 Peter 2:11. It conveys not only the affection we naturally have for one another (see Romans 13:8), and not just the love we are bound to return to those who love us (see Matthew 5:46), but that special love that we owe to those who are with us in Christ, which is always expressed as *agape* in Scripture.

The second reason for Jude's writing testifies to his great love and care for his readers: **Although I was very eager to write to you.** He speaks as if nothing else mattered to him but their spiritual welfare and how he could help their faith. When he adds **to write to you**, this also shows his concern for them. He writes to them even though he was separated from them, even though he could not speak to them.

The third reason he gives to show his readiness to help them, which is also the subject he wants to write to them about, is **the salvation we share**.

I have commented on the first part of the reason why this letter was written, Jude's earnestness in wishing to promote his readers' good. I now come to the second reason for the writing of this letter: the urgency of the prevailing circumstances. **I felt I had to write and urge you.** This shows that this letter was not only written out of the strength of Jude's own love for them but because of the present situation in which they stood. The school of Simon, the Gnostics, and some other heretics were trying to cut them off from the truth, and that is what Jude is referring to. This meant that action had to be taken at once, as is clear from the next verse. Exhortations were needed, and Jude provided them.

Jude clearly states the theme of his letter: **to . . . urge you to contend for the faith that was once for all entrusted to the saints.** The verb in the Greek means to "contend earnestly." The object of all this effort is **for the faith that was once for all entrusted to the saints.** The word **faith** may be taken either for the teaching of faith or for the grace of faith. Both are too good to be lost—either the Word that we believe or the faith by which we believe. The former is intended. **Faith** here means sound teaching that is to be absorbed and believed for salvation, which Jude insists they must contend for, so that they may preserve it safe and sound for future generations.

This faith is described, first, by how it is conveyed. It was **entrusted** to them. It was given to them so that they might keep it. It is not an invention they made up, but something they were given. It is not discovered by us but is entrusted to us by God himself and given to us so we will keep it safely for posterity. It is like the oracles of God in the Old Testament that were given by God to the Jews for safe keeping (see Romans 3:2). Second, the moment in history when this faith was given is mentioned. It was given **once,** and it will never be altered or changed. It was given **once for all.** Third, the apostle mentions to whom this faith was given: **to the saints.** Jude calls the members of the church by a title that is commonly used in Scripture.

Notes on Verse 3

Note 1. **Dear friends.** From this we note that Christians should love each other. I give three reasons for this.

1. There are no better grounds for loving one another than that they are members of the same body (see 1 Corinthians 12). They are brothers born in the same womb, living in the same family. Surely no division could occur in the same body. Who would use an arm to cut off a leg, or a hand to scratch out the eyes? They are members of each other. This is the relationship in which Christ has placed us. He has not only called us into a family but into a body (see Colossians 3:15).

"There is one body and one Spirit—just as you were called to one hope when you were called—one Lord, one faith, one baptism; one God and Father of all, who is over all and through all and in all" (Ephesians 4:4-6). First of all there is "one body." People who suck out all the nourishment for themselves are not members of this body. Again, if one member lacks something or is out of joint, the whole body suffers. Next we are told there is "one Spirit." Friends speak as if they lived by one common soul, but here is the reality of this. All believers have the same Spirit. What is able to divide us if we have the same Spirit? We also have "one hope." Cannot the earth contain those who expect to live in the same heaven? Luther, Cranmer, Hooper, Ridley, and Saunders will all be together in heaven. In other relationships there may be many divisions because they have different aspirations that often conflict with each other. But here you have one heaven and one hope. There may be a difference in the degree of glory, but nothing that anyone can be proud of or envious about. How will bitter spirits look on each other when they meet in glory? Then comes "one Lord." We are in the same family. How will you look God in the face if you "begin to beat his [God's] fellow servants" (Matthew 24:49)?

Then comes "one faith." There may be different understandings, but the faith is the same. All should agree about the essentials of the faith. The enemies of the church, though divided in interests and opinions, yet, because they agree in their common hatred of the saints, work together. Gebal, Ammon, Amalek, the men of Tyre, and others all conspired against Israel (see Psalm 83). They were like Samson's foxes. Although they faced in different directions, their tails were tied together, and they ran together and set fire to the cornfields. Should not God's people agree with each other since all profess the same faith? The next consideration is "one baptism"—that is, one badge of profession. Jacob's sons were divided because only one son had a coat of diverse colors, a special token of affection. But no one has a special and privileged call from heaven that makes him or her superior to the rest of the brethren.

Lastly, we have "one God and Father of all." We all worship the same God. Nothing divides people so much as having different objects of worship. It is extremely provocative for one person to scorn what another adores. That was the plea made to Joseph: "I ask you to forgive your brothers the sins and the wrongs they committed in treating you so badly" (Genesis 50:17). Thus we see that we have better grounds for love than others have.

2. Nobody can have a higher motive than the love of Christ. "Live a life of love, just as Christ loved us" (Ephesians 5:2). The pagan world never understood this motive. None are affected with Christ's love except those who have an interest in it. Therefore Christ expects more love from Christians than from others. "If you love those who love you, what reward will you get? Are not even the tax collectors doing that?"

(Matthew 5:46). Tax collectors were thought of as the most vile people of all in society, the most unworthy men of their age. But a tax collector loved a fellow tax collector. Therefore, a Christian who is acquainted with Christ's love for strangers and for enemies should take care that he loves in an excellent and pure way. The world is not familiar with Christ's love and therefore only loves its own, but we are acquainted with it, and therefore we should love others. "As I have loved you, so you must love one another" (John 13:34). Jesus Christ came from heaven not only to repair and preserve the notions of the Godhead by the greatness of his sufferings, but to give us a more exact pattern of love and to instill this love between man and man.

3. Nobody has a greater charge. Christ calls it his "new commandment" (John 13:34). "A new commandment I give you: Love one another." Why is this "new" since it was as old as the moral law or the law of nature? The answer is that it is called "new" because it is excellent, like a new song, or rather because it was solemnly and especially renewed by him and commended to their care, for new things and new laws are much esteemed and prized, or enforced by a new reason and the example of his own death. "And this is his command: to believe in the name of his Son, Jesus Christ, and to love one another as he commanded us" (1 John 3:23). It is made equal with faith. All the Scriptures aim at "faith and love." Christ's dying charge, the great charge he left shortly before his death, was, "This is my command: Love each other" (John 15:17). Speeches of dying people are held in high honor, and especially the charge of dying friends. Joseph's brothers, fearing that he might remember the injuries they had previously inflicted on him, made use of this plea: "Your father left these instructions before he died . . ." (Genesis 50:16). Let us fulfill the will of the dead. When Christ took leave of his disciples, he left this as his last charge. Shall I slight his last commandment, his dying charge? It should be the distinguishing characteristic of Christ's disciples. "All men will know that you are my disciples if you love one another" (John 13:35).

Application. Christ's love encourages us to love. Why should those who are going to meet in the same heaven be estranged from each other? Certainly such a thing comes from the evil one. About two things God's people can agree easily enough—about glory then and about misery now. Ridley and Hooper did this in a prison. May we work for love and for meekness. I will give you a few pointers about this.

1. Honor the least manifestation of Christ's love wherever you find it. If anyone is to despise others for their meanness, it would be more proper for God to do so than for any man. But God will not despise "a smoldering wick" (Matthew 12:20). You do not know what spark of glory and divine nature may lie hidden under smoke or the covering of darkness. Christ loved the young man who only had some understanding about

God: "Jesus looked at him and loved him" (Mark 10:21). How much more should you show love toward others when you find any weak appearances of Christ, even if they do not come up to your standards.

2. Do not let differences of opinion divide you. It would be good if believers were of one heart and mind about everything; but if they differ, may they cherish others for what they have that is of God. In a great organ the pipes are different in size, but this makes the harmony and melody sweeter. Many people love to speak of religion as if there were nothing of God to be found except in their own sphere. It is natural to do this. We want to be unique, gaining a reputation for piety, orthodoxy, and right worship.

3. Beware of allowing love to degenerate into compliance. There is "the unity of the Spirit" (Ephesians 4:3), and there is being "yoked together with unbelievers" (2 Corinthians 6:14). There are cords of love, and there is a chain of antichristian interests, and you must be careful to make a distinction between the two. There are evil alliances that are not of God, which you must be aware of in case you join other people, depart from God, and turn love into compliance. The image crumbled to pieces when the toes were a mixture of iron and clay (see Daniel 2). Love may forbear the profession of some truths—there is a valid time for private faith—but it must not give in to error.

4. Some people are so vile that they will hardly come within the circle of Christians. These people are the open enemies of Christ and seek to destroy the foundations of religion. "If anyone comes to you and does not bring this teaching, do not take him into your house or welcome him" (2 John 10). Vile wretches must know that the church is completely opposed to their practices. Elisha would not have looked on Jehoram had it not been for Jehoshaphat (see 2 Kings 3:14). When people rage against Christians and are directly opposed to Christ's ways or run into damnable errors, it is a wrong compliance to countenance them in any way.

Note 2. **I was very eager.** From these words note that it is not enough to do good, but we must do good with work and care and diligence. "Our people must learn to devote themselves to doing what is good" (Titus 3:14). It is not enough to admonish one another, for we must consider and study one another's characters so that we may offer Christian fellowship in the most useful way. So we read in Romans, "Be careful to do what is right in the sight of everybody" (12:17). So for ministers, it not enough to emphasize what they are most well versed in or what just comes to hand, but to study what will be most conducive to the ends of their ministry. "Do your best to present yourself to God as one approved, a workman who does not need to be ashamed and who correctly handles the word of truth" (2 Timothy 2:15). Measure your Christian attitude to other people by that yardstick. The spirit is most pure not only when you do good, but when you do it with care and diligence. Wicked people may stumble on good, but they do not study to do good. Natural spirits may be moved to pray, but they are not alert and do not keep on praying (see Ephesians 6:18). That is, they do not take care to keep their hearts awake and to pray about the present necessities. Many people may do what is useful for the church, but they do not watch out for opportunities to serve and make it their aim to be of service whenever they can.

Again, do not be so carried away by the world that you are unable to do good deeds. "So I will very gladly spend for you everything I have and expend myself as well" (2 Corinthians 12:15). We cannot spend our time in any better employment. So we must give out light, even if we burn down to the socket or, like silkworms, die in our work. "But even if I am being poured out like a drink offering on the sacrifice and service coming from your faith, I am glad and rejoice with all of you" (Philippians 2:17). Taking the greatest pains and care, even if it is to our own personal detriment, should not displease a generous heart. Certainly this expression, **I was very eager**, is one that will shame us. Jude sought opportunities to serve Christ, but we often fail to use those opportunities for service that are presented to us. Love will make us search out and devise ways of doing good.

Note 3. **To write to you.**

1. Jude expressed his love in a letter when he was unable to pay a visit. Holy men take every opportunity to do good. Whether they are present or absent, they still have the saints on their minds and write to them when they are unable to speak to them. Ambrose alludes to Zechariah, who wrote when he was struck dumb. Many people would have used Jude's readers' absence as a reasonable excuse not to bother anymore, as if they had providentially been told to take their ease. Yet godly people would not be satisfied with behaving in such a way but would use every means at their disposal to promote others' spiritual welfare. A willing mind will never lack opportunity to do good, and those who have a heart to do good are certain to find an occasion to express their concern.

2. Writing is a great help in promoting salvation. In this way we speak to people who are absent as well as to posterity. In this way the oracles of God are recorded publicly and are preserved without the danger of corruption that they would run if they were left to the uncertainty of verbal tradition. Writing also enables errors to be publicly refuted and is a testimony against them passed on to future generations. Speech is transient, but writing remains. So Christ tells his apostles that they should "go and bear fruit—fruit that will last" (John 15:16). Apostolic teaching that has been committed to writing remains as a constant rule of faith and a guide to godly behavior. The public expositions of the church, recorded in writing, enable us to understand the dispensations of God in every age. They tell us what kind of light they enjoyed, how God's truths were opposed,

and how the church overcame such attacks. Finally, through writing the streams of salvation are conveyed to every family, just as a public water supply is conveyed to all through pipes. Where there is poor public preaching, people are able to turn to the written word for instruction. Writing is used by the church to refute error in a public and lasting way. It is a public monument of concern for the truth.

The Earl of Derby accused Bradford of doing more harm through his writing than through his preaching. Hezekiah's servants were commended for copying out the proverbs of Solomon: "These are more proverbs of Solomon, copied by the men of Hezekiah king of Judah" (Proverbs 25:1). People who engage in such service deserve to be commended and cherished, not censured. I confess that there is no end of books. Pride and ambition may make many people write books, and they should be discouraged from doing this. But writing is a more public way of teaching, though people should not engage in it without a call from God. Jerome has good advice on this point: "Do not be too hasty to write; for what is prepared for public instruction needs to be prepared with great deliberation." The vestal virgins took ten years over their preparations, ten years in practicing their good deeds, and ten years in teaching other people. Great abuses take place when every aspiring teacher intrudes his ideas on the world. But if this abuse is removed, writing can be very beneficial to the church, so that people may be provided with books of substance in every age. Controversial teaching is hard to assess in public debate but can be mulled over to our benefit if it is written down. Tertullian wrote his treatise against the Jews in case the uproar caused by public debate should eclipse the truth.

Note 4. **The salvation we share**. The apostles, in their private and personal letters, were very spiritual. When they wrote about ordinary matters, as in Paul's letter to Philemon, they were still prepared to pass on spiritual lessons in their writing. Those letters should be welcomed by us.

But what is this **salvation we share**? I suppose it means the salvation that Jude and his readers and all the saints were concerned about. This expression may possibly be thought of as being an indication of the apostle's meekness. Although he was an apostle, and his readers were not, yet he and they had a common salvation. Captains may endear themselves to their troops by saying, "Fellow soldiers" since they are engaged in one common war. But the phrase may also point to Jude's concern about his readers' salvation, which he would care about, as well as his own salvation. The saints carry a joint calling to heaven. They are all partners, and salvation is common to them all. Since Jude had a faith and salvation just as they did, he was willing to write to them in order to establish them in the truth.

The salvation of God's people is common to all believers.

1. They are all chosen by the same grace. There is no special reason why

Paul should obtain mercy rather than John and Andrew and Thomas. Free grace is available to them all. There may be a difference in the creature, as John and Andrew may have a different disposition from Paul and Peter, but God's motives in choosing them are the same.

2. They have the same Christ. "Salvation is found in no one else, for there is no other name under heaven given to men by which we must be saved" (Acts 4:12). "Jesus Christ is the same yesterday and today and forever" (Hebrews 13:8). In all ages the church has been saved by Christ. None of God's holy followers had a more worthy Redeemer than we have. Christ gave the same ransom to purchase heaven for me and you and the others. Under the law the rich and the poor had to give the same ransom: "The rich are not to give more than a half shekel and the poor are not to give less when you make the offering to the LORD to atone for your lives" (Exodus 30:15). In the same way, the price of Christ's blood was equal for all souls.

3. You are justified by the same Righteous One as other people are. "This righteousness from God comes through faith in Jesus Christ to all who believe. There is no difference, for all have sinned and fall short of the glory of God, and are justified freely by his grace through the redemption that came by Christ Jesus" (Romans 3:22-24). In sanctification there are degrees, but in imputed righteousness all are equal. None of the saints has finer clothes than you. There is a difference in degrees of faith, which receives this righteousness, but there is no difference in the righteousness itself. A giant and a strong man can hold a jewel, but so can a child. The jewel is the same. A strong man may hold it in his hand, but the jewel does not become less valuable in the hand of a child. So here the righteousness is the same, while faith may not be the same.

4. As we have the same privileges, so we all have to follow the same way. Each person has to do this by faith, and the faith of the weakest person is just as acceptable to God as the faith of the strongest. "Simon Peter, a servant and apostle of Jesus Christ, To those who through the righteousness of our God and Savior Jesus Christ have received a faith as precious as ours" (2 Peter 1:1). This faith has the same nature and value for everyone, although not every man is an apostle.

5. They are all under the same rule and direction. "Peace and mercy be to all who follow this rule, even to the Israel of God" (Galatians 6:16). The paths of error are numerous, but there is only one path that leads to heaven.

6. They are all in one mystical body, ministering to one another. "He has lost connection with the Head, from whom the whole body, supported and held together by its ligaments and sinews, grows as God causes it to grow" (Colossians 2:19). The head is the fountain of all vital influence, but the joints minister and convey the food to different parts of the body.

The whole body is still making progress and growing up to perfection, and as members of the same body they are helping one another continue in fellowship with the same Spirit or by the continuity of the parts make way for the quickening of the soul.

Application 1. It shows care for others if we promote salvation both in ourselves and in others. We should rejoice over other people's faith as well as over our own. ". . . that you and I may be mutually encouraged by each other's faith" (Romans 1:12). Paul's faith was a comfort to the Christians at Rome, and their faith comforted Paul. Out of overflowing love and charity Paul also said, "For I could wish that I myself were cursed and cut off from Christ for the sake of my brothers, those of my own race, the people of Israel" (Romans 9:3-4).

Application 2. This shows how inappropriate it was for religion to be confined to a cloister or wrapped in a black garment or consigned to what was called a religious house. Oh, how far this was from the modesty of the apostles! Peter called the faith of ordinary Christians "a faith as precious as ours" (2 Peter 1:1), and Jude speaks of **the salvation we share**. The Jews who lived before them confined God's choice to their nation. They could not bear to hear about salvation among the Gentiles or of a righteousness that came to everyone and on all who believe. We are envious by nature and want to appropriate common favors to ourselves. The church of Rome seeks to bring the whole world under their law and confine truth and faith and salvation within the precincts of their churches. They seize the keys of heaven and open the gate to whomever they wish. Now God has broken down all enclosures that attempt to build up a new wall of separation. Corrupt human nature does not want other people to share the same privileges that we have. People value their lesser differences and the particular opinions they have taken up as if only those of their own party and persuasion could be saved; it is our nature to treat our own opinions as holy, and not to admit that anyone is good unless they agree with us in everything. There were divisions at Corinth. Even the people who said, "I follow Christ" made themselves into a faction (see 1 Corinthians 1:12). They arrogated Christ to themselves. So Paul the apostle writes to them and says, "To the church of God in Corinth, to those sanctified in Christ Jesus and called to be holy, together with all those everywhere who call on the name of our Lord Jesus Christ—their Lord and ours" (1 Corinthians 1:2). We are apt to be harsh toward those who differ from us and to be happy only with those who share our opinions. Beware of hurting your Christian brother. "Why do you look down on your brother?" (Romans 14:10). Since God has made him a Christian, why do you make nothing of him? And why do you make another religion out of all your private opinions as if nobody could be a saint or a believer unless they thought exactly as you do? Beware that you do not fence in the common salvation; enclosures are against the law.

Application 3. This shows that there are not several ways to heaven, as there is but one common salvation for all the elect and one common faith, as the apostle Paul says: "To Titus, my true son in our common faith" (Titus 1:4). There are some libertines who think a person may be saved in any religion, so long as he does not walk away from the light he has. Do not flatter yourselves. All the elect are brought to heaven in the same way, whether they are Jews or Gentiles, free men or slaves. There is a good, old way that if we miss, we are sure to perish. "Stand at the crossroads and look; ask for the ancient paths, ask where the good way is, and walk in it, and you will find rest for your souls" (Jeremiah 6:16).

Application 4. This tells us who are the best people to deal with in matters of religion. Those who are truly religious can call it a common salvation—that is, common to them along with others. They have a share in it and so are the best people to defend it. Differences are aggravated when worldly people meddle in religious controversies. The people who are most likely to show the most zeal and love are those who can say that your salvation is their salvation. So in the next verse we read that they **change the grace of our God into a license for immorality** (verse 4). Those who have an interest in grace cannot bear to see it abused.

7. This **salvation we share** stops us from being scornful of the lowest Christians. They have as good a hope through grace as you have in Jesus Christ; all are one—master and servant, rich and poor. Onesimus, a poor slave on the run, once he was converted, was called by Paul "my son" (Philemon 10) and "a dear brother" (Philemon 16). There are differences in earthly relationships, but insofar as our common faith and common salvation are concerned, we are all one.

Note 5. **I felt I had to write and urge you.**

1. Observe from this that necessity is a time for duty, necessity is God's season to work, and therefore it should be ours as well. "In this you greatly rejoice, though now for a little while you may have had to suffer grief in all kinds of trials" (1 Peter 1:6). Duties are best carried out when we see that they are necessary. Things that do not matter are done halfheartedly. The creatures' duty toward God begins with a sense of their own needs. "If any of you lacks wisdom, he should ask God" (James 1:5). Take this hint for prayer and for other services. If there is a need, do not forget to call on God. When David was troubled by his conscience, he could not find peace until he had confessed his sins to God: "For day and night your hand was heavy upon me; my strength was sapped as in the heat of summer. Then I acknowledged my sin to you and did not cover up my iniquity. I said, 'I will confess my transgressions to the LORD'—and you forgave the guilt of my sin" (Psalm 32:4-5). Silence will cause roaring,

and a restraint on prayer produces anxiety. Again, if there is a need, do not forget to call on men by exhortation and counsel, especially when you see things daily deteriorate and can cope with them no longer. Paul "was greatly distressed to see that the city was full of idols" (Acts 17:16). When we see crowds of people falling into error and traveling along paths that lead to destruction, is that not the time to speak up? Men may say we are bitter, but we must be faithful. They also say the doctor is cruel when they are seriously ill. Can we see another perish and remain quiet?

2. Note again that ministers must concentrate on those doctrines that are most needed. It is only a cheap zeal that focuses on yesterday's errors that are no longer believed. We are to consider what the present age needs. What use was it in Christ's day to mention the rebellions of Korah, Dathan, and Abiram without citing current rebellions? Or why should we now go into the causes of Henry VIII's divorce but not issue exhortations about present behavior? What benefit would that be to our present congregations? Usually when we reflect on the guilt of our times, people want us to preach general doctrines of faith and repentance. But we may answer, "It is necessary for us to exhort you in this way." What is the purpose of arguing about the truth of the Christian religion against pagans when you have so many people trying to bring in corrupt ways among yourselves? In a country audience what is the point of speaking against the Socinians when there are drunks and atheists in need of other teaching? Only God can teach us the difficult skill of delivering what is necessary at a particular time.

3. Again observe that the need of the early church brought about the complete canon and the rule of faith. We are indebted in part to the seducers of that age for the Scriptures' being so full. We would be without many letters if it had not been for them. Thus God can bring light out of darkness and through errors can make way for the discovery of truth.

Note 6. **I . . . urge you to contend for the faith that was once for all entrusted to the saints.** This faith is said to have been **entrusted.** Observe that faith is a gift. "For it has been granted to you on behalf of Christ not only to believe on him . . ." (Philippians 1:29). "For it is by grace that you have been saved, through faith—and this not from yourselves, it is the gift of God" (Ephesians 2:8). We cannot obtain grace by ourselves. It is easy to just think about Christ's death, but to bring the soul and Christ together needs the power of God: ". . . his incomparable great power for us who believe . . . his mighty strength" (Ephesians 1:19). We cannot merit this, so it is a gift. God bestows it on those who can give nothing for it. Deeds done before conversion do not convince God, and good deeds done after conversion do not in themselves satisfy God. So let us thank God for his mercy in the covenant of grace. Christ too is a gift: "If you knew the gift of God . . ." (John 4:10). His righteousness also is a gift: "Again, the gift of

God is not like the result of the one man's sin" (Romans 5:16). And faith, which receives this righteousness, is a gift, so that everything is received by grace. This teaches us where to go for faith—we must seek it from God, as his gift. All the efforts of a creature will never achieve it.

But are we not meant to use the means of grace, such as prayer and meditation and listening? I answer, yes.

1. God gives faith through the means of grace. "With the measure you use, it will be measured to you—and even more" (Mark 4:24). According to the measure of our hearing, if the Lord is going to work in us, is the measure of our faith. "The Lord opened her [Lydia's] heart to respond to Paul's message" (Acts 16:14). God stirs us up to receive the means of grace, and as we are taught about salvation we are drawn to God. "No one can come to me unless the Father who sent me draws him, and I will raise him up at the last day. It is written in the Prophets: 'They will all be taught by God'" (John 6:44-45).

2. Although faith is God's gift, human endeavors are still necessary, for supernatural grace does not exclude the ordinary and natural graces. Faith is planted in us by God; so we should be very careful how we use the means of grace.

Note 7. This faith is said to have been **once for all entrusted** to believers. This also applies to grace, for where grace has been planted, it cannot be finally and totally destroyed. Rather, it is continually fed by the care and faithfulness of God. "He will keep you strong to the end, so that you will be blameless on the day of our Lord Jesus Christ" (1 Corinthians 1:8). "The one who calls you is faithful and he will do it" (1 Thessalonians 5:24). "He who began a good work in you will carry it on to completion until the day of Christ Jesus" (Philippians 1:6). And hypocrites who fall away after professing for a long time that they were Christians are seldom "brought back to repentance" (Hebrews 6:6; see also 2 Peter 2:21). Here is comfort for God's people, who are attacked by so many evil desires and temptations. They think they cannot withstand such onslaughts. But they have been given faith, and where it has genuinely been given, there is no need for a second gift. This is a warning for us. Faith is a precious jewel. If it is deliberately neglected, it is not easily regained.

Consider the people to whom it is given. "Not everyone has faith" (2 Thessalonians 3:2). "And even if our gospel is veiled, it is veiled to those who are perishing" (2 Corinthians 4:3). Faith is given to the saints, to those who are chosen, so that they may be saints who show the excellency of faith, which is a special mercy. Believers through faith have an interest in Christ and therefore must be made holy. Christ's blood cleanses us (see 1 John 1:7), and his blood sanctifies us (see 1 Corinthians 6:11). Faith itself has a cleansing and purifying characteristic: "he purified their hearts by faith" (Acts 15:9). Faith applies the blood of Christ to us. The hand of the person washing our clothes is as important in making the clothes clean as the soap that does the actual cleaning. Faith waits for the Spirit. Faith comes from God's love. Faith and sin are like the poison and the antidote, which always work on each other, until faith gains the upper hand. So then, is your faith sanctifying? Strong convictions about grace and a loose life will not do. We may not be completely clean and holy, but we should wholeheartedly desire to be more holy. "Create in me a pure heart, O God, and renew a steadfast spirit within me" (Psalm 51:10). "What a wretched man I am! Who will rescue me from this body of death?" (Romans 7:24). "Oh, that my ways were steadfast in obeying your decrees" (Psalm 119:5). In addition to groans, there will be struggles against sin. A child of God may fall into sin but cannot rest in it and lie down in it with a clear conscience. Peter and David both fell, but they had no peace until they were reconciled to God. You may know this through the general disposition of your own heart. What does your heart incline toward? "My heart is set on keeping your decrees to the very end" (Psalm 119:112). Is your heart inclined constantly toward God? "Now devote your heart and soul to seeking the LORD your God" (1 Chronicles 22:19). Is your heart devoted in this way?

Note 8. **To the saints.** This may refer to the apostles, to whom was delivered the responsibility of spreading this faith. Or it may refer to the church, to whom this faith was delivered, and whose members are called saints. Note that saints are devoted to acknowledging, spreading, and defending the truth. The Christian faith was delivered *to* saints and *by* saints, and no one receives it so willingly, defends it more zealously, and keeps it so faithfully as they do.

1. The men whom God's Spirit used to write down the Scriptures were holy people. "For prophecy never had its origin in the will of man, but men spoke from God as they were carried along by the Holy Spirit" (2 Peter 1:21). ". . . which was not made known to men in other generations as it has now been revealed by the Spirit to God's holy apostles and prophets" (Ephesians 3:5). These men were the most suitable instruments to bring to birth an external witness to the Word. Surely they would not do anything for themselves or pass on their own thoughts about the world as if they were the oracles of God.

2. Only holy people should preach the faith—*sancta sanctis*, holy men for holy things. It is a holy faith, and it must be managed by holy people. "Depart, depart, go out from there! Touch no unclean thing! Come out from it and be pure, you who carry the vessels of the LORD" (Isaiah 52:11). The people who carried the vessels and utensils of the temple from Babylon were ordered to be clean. God purified Isaiah when he sent him to reprove the people of Israel: "With it [a live coal] he touched my mouth and said, 'See, this has touched your lips; your guilt is taken away and

your sin atoned for'" (Isaiah 6:7). The priests who served before the Lord had to wash in the great bronze basin (see Exodus 30:18-21). Regeneration is the best preparation for the ministry. The Levites cleansed themselves first, and then they cleansed the people (Nehemiah 12:30). Ministers' lives can build up or destroy people's faith. People notice the way God's servants live their lives.

3. Only holy people are fit to defend the Gospel publicly. They speak with power, from the heart and inner experience. Worldly people stir up trouble and exacerbate differences between Christians. The saints contend best for the saints' faith: "For we cannot do anything against the truth, but only for the truth" (2 Corinthians 13:8). Zeal in worldly people is like fire in straw; it catches fire quickly but goes out quickly. But zeal in godly people is like fire in wood—it burns for a long time.

4. Nobody receives the truth more readily than saints do. Holy people are the best people to understand what has been written down by holy people. God reveals himself to those who are close to him. "The Lord confides in those who fear him; he makes his covenant known to them" (Psalm 25:14). Holy hearts are not clouded with the mists of evil desires and selfish interests. Where there is purity, there is brightness. The mind that is separated from evil things is fit to receive spiritual mysteries. Paul saw God most clearly when he was blind to the world.

5. Nobody retains the truth so well as holy people. Manna was kept in a golden vessel, and truth is best kept in a pure soul. "They must keep hold of the deep truths of the faith with a clear conscience" (1 Timothy 3:9). Truth does not blunt the mind but sharpens it. Those who lack grace have the worst spiritual insight. "But if anybody does not have them [faith, goodness, knowledge, self-control, perseverance, godliness, brotherly kindness, and love—verses 5-7], he is nearsighted and blind, and has forgotten that he has been cleansed from his past sins" (2 Peter 1:9). An unclean cup pollutes any liquid that is poured into it, and a worldly heart perverts the faith.

Verse 4

Commentary on Verse 4

For certain men whose condemnation was written about long ago have secretly slipped in among you. They are godless men, who change the grace of our God into a license for immorality and deny Jesus Christ our only Sovereign and Lord.

Jude has made his way into his readers' affection with his greeting. In this greeting, like the greetings of the other apostles, he prays for their spiritual welfare. In verse 3 Jude had exhorted them to defend the truth. Now Jude gives his reason for giving this exhortation. It is on account of false teachers who had cunningly called themselves Christians. Since Jude was faithful to the Gospel, he had to warn them of the danger his readers were in. This whole letter is given over to describing these heretics, and their sins and the punishment that waited for them. They are described in four ways in this verse. First, by the way they entered the church: they **secretly slipped in among you**. Second, by their condition before God: **men whose condemnation was written about long ago**. Third, by the disposition of their spirits: **who change the grace of our God into a license for immorality**. Fourth, by denying the nature of and work of Jesus Christ: **deny Jesus Christ our only Sovereign and Lord**.

First, let us start with the description of their entry into the church. This was done **secretly**. They **slipped in among you**. Some people say these people are not mentioned by name because they were such unworthy people, or rather that it was unnecessary since they are described so clearly. This was the normal practice of the apostles, who spoke more against doctrines than against people in order to suppress the sin.

Second, these seducers are described by their state before God—**whose condemnation was written about long ago**—that is from all eternity. *Progegrammenoi* (**written**) some translate as "before ordained," but the word means "written as in a book." It is usual in Scripture to compare God's decrees to a book. Christ said, referring to God's decree for his world mission, "To do your will, O my God, is my desire; your law is within [that is, written in] my heart" (Psalm 40:8). This metaphor shows that these decrees are as certain and definite as if they had been written down in a book. These men's condemnation was said to be **written about long ago** to show that although they crept in unawares into the church, they were not unknown to God. They came to his notice before they infiltrated any church with their evil. It is also said that they were written down in God's book for judgment: **whose condemnation was written about long ago.** The meaning of this section of the verse is that these people will bring just condemnation on themselves because of their own sins and errors.

Third, we come to the part of the description that says, **they are godless men.** The word **godless** means "without worship." It is sometimes used of pagans and people who live without the knowledge of the true God and so do not worship him. At other times this word is used of wicked people who may acknowledge the true God but live their lives as if they did not possess this knowledge. In order that we may find out who these men are, let us see what the nature of ungodliness is. Ungodliness is a sin that is often spoken about, but few people know what it means. The word, as I just said, means "without worship." Worship is the chief important activity for people to be engaged in. In worship a created person shows his respect for God. In this sense it stands for the whole subjection and obedience that we owe God, and when any part of that service, respect, or honor is denied or withheld, we are guilty of ungodliness.

That pagans and men outside the church are said to be **godless** is also taught by Peter. "For it is time for judgment to begin with the family of God; and if it begins with us, what will the outcome be for those who do not obey the gospel of God?" (1 Peter 4:17). The unjustified state is described as a godless state. The apostle Paul, when he refers to Abraham and David being justified, states that the Lord is the One who justifies. "However, to the man who does not work but trusts God who justifies the wicked, his faith is credited as righteousness" (Romans 4:5). This expression is used because the Jews were divided into three kinds of people. There were the ungodly, the just, and the good. Or to use their own terminology, there were *reshagnim*, the wicked or violent; the *tsidikim*, the just; and the *chasidim*, the good or the bountiful. Now, says the apostle Paul, one would hardly die for a righteous man (see Romans 5:7), that is, for a man of rigid innocency; but for the good man, that is, the bountiful, the useful, a man would even dare to die. But Christ died for us when we were *reshagnim*, sinners and God's enemies.

Godlessness also implies breaking the law from the first table of commandments. "The wrath of God is being revealed from heaven against all the godlessness and wickedness of men who suppress the truth by their wickedness" (Romans 1:18). Here all sin is spoken of as being "godlessness" or "wickedness." It is godless in its duty toward God and wicked in its duty toward men. "The grace of God . . . teaches us to say, 'No' to ungodliness and worldly passions" (Titus 2:11-12). Here sin is spoken of as "ungodliness," and "worldly passions." In this sense sin may be described as not giving God his right and due honor, as the first commandment lays down.

Fourth, the next clause in the text describes seducers as those **who change the grace of our God into a license for immorality**. I will now mention four things about this.

1. First, there is their dirty and brutish way of living, which is implied by the words **a license for immorality**. In the Greek the word for **immorality** is *aselgeian*. It is the word used to denote luxury and the impurities of lust. It is derived from *alpha*, an augmentative particle, and *Selga*, the name of a town in Pisidia, according to Suidas. The people who lived in Pisidia were notorious for sodomy and other unnatural acts that cannot be mentioned in Christian company. Those people followed the school of Simon. The Nicolaitans, the Gnostics, and other impure heretics of that age indulged in all kinds of promiscuity with other people, as some people in our own age are indulging in. They had no respect for marriage and behaved like wild animals giving themselves over to all kinds of unnatural lusts, which we will mention later on.

2. Second, we touch on the occasion and encouragement of this immorality, which has to do with **the grace of our God**. "For the grace of God that brings salvation has appeared to all men" (Titus 2:11). The part of the Gospel these people abused was the teaching about Christian freedom and Christ's free justification of us. You may by analogy extend these words to include all of the teachings of the libertines.

3. God's grace was abused by these people. It is difficult to imagine that things that are so far from God's grace should be mentioned in the same breath as God's grace. This is clear from the word **change**. These are **godless men, who change the grace of our God** . . . The Greek word used here for **change** is *metatithentes*, which indicates that something is transferred away from its original purpose. They violated the teaching of grace in order to justify their filthy lusts and worldly pleasures.

4. You have a hint about the reason the apostle writes against these people with such zealous indignation in the word **our**. Note: **. . . who change the grace of our God**. It is as if he were saying, "That grace whose sweetness *we* have tasted, whose power *we* have felt, the grace of that God who has been so kind to *us* in Christ, whose glory *we* are bound to promote—shall we see *our* God, and that grace on which all our hopes stand, be abused in such an unclean way?"

I come now to the last part of their description. **They . . . deny Jesus Christ our only Sovereign and Lord**. Observe their sin: **they deny**. Note the object of their denial: **Jesus Christ**.

Deny. This is done either openly or secretly. It is done openly when Christ is clearly renounced and opposed; and it is done secretly when Christ is denied either by the filthy conversation of Christians or by heretical insinuations that attack his person and nature from a distance. Both are meant here. Although they denied Christ, they pretended not to. This Christ whom they denied is described by his relation in the world: the **only Sovereign** or ruler. He is also described as **our . . . Lord.** Jude says **our** partly to show that this was the title Christ bore in relation to the church, they being his special people by his Father's gift and his own purchase; and partly to awaken their zeal by a consideration of the interest they had in this Lord thus denied. The word **Lord** applies to Christ's role as mediator. "For even if there are so-called gods, whether in heaven or on earth (as indeed there are many 'gods' and many 'lords'), yet for us there is but one God, the Father, from whom all things came and for whom we live; and there is but one Lord, Jesus Christ, through whom all things came and through whom we live" (1 Corinthians 8:5-6).

We must discuss also the name **Jesus Christ.** The word **Jesus** is explained by Matthew: "You are to give him the name Jesus, because he will save his people from their sins" (Matthew 1:21). It implies that Christ's lordship will be used for the salvation of the church. The other word, **Christ**, means "anointed," which indicated his designation from God to be king, priest, and prophet. I mention the meaning of these names because I believe the apostle wanted to give his readers a summary of the Christian doctrine concerning the person, natures, and offices of Jesus Christ, all of which were one way or another impugned by the seducers of that age.

Notes on Verse 4

Note 1. **Secretly slipped in among you.** What does this mean?

1. It may imply that they came into the church in a kind of disguise. Wicked men are able to infiltrate the best churches. God permits this not just to harden them but to work in us through our troubles and trials. "This matter arose because some false brothers had infiltrated our ranks to spy on the freedom we have in Christ Jesus and to make us slaves" (Galatians 2:4). The opponents of Jerusalem said, "Let us help you build because, like you, we seek your God" (Ezra 4:2). But their intention was to hinder the work. Simon Magus managed to get himself baptized (see Acts 8), just as thieves try to gain access to a house so they can steal from it as soon as the owner has gone to sleep. From this you can learn that you must be more diligent about whom you allow to enter into your church

fellowship. No dangers are as great as those brought about by false brothers. We desire to fill a church with people, but we do not fill a house with thieves. Wicked people always make trouble. It is easy to fill a church by not exercising any discipline among people. The church loses its strength when it increases its breadth, just as a river does. Zeal sometimes decreases as the numbers increase. After wicked men have caused a great deal of trouble, we wish we had been more strict. In the Acts of the Apostles we read, "No one else dared join them, even though they were highly regarded by the people. Nevertheless, more and more men and women believed in the Lord and were added to their number" (Acts 5:13-14). This was said after Ananias and Sapphira suddenly died. That terrified the hypocrites but brought in more and more sound believers. "No one else dared join them" refers to people like Ananias and Sapphira, who were believers on the outside but had evil hearts. Others saw what God had done to that sinful couple, and they were frightened away. When a church is strict about its membership, hypocrites will not wish to join it, but sound believers will be eager to join.

What is the rule we should go by? Is it outward profession? My answer to this is that outward profession does give us a *general* indication about a person's state. We can judge people insofar as we are able to discern their hearts. These people entered the church by underhanded methods. If the church had known about them or was wary about them as they should have been, the harm they did might have been avoided. Bellarmine himself states that the intention of the church is only to gather believers into a body, and if it knows about the wicked and unbelieving, it would not admit them. If they are allowed in by mistake, the church can then oust them. It is good to be strict so that the church is spared the evils that allowing these people into the church always brings.

2. **Secretly slipped in among you** can note their intrusion or invasion in the office of preaching. False teachers usually arrive without being invited. They are prone to error because they are not called by God. Christ, when he was praying for a blessing on the apostles' work, said, "As you have sent me into the world, I have sent them into the world" (John 17:18). People who are not prepared to submit their gifts to public scrutiny should be regarded with suspicion. So ask yourself, how did these false teachers arrive? Did they creep in? Or were they solemnly admitted? When men are out of their place, they bring turmoil and not a blessing to the church.

3. The two previous interpretations may be allowed, but I prefer a third one. These false teachers creep into people's hearts and affections by plausible pretenses and insinuations, instilling their errors drop by drop before they are noticed. They pretend to be friends of truth and piety. I prefer this interpretation partly because Jude says they **secretly slipped in** among

them. No mention of any office or church is made. I also incline to this view because I do not think Jude's letter is just an abridgment of Peter's second letter. The similarities between the two letters are easily seen by comparing them with each other. Second Peter says, "But there were also false prophets among the people, just as there will be false teachers among you" (2:1). From this we observe that false teachers mask their erroneous teaching, so that we welcome it without realizing what we are doing. The apostle Paul speaks about the "cunning and craftiness of men in their deceitful scheming" (Ephesians 4:14). They engage in numerous deceptions, and I will just mention a few of them.

a. Sometimes they pretend they are stricter than everybody else. "Do not let anyone who delights in false humility and the worship of angels disqualify you for the prize. Such a person goes into great detail about what he has seen, and his unspiritual mind puffs him up with idle notions" (Colossians 2:18). Papists engage in rigorous observations and outward mortifications.

b. Special meekness. They pretend to be full of love and kindness, but they are really wolves. "Watch out for false prophets. They come to you in sheep's clothing, but inwardly they are ferocious wolves" (Matthew 7:15). Absalom stole people's hearts by using this trick.

c. A superior gospel. Paul warns against "turning to a different gospel" (Galatians 1:6) or turning to a "Jesus other than the Jesus we preached" (2 Corinthians 11:4). They were not to turn to any other gospel of their own making.

d. Self-denial. Some false teachers at Corinth tried to disgrace Paul. "And I will keep on doing what I am doing in order to cut the ground from under those who want an opportunity to be considered equal with us in the things they boast about" (2 Corinthians 11:12). They gloried in their own preaching.

e. Greater learning and new and superior ideas. "Timothy, guard what has been entrusted to your care. Turn away from godless chatter and the opposing ideas of what is falsely called knowledge" (1 Timothy 6:20).

Application 1. We cannot see the precise beginning of errors because they are brought in secretly. "This title was written on her forehead: MYSTERY . . ." (Revelation 17:5). A leak may not be discovered until the ship is about to sink. The origin of evil is like the source of the Nile—it is hidden and obscure.

Application 2. We see how odious this error is. It does not dare to array itself in its own colors, and it is ashamed to show its face. When Satan plans to instill his errors, he chooses the most subtle instruments. Satan made use of the serpent before he tempted Eve. "Now the serpent was more crafty than any of the wild animals the LORD God had made" (Genesis 3:1). The Lord chooses the plainest instruments. Truth is so appealing in itself that it does not need to be dressed up in different colors. "Now this is our boast: Our conscience testifies that we have conducted ourselves in the world, and especially in our relations with you, in the holiness and sincerity that are from God. We have done so not according to worldly wisdom but according to God's grace" (2 Corinthians 1:12).

Application 3. This tells us why those who are over you in the Lord insist on these things. It is because of "godly jealousy" (2 Corinthians 11:2). We must bark when we see a wolf, even when he is disguised in sheep's clothes. We only encourage him through our silence and negligence. "But while everyone was sleeping, his enemy came and sowed weeds among the wheat, and went away" (Matthew 13:25).

Application 4. This encourages you to be judicious and watchful. You need to have a sound faith so you can tell the difference between good and evil. "Solid food is for the mature, who by constant use have trained themselves to distinguish good from evil" (Hebrews 5:14). Credulity is soon abused. "A simple man believes anything, but a prudent man gives thought to his steps" (Proverbs 14:15). It takes a great deal of skill to be a thorough Christian. There is a great deal of sophistry and cunning all around us. If you follow the latest fashion, you are in danger of opposing God; and if you accept the received customs, you may be welcoming error. You need watchfulness and not just discernment. It is not a good idea to drink too freely from fountains that may be polluted. Do not let your affections control your judgments. We admire the person and his gifts, and we easily swallow his teaching. "Dear friends, do not believe every spirit, but test the spirits to see whether they are from God" (1 John 4:1). "Test everything" (1 Thessalonians 5:21). When there is counterfeit gold in circulation, we use a touchstone. Truth loses nothing by being tested; and you will lose nothing by testing truth, for your affections can then build on solid ground. No man is infallible. That is why everything must be tested.

Note 2. **For certain men whose condemnation was written about long ago.**

1. Divine decrees include people and not just people's actions. I mention this because many people say that God's decrees only apply to events and actions, but here we see that they apply to people as well. We have no reason to water this down when Scripture speaks about it so clearly.

2. Again, from **was written about**, observe that God has his books and registers, in which people, actions, and the eternal estates of all people are recorded. On judgment day these books will be opened. "And I saw the dead, great and small, standing before the throne, and books were opened. Another book was opened, which is the book of life. The dead were judged according to what they had done as recorded in the books" (Revelation 20:12). So it should be our great concern that our names are

written in "the book of life." There is no greater privilege than this. "Do not rejoice that the spirits submit to you, but rejoice that your names are written in heaven" (Luke 10:20). This is a word of warning to us, for everything we say is kept on record. "Then those who feared the LORD talked with each other, and the LORD listened and heard. A scroll of remembrance was written in his presence concerning those who feared the LORD and honored his name" (Malachi 3:16). Every thought we have had is also recorded. "Therefore judge nothing before the appointed time; wait till the Lord comes. He will bring to light what is hidden in darkness and will expose the motives of men's hearts" (1 Corinthians 4:5). All our actions are also recorded (see Jeremiah 17:1).

3. Again, notice that God does not act rashly about everything concerning the judgment of sinners but acts by foresight and preordination.

4. Also note that no one ever perverted God's truths except to their own loss. They were ordained to this judgment; that is, their sins brought this ruin on them. We toy with opinions but do not consider that damnation is the end of them. The way of truth is the way of life, and the way of error is the way of death.

5. Heresies and errors do not come about by chance but according to God's preordination and foreknowledge. There are two reasons for this. First, nothing can happen without God's will, and, second, nothing can happen that is against God's will.

a. Nothing can happen without God's will. "Are not two sparrows sold for a penny? Yet not one of them will fall to the ground apart from the will of your Father" (Matthew 10:29). If a sparrow cannot fall to the ground without the permission of our heavenly Father, that is, it cannot be taken and killed without God's allowing it, then nothing can be imagined that God did not foresee or that he could not have stopped. There is nothing that is too small for the Lord to know about; there is also nothing so evil that he cannot bring good out of it. If you take anything out of God's providential care, you weaken the creature's respect for God. If Satan is allowed to do just as he likes, with God reduced to being a mere spectator, then the devil-worship of the pagans would seem to be rational. Their custom was first of all to appease angry gods, in case those gods should hurt them, and then to invoke the more favorable circumstances.

b. Nothing can happen that is against God's will. If this were not the case, God would have made creatures that were beyond his control. Things may be against God's revealed will but not against his secret will, for that would make God impotent and weak. Things that are most against his revealed will fall into the category of being under the ordination of his secret will. So while men break God's commandments, they fulfill God's secret will. God's revealed will shows what *should* be done, his secret will what *will* be done. Briefly, the concurrence of God in and about the errors of men may be thought of in two ways. First, God denies grace and light, which might sanctify. God is no man's debtor, and he may do with his own according to his good pleasure. "Don't I have the right to do what I want with my own money? Or are you envious because I am generous?" (Matthew 20:15). God is not bound to give grace at all, and so his goodness is not affected if he passes over some people.

Second, God leaves enough difficulties in the world that men who are not satisfied may become hardened. "He [Jesus] told them, 'The secret of the kingdom of God has been given to you. But to those on the outside everything is said in parables so that, 'they may be ever seeing but never perceiving, and ever hearing but never understanding; otherwise they might turn and be forgiven!'" (Mark 4:11-12). This means they will be punished for their willful blindness and hardness. Corrupt nature stumbles at God's plainest ways. The Word is clear enough to those who have a mind to understand it, and yet so difficult for those who harden their hearts. The Lord himself says, "I will put obstacles before this people" (Jeremiah 6:21). This indicates that God will allow them to stumble over their own prejudices.

Third, God leaves them to follow the devices of their own hearts. God does not bend their wills or compel them to do anything against their wills. God does not infuse evil into them but simply allows them to follow the worldly bent of their corrupt ambitions. "Ephraim is joined to idols; leave him alone!" (Hosea 4:17). "Finally, a spirit came forward, stood before the LORD and said, 'I will lure him.' 'By what means?' the LORD asked. 'I will go out and be a lying spirit in the mouths of all his prophets,' he said. 'You will succeed in luring him,' said the Lord. 'Go and do it'" (1 Kings 22:21-22). "So I gave them over to their stubborn hearts to follow their own devices" (Psalm 81:12). God does not prevent them from being wicked. God even permits this, so that His wise counsels may be fulfilled.

Fourth, God orders this for good and so brings glory to his name. "But I have raised you up for this very purpose, that I might show you my power and that my name might be proclaimed in all the earth" (Exodus 9:16). Great shakings and tumults reveal God to the world. God not only advances his name and reveals the glory of his providence in protecting the church, but he makes the truths that are questioned shine even more strongly. And all this is done despite Satan's attacks. This is like a torch being waved in the wind so that it shines more brightly. In such times people should study and love the truth more; doctrines should be accepted on trust but also through sound conviction. "No doubt there have to be differences among you to show which of you have God's approval" (1 Corinthians 11:19). A strong wind separates the solid grace from the lighter chaff. This is a way to engage our dependence on God for knowledge and instruction. Christ's prophetic office would lie idle and useless if the chains of consent were not sometimes broken and different interpretations made by different people. A case in point is the difference the Jews and Samaritans had over the correct place for worship. The Samaritan woman asked Christ about this: "Our fathers worshiped on this mountain, but you Jews claim that the place where we must worship is Jerusalem" (John 4:20).

Again we see that God's enemies are rightly punished as a result of God's allowing error to occur. "But if anyone causes one of these little ones who believe in me to sin, it would be better for him to have a large millstone hung around his neck and to be drowned in the depths of the sea. Woe to the world because of the things that cause people to sin! Such things must come, but woe to the man through whom they come!" (Matthew 18:6-7). Note that Eli's sons "did not listen to their father's rebuke, for it was the LORD's will to put them to death" (1 Samuel 2:25). By their own voluntary sins God brings them to their just ruin and condemnation. God leaves them alone to wallow in their sins and to reject salvation.

Application 1. Here is comfort for those who take note of the affairs of Zion. All the confusion and troubles that are in the church are ordered by a wise God. He will bring some good out of them, some glory to his name, in which the saints can rejoice as if it was benefiting them. The church will derive some good from such occurrences. Have you not been strengthened in the truth? Have you not been forced back to a more frequent reliance on Christ, in whom are hidden all the treasures of wisdom and knowledge? Have you not seen more of God's providence displayed in these tumults?

Application 2. This keeps fear in check. It shows that everything is in the hands of a good God. As God tests you to see what you will do, so you must wait on God to see what he will do. In everything and through everyone God will complete his work at the right time.

Application 3. This shows the wickedness of those people who attempt to turn people into atheists by their erroneous teaching. When the church is split into so many factions, men deceive it as if there were no God and as if the whole Gospel were a fairy tale. It is for this reason that Christ prayed: "My prayer is . . . that all of them may be one, Father, just as you are in me and I am in you. May they also be in us so that the world may believe that you have sent me" (John 17:20-21). In this way they would not think Christ was an imposter. We usually find that in these situations we are haunted by thoughts of atheism. But there is little reason for this, as all these things were known about beforehand by God and predicted by God. "No doubt there have to be differences among you to show which of you have God's approval" (1 Corinthians 11:19). "You will hear of wars and rumors of wars, but see to it that you are not alarmed. Such things must happen, but the end is still to come" (Matthew 24:6). We never see so much of God and the beauty of discovered truth as when errors abound. In fact, if there were no errors we might think something was wrong. When all things run smoothly and when there is total agreement about everything and nothing is ever questioned, our strength is not tried. "And the words of the LORD are flawless, like silver refined in a furnace of clay, purified seven times" (Psalm 12:6).

Application 4. This is a basis for prayer in times of delusion. "Lord, this was ordained by you in wisdom. Let us discern your glory in it and through it more and more." The church argues that there was not only Pilate's malice and Herod's malice but God's hand in the crucifixion of Christ. "They did what your power and will had decided beforehand should happen" (Acts 4:28). *Lord, we know that your counsel is in it and that your counsel still brings about good.* God loves to be owned in every providence and to be entreated to fulfill his own decrees.

Application 5. This tells us how foolish it is to think that God does not see our every sin. Surely he sees them, for he foresaw them before they were committed, yes, from all eternity.

Note 3. **For certain men whose condemnation was written about long ago**. From all eternity some people were decreed to come into judgment or condemnation because of their sins. As this is one of the texts that theologians use to prove the general doctrine of reprobation, I shall now, first, open up this teaching; second, demonstrate its truth; third, vindicate it; and, fourth, apply it. In the first you will understand its nature, in the second you will see the reasons for believing it, in the third its righteousness, and in the fourth the benefit of this decree.

1. The nature of the teaching of reprobation.

a. It is an eternal decree. God's eternal acts are one with his essence and so are before all time. "For he chose us in him before the creation of the world" (Ephesians 1:4). In the same way unregenerate sinners were made reprobates. "Yet, before the twins were born or had done anything good or bad—in order that God's purpose in election might stand: not by works but by him who calls—she was told, 'The older will serve the younger.' Just as it is written: 'Jacob I loved, but Esau I hated'" (Romans 9:11-13). Election and reprobation are not things that belong to yesterday, that follow the acts of creation, but are from all eternity.

b. There is a decree and preordination, not only a mere foresight about those who perish. Some Lutherans say it is right to apply predestination to the elect, but as far as the reprobate are concerned there is only foreknowledge. They say there is no preordination in the case of the latter as this would make God the author of the creatures' sin and ruin. But these men fear where there is nothing to be frightened of. The Scriptures show that the greatest evil of all did not occur just with God's foreknowledge but "by God's set purpose and foreknowledge" (Acts 2:23). It was not only foreknown but was unchangeably ordained and determined.

c. This decree from God is founded in his own goodwill and pleasure, for there is nothing higher and greater than God. Therefore it is a great error to suppose that anything existed before his will or above his will or without his will. All of God's actions begin in himself, and his will is the supreme cause of everything. "Yes, Father, for this was your good pleasure" (Matthew 11:26). Jesus Christ gave no other reason why God had "hidden these things from the wise and learned, and revealed them to little children" (Matthew 11:25). "Therefore God has mercy on whom he wants to have mercy, and he hardens whom he wants to harden" (Romans 9:18). This does not occur from God's foresight of our wills receiving or rejecting the grace offered to us, for then human will would be superior to one of God's acts.

d. In this matter of reprobation, passing over and pre-damnation must be carefully distinguished. In election God has decreed to bestow grace and then glory. God's passing over is merely from his own good pleasure. But pre-damnation presupposes consideration of the creatures' sin. Both these parts of the decree are clearly set out in the Word. Passing by is seen in Revelation 17:8: "The beast, which you saw, once was, now is not, and will come up out of the Abyss and go to his destruction. The inhabitants of the earth whose names have not been written in the book of life from the creation of the world will be astonished when they see the beast, because he once was, now is not, and yet will come." Pre-damnation is spoken of here. "For God did not appoint us to suffer wrath but to receive salvation through our Lord Jesus Christ" (1 Thessalonians 5:9).

e. Those who are passed over or not written in God's book never attain saving grace. It is not given to them. "The knowledge of the secrets of the kingdom of heaven has been given to you, but not to them" (Matthew 13:11). It is said to be hidden from them. "At that time Jesus said, 'I praise you, Father, Lord of heaven and earth, because you have hidden these things from the wise and learned, and revealed them to little children" (Matthew 11:25). They may have common gifts or be under a common work of the Spirit that leaves them without any excuse. But because the Lord has passed them by, effectual grace is not given to them, without which they cannot believe and be saved. "But you do not believe because you are not my sheep" (John 10:26). These people are not elected by God the Father. Saving grace runs in the channel of election. "When the Gentiles heard this, they were glad and honored the word of the Lord; and all who were appointed for eternal life believed" (Acts 13:48). God's special gifts are dispensed according to his decrees.

f. Men who have ignored God, who are devoid of saving grace, freely and of their own accord fall into those sins that make them suffer the just wrath of God. "What then? What Israel sought so earnestly it did not obtain, but the elect did. The others were hardened, as it is written: 'God gave them a spirit of stupor, eyes so that they could not see and ears so that they could not hear, to this very day'" (Romans 11:7-8). Freely and of their own accord they brought judgment and ruin on themselves. "All inhabitants of the earth will worship the beast—all whose names have not been written in the book of life belonging to the Lamb that was slain from the creation of the world" (Revelation 13:8). These people turn to anti-Christian defilements and pollutions.

g. God's decree concerning such people is immutable. It is not rescinded or annulled but is fully executed and accomplished in the damnation of the sinner. The Lord's counsels are all unchangeable concerning election. "Nevertheless, God's solid foundation stands firm, sealed with this inscription: 'The Lord knows those who are his,' and, 'Everyone who confesses the name of the Lord must turn away from wickedness'" (2 Timothy 2:19). "Because God wanted to make the unchanging nature of his purpose very clear to the heirs of what was promised, he confirmed it with an oath" (Hebrews 6:17). The Lord's counsels are all unchangeable concerning reprobation. No reprobate can ever be an elect person, nor can an elect person be a reprobate. "What he tears down cannot be rebuilt; the man he imprisons cannot be released" (Job 12:14). "But he stands alone, and who can oppose him? He does whatever he pleases" (Job 23:13). In God's book no names are added or deleted. Since the number of the elect is definite and certain, there cannot be more and there cannot be less. This is also true about the reprobate.

h. This eternal, irrevocable purpose of God of leaving sinners to themselves, that through their sins they come into judgment, is for God's glory. "What if God, choosing to show his wrath and make his power known, bore with great patience the objects of his wrath—prepared for destruction?" (Romans 9:22). All God's decrees, works, and providence reveal more about God in the sight of the creatures.

2. Let me now demonstrate that there is such a decree from the Scriptures, for reason has no place here. I will mention three verses that describe this clearly. The first is, "For God did not appoint us to suffer wrath but to receive salvation through our Lord Jesus Christ" (1 Thessalonians 5:9). This clearly implies that some people are appointed to be under God's wrath. The second verse comes in 1 Peter 2:8, where the apostle speaks about some people who were disobedient and refused Christ: "'A stone that causes men to stumble and a rock that makes them fall.' They stumble because they disobey the message—which is also what they were destined for." The third verse is in Proverbs: "The LORD works out everything for his own ends—even the wicked for a day of disaster" (16:4). This shows that both creation and predestination were for God's

glory, and Jude specifies the facet of predestination that applies to the wicked because this is the hardest to accept and believe.

I will now mention some of the reasons why God has chosen some and appointed others because of sin to come into judgment. It is not possible to fully fathom God's judgments. "Oh, the depth of the riches of the wisdom and knowledge of God! How unsearchable his judgments, and his paths beyond tracing out!" (Romans 11:33). We must stand in awe of God's teaching, for we are not able to understand it. But insofar as God has revealed his will, we may clearly judge that it is for the discovery of his justice and mercy. Neither of these two aspects of God's character could have been found out by the world had it not been for this double decree from God, in which some are saved and others are left to their own ruin. If grace was given to everyone, how could the world know that God was sovereign? Also, if everyone was pardoned, how could the world know that God was just? In election God demonstrates his sovereignty. ". . . to the praise of his glorious grace, which he has freely given us in the One he loves" (Ephesians 1:6). It is through love that we enjoy grace, and it is through elective love that we enjoy it at all. In reprobation God demonstrates his sovereignty, the severity of his justice, and the power of his wrath. "Consider therefore the kindness and sternness of God: sternness to those who fell, but kindness to you, provided that you continue in his kindness. Otherwise, you also will be cut off" (Romans 11:22). In choosing one and leaving the other, God demonstrates his freedom and shows that he does not act out of servile necessity. He also shows his severity in the eternal pains of those who perish in their sins.

3. Let me vindicate this doctrine, which in the eyes of some seems to tarnish God's justice. Some people also think this doctrine infringes on human comfort and even removes any duties toward God. This doctrine clearly needs some clarification. Reason cannot easily digest this strong meat, partly because we are prone to discount what we cannot understand, and partly because this doctrine checks worldly ease and security. This worldly ease usually feeds on the presumption that the God who has made us will save us and that he will not damn his creatures but will save everyone. So we are startled to learn that grace flows in a much narrower channel than we had thought. This is the case because man is loath to submit to the absolute lordship and sovereignty of God, not wanting to acknowledge that he disposes of his creatures according to his own pleasure. Our ambition is to be lords of ourselves. People desire to be like God, and they object to the idea that they can be like wild animals who can be captured and destroyed. For all these reasons they are loath to welcome this doctrine; so it needs to be clarified.

a. As far as your attitude toward God is concerned, you may not pollute and stain his excellency with impure and wrong thoughts about him. You will say, "Is God just if his will and pleasure ordains his creatures to condemnation? Do not the reprobate have grounds for complaint if God has passed a decree upon which their condemnation will infallibly follow?"

I answer, first, that our understanding is not the measure of God's justice but of our own desires. Things may be just even if the stated reasons behind this justice do not appeal to us. Human reason becomes giddy by peeping into the deep decrees of God. Our role is not to argue about this but to wonder at it. God's freedom is a riddle for our reason, because although we are not willing to be bound by laws, yet we expect God to be bound by them. God's actions must not be measured by any external rule. Things are good because God wills them, for his will is justice itself.

Second, the election of some people and the passing by of other people is not an act of justice but of dominion. God is not judge here but lord. It is a matter of favor, not of right or wrong. Condemnation of a man for sin, or punishing a man for sin, is an act of justice. But to have mercy or not to have mercy depends solely on God's will; otherwise it would follow that God was a debtor to man. Justice presumes indebtedness or that something is owed. The elect can speak of undeserved grace, and the reprobate can speak of deserved punishment. When we are not bound to do good, if we act according to pleasure, no injury is handed out, as invitations and preferments are then all acts of favor. We cannot allow anyone to challenge a right. The good man in the parable pleaded: "Don't I have the right to do what I want with my own money?" (Matthew 20:15). The Lord may rightly say that grace belongs to him, and so he will give it to whom he wishes, as he is not bound to give it to anyone.

b. I will now move on to the second objection—whether this doctrine impinges on our comfort and discourages men from looking after their salvation. "If I am elected, I shall be saved; if I am not elected, I shall be damned"—this is how they reason. They say, "And how will you stir up the negligent and encourage the distressed in the light of the doctrine you have taught?"

I answer, first, that this objection is only a misplaced scruple. It needs to be condemned rather than answered. God's secret is linked to his own actions and his revealed will to us. We must not look to God's will in the depths of his counsel but to his precepts. We are not to look at what God will do himself, but at what he wants us to do. God has said that we should believe in Christ and so be saved. That is our rule. A doctor offers a cure to everyone who comes to him. Only a madman would object to such an opportunity and say, "I am not sure that I am included in this invitation." If we were about to be drowned in deep waters, we would not debate about whether the rescuers were intended for us. We would just climb into the lifeboat and thankfully take hold of what was offered.

Second, this doctrine gives no grounds for despair because reprobation is a sealed book. None of us, for the present, knows about our reprobation, nor should we believe that we are reprobates. We are called on to use the means of grace so we may be saved. It is not those who fall into sin that are reprobates, but only those who persist in sin to the end of their lives. So it is no good saying, "I am a sinner, and therefore I am a reprobate; it is midnight, therefore it will never be day." This is a book sealed with seven seals, and only the Lamb can open it.

Third, the opposite opinion presents even more difficulties. What comfort can anyone have in universal redemption? A person cannot take comfort in what is common to good people and to bad people, to those who will be damned and to those who will be saved. All comfort derives from a practical syllogism. This is the syllogism according to the doctrine of universal grace: Christ died for all people; I am a person; therefore Christ died for me. In this case humanity is the basis for claiming salvation. Such an argument produces no comfort. How can I, according to that opinion, derive comfort from Christ's death, when some people may be damned who have an interest in it?

c. The next objection is: How can God call those he has passed by in the counsels of his will to believe in him if he never intended to give them grace and without it they cannot believe? I answer, God may require people to believe even though he never intended to give them faith. For there is a great deal of difference between his decree and his law. God's law shows what *must* be, his decree what *will* be. God never said that all *will* believe, but he has said that all *must* believe. He says this again and again. "And pray that we may be delivered from wicked and evil men, for not everyone has faith" (2 Thessalonians 3:2). This Gospel does not say that this person or that person will be saved, but "whoever" believes will be saved. Just as it can be rightly said of the apostles John or Thomas or any elect person, "If you do not believe, you will be damned," so surely it may be said to a reprobate, to Judas Iscariot or any other, "If you believe, you will be saved." If reprobates have the same opportunity as the elect in the general offer of grace, they have no excuse. Although the elect receive salvation by special grace, yet the reprobate reject it without good reason and so voluntarily turn their back on God's own mercies. So much for the vindication of this doctrine.

Application 1. I will now apply this teaching. The elect should stand in awe of God's love for them, for some people are passed by. Our mercies are not everyone's mercies. God's purpose was "to make the riches of his glory known to the objects of his mercy" (Romans 9:23). If God had passed us by, we could not have blamed God's love. If God had punished us eternally, we could not have blamed God's justice. God is just as concerned with others as he is with you. "For every living soul belongs to me"

(Ezekiel 18:4). He was their Creator as well as yours, and we are all involved in the same condemnation. God saw as much original sin in them as he saw in you. We lay in the same polluted mass. Oh, that free grace should make such a difference. God had as much reason to choose Judas Iscariot as to choose you. "Was not Esau Jacob's brother?" (Malachi 1:2). In every way we are like Judas Iscariot, except in God's choice of us. When men make choices, they do so on the basis of what is valuable. Who would choose warped timber to build a magnificent house? Yet the Lord singles out the worst and most depraved natures to mold them into a people for himself. How often God has made a distinction between you and others. "One will be taken and another left." One person is taken to grace, and another person is left to perish in his own ways. Other people may have been hardened by the same sermon through which you were converted. Oh, how ravishing is the sight of God's love in election and the distinct courses of his providence.

Application 2. This teaching makes us diligent in making our election certain, so that we may not be fearful about being one of the reprobates. The great question that occupies your soul is whether you are ordained to eternal life or not. If you are negligent and careless, and if you refuse to use the means of salvation, the case is decided, and it will bring you no comfort. "Then Paul and Barnabas answered them boldly: 'We had to speak the word of God to you first. Since you reject it and do not consider yourselves worthy of eternal life, we now turn to the Gentiles'" (Acts 13:46). Lazy, careless, worldly people only bring despair upon themselves. There are some steps that bring about the decree of reprobation. For example, acting like a drunkard in being totally obstinate to the counsels of the Word, being people given over to the spirit of error, always neglecting the means of grace, and hardening oneself against the means of grace are all indications of an evil heart. People may recover from a physical illness, but their souls may be close to death. So beware that you are not among those who through sin are ordained to come to judgment. Eli's sons did not listen to the advice of their father because the Lord intended to kill them.

Note 4. **They are godless men.** Let me explain this with four thoughts that are the basis of all religion. (1) God is, and he is one. (2) God is not like anything we can see, as he is something more excellent. (3) God cares about human affairs and judges justly. (4) The same God is maker of all things. These four principles match the first four commandments. In the first we have the unity of God; in the second, God's invisible nature, and so images are forbidden. "Then the LORD spoke to you out of the fire. You have heard the sound of words but saw no form; there was only a voice" (Deuteronomy 4:12). The third principle concerns God's knowledge of human affairs, and even men's thoughts, and that is the basis of an oath. The third commandment forbids perjury, and in an oath God is invoked as witness, mainly of the heart, in which his omniscience is acknowledged and appealed to as a judge and avenger, in which his justice and power are acknowledged. The next principle, that God is Creator and governor of all things, is established by the fourth commandment. The Sabbath at first was instituted to remember the creation of the world.

We deduce practical things from these principles. God alone is to be worshiped, obeyed, honored, and trusted. Insofar as we place our confidence in anything else or are ignorant of God's excellency or deny God by not worshiping him or by not serving him or by serving him in an unworthy way, superstitiously, carelessly, hypocritically, or by having wrong thoughts about his essence, or by excluding the dominion of his providence, or by not calling on his name, we are guilty of godlessness.

God is to be acknowledged as (1) the first cause, (2) the highest good, (3) the supreme truth and authority, and (4) the last end.

1. God is to be honored as the first cause. He gives life to everything and does not have his being from anything. And so if we do not trust in him, or if we trust in any creature rather than God or do not acknowledge his providence or the effects of his mercy, justice, and power, or do not acknowledge his dominion in all events and sanctify the things that we use by asking him in prayer to bless them, we are guilty of godlessness.

2. God is to be acknowledged as the highest good. So if we do not know him and if we do not often think about him, delight in communion with him, fear to offend him, or take care to please him, this neglect and contempt for God is godlessness.

3. God is to be acknowledged as the supreme truth and authority. Therefore, if we are not moved with his promises, threats, or counsels, as the Gentiles were moved with the oracles of their gods, or as were God's people of old, when that dispensation was in use, with a voice from heaven, and do not submit to him, reverence him in worship, or subject our hearts and lives to his laws, it is godlessness.

4. God is the last end. Therefore, if in all of our actions, spiritual, moral, natural, even those of the smallest consequence, we do not aim at God's glory, that is godlessness.

I will now use these four headings as I expand this argument.

1. First, let us consider God as the first cause.

a. Ignorance is a branch of godlessness. I mention it first as it is the cause of all disorder in worship or behavior. "Dear friend, do not imitate what is evil but what is good. Anyone who does what is good is from God. Anyone who does what is evil has not seen God" (3 John 11). Right thoughts about God are the fuel that keeps the fire of religion going, which would otherwise soon decay and be extinguished. Generally speaking, people are ignorant about God. They know him as those born blind know fire. They know there is such a thing as fire because it keeps them warm, but what it is they cannot say. So the whole world and conscience proclaim there is a God. The blindest people can see that, but they know little if anything about God's essence, as he has revealed himself in his Word. The Athenians had an altar on which was inscribed, "TO AN UNKNOWN GOD." In the same way many Christians go on in a track of customary worship and so worship an idol rather than God. So Christ told the Samaritan woman, "You Samaritans worship what you do not know" (John 4:22). It is usually the case that people in a dark and blind superstition conform to the worship of their place, not considering why or whom they worship. Gross ignorance is a sign of no grace, for God has no child so little that he does not know his father. "They will all know me, from the least of them to the greatest" (Jeremiah 31:34). Some have a better education than others, greater aids and advantages of ability or instruction, but they all have a necessary knowledge of God.

Gross ignorance is also a pledge of future judgment. "This will happen when the Lord Jesus is revealed from heaven in blazing fire with his powerful angels" (2 Thessalonians 1:7). Many poor, ignorant creatures are harmless and do no wrong. Oh, but they do not know God, and that is wrong enough; God will avenge this. To be ignorant of the God who made them has much more serious consequences than you are aware of. "Those who do not know God" refers to pagans, who "do not obey the gospel of our Lord Jesus" (1 Thessalonians 2:8). If there is going to be vengeance for pagans, who have no other apostles sent to them but those apostles of sun, moon, and stars and have no books in which they can study about God except for showers of rain and fruitful seasons, if there is vengeance on them because they did not see and own a first cause, what is there for those who close their eyes against the light of the Gospel? Surely to be ignorant now is a much greater sin than we imagine.

b. We are being ungodly when we do not depend on God. Trust and dependence is the basis of all communication between us and God. It is the best way to show respect and pay homage to the Creator and first cause. When people put their trust in other people or in their possessions rather than in God, they rob God of his special honor. Job clearly states that this sin exists. "If I have put my trust in gold or said to pure gold, 'You are my security,' if I have rejoiced over my great wealth, the fortune my hands had gained, if I have regarded the sun in its radiance or the moon moving in splendor, so that my heart was secretly enticed and my hand offered them a kiss of homage, then these also would be sins to be judged, for I would have been unfaithful to God on high" (Job 31:24-28). Job, to vindicate himself from hypocrisy, listed the sins that hypocrites usually commit. Among these sins is to put "trust in gold." People often think gold is the staff of their lives and security for their posterity. When their trust is captured in this way, they are diverted away from trusting God. This is a common sin, but not often taken into account.

The great danger of riches is putting any trust in them. "At this the man's face fell. He went away sad, because he had great wealth. Jesus looked around and said to his disciples, 'How hard it is for the rich to enter the kingdom of God!'" (Mark 10:22-23). When people are ensconced in their home, they think they are safe, secure against whatever may happen, and so God is put to one side. Wealth breeds a false sense of security. So "greed" is called "idolatry" (see Colossians 3:5), and a "greedy person" is called an "idolater" (see Ephesians 5:5). This is the case not so much because of his love for money, but because of his *trust* in money. Many who smile at the vanity of the Gentiles who worshiped stones and idols made out of gold and silver do worse things as they place their trust in their possessions.

c. We are being ungodly when we do not observe God's providence. The blind world sets up an idol called chance and does not acknowledge God as swaying all things by his wisdom and power. In afflictions they think they are just experiencing a piece of bad luck. "Send it [the ark of the Lord] on its way, but keep watching it. If it goes up to its own territory, toward Beth Shemesh, then the LORD has brought this great disaster on us. But if it does not, then we will know that it was not his hand that struck us and that it happened to us by chance" (1 Samuel 6:8-9). "O LORD, your hand is lifted high, but they do not see it. Let them see your zeal for your people and be put to shame; let the fire reserved for your enemies consume them" (Isaiah 26:11). They view instruments and secondary causes as if God is an idle spectator and has no hand in what happens to us. Job had a better understanding than this, as he showed when he said that the Lord gives and the Lord takes away. He did not just look for help *against* the Chaldean, the Sabean, the thief, but *from* the Lord. In all afflictions we should look beyond the creature and not complain about bad fortune, chance, the stars, or anything like that. We should look to God for help.

It is ungodly not to see God in all our mercies. Wicked people receive blessings and never look up to God. They live by God's mercy every moment of their lives. Their life and breath come from God, but they do not give God a thought. As pigs eat acorns and never look up to the oak tree they have fallen from, so humans do not look beyond the hand from which they daily receive mercies. But God's children are like chicks that sip a little food and then look up. The Lord complained about Israel, "She has not acknowledged that I was the one who gave her the grain, the new wine and oil, who lavished on her the silver and gold—which they used for Baal" (Hosea 2:8). There is no greater sign of an ungodly spirit than this profane ingratitude. God expects us to acknowledge him as the giver of all good things that we enjoy. Other creatures live on God's mercies, but they are not capable of knowing the first cause as we are. Idolatry and atheism would never have crept into the world if men had considered who it is that blessed them with food every day. "In the past, he [God] let all nations go their own way. Yet he has not left himself without testimony: He has shown kindness by giving you rain from heaven and crops in their seasons; he provides you with plenty of food and fills your hearts with joy" (Acts 14:16-17). Certainly nothing feeds piety like constantly showing reverence to God and thanking him for food each time we eat and drink and enjoy any new mercy from him. But alas, we usually forget God when he remembers us most. God is not dishonored more than when we eat and drink and take pleasure in our outward comforts without giving him a second thought.

d. We are revealing our ungodliness when we do not acknowledge God's dominion in everything that happens. We steal from others if we use their possessions without asking them; so we are acting in an ungodly way if we make use of people or food or anything else without making it holy through the Word and prayer. "They forbid people to marry and order them to abstain from certain foods, which God created to be received with thanksgiving by those who believe and who know the truth. For everything God created is good, and nothing is to be rejected if it is received with thanksgiving, because it is consecrated by the word of God and prayer" (1 Timothy 4:3-5). We should also consult God about everything. "You ought to say, 'If it is the Lord's will, we will live and do this or that'" (James 4:15). We forget to bid ourselves "good speed" when we do not acknowledge the dominion of God in all these instances. "In all your ways acknowledge him, and he will make your paths straight" (Proverbs 3:6). God's children do not dare to take any decisions without first consulting him.

2. Second, we must acknowledge God as the highest good or we are being ungodly.

a. We are being ungodly if we do not often think about God, for God is not far from each one of us (see Acts 17:27). But although God is not far from us, we are far from God. He who is everywhere is seldom found in our hearts. We are not as close to ourselves as God is to us. Who can breathe for a minute if God is not with him? He is within us and round about us revealing his power and goodness, but we are so distant from him in our minds and affections. How many trifles occupy our minds! But the Lord can seldom find any room there. "In his pride the wicked does not seek him; in all his thoughts there is no room for God" (Psalm 10:4). When thoughts about God rush into our minds, they are like unwelcome guests whom we want to get rid of. Wicked men abhor thoughts about God, because the more they think about God, the more they tremble, as the devils do. Therefore the apostle Paul says, "although they knew God, they neither glorified him as God nor gave thanks to him, but their thinking became futile and their foolish hearts were darkened" (Romans 1:21). This is a long way from behaving like God's children.

David said, "May my meditation be pleasing to him, as I rejoice in the LORD" (Psalm 104:34). Thinking about God is a spiritual feast for a gracious soul. Nobody deserves our thoughts more than God, and there is no better way to occupy our mind. God thought about us before the creation of the world, and he continues to think about us still. Therefore, it shows great ingratitude if we do not think about God. When we hate a person, we cannot stand looking at him; the hatred of the mind is shown by the way it turns its thoughts away from people it hates.

b. We are being ungodly if we do not delight to have communion with God and are not honoring him as the highest good. Friends love to be in each other's company. It is certainly good for us to draw near to God to strengthen the friendship we have with him. God has appointed the ordinances of Bible reading and prayer, which are, as it were, a dialogue between God and the creature. In the Bible God speaks to us, and in prayer we speak to God. God tells us his mind and will through the Word, and we ask for God's grace as we pray. In prayer we make our requests, and in the Word we have God's answer. So then, when people neglect public or private prayer or other opportunities of listening to God, they are guilty of godlessness. In this way they cut off their communication with God, especially if they neglect to pray. For prayer is a duty in which we should engage all the time. It is a sweet diversion in which the soul enjoys God in private. Therefore to neglect prayer is to behave like an atheist. "All have turned aside, they have together become corrupt; there is no one who does good, not even one. Will evildoers never learn—those who devour my people as men eat bread and who do not call on the LORD?" (Psalm 14:3-4). When people are disinclined to come into God's presence because of their love of pleasure and worldly desires, they commit a grave sin. Our comfort and peace is dependent on frequent communion with God. When family worship is neglected, God is not being treated as the highest good. The heathen are described as "the peoples who do not call on your [God's] name" (Jeremiah 10:25). In many places there is no worship and prayer in the family, from the start of the week until the end of the week. But the home should be like a church. Pigs who live outside the house night and morning are looked after, but no time is found to invoke God's name at any time during the day. Are such people any better than pagans?

c. If we do not live in fear of offending God, we are being ungodly. God wishes to be served with every affection. Love as well as fear is to be made use of in the spiritual life. "Since we have these promises, dear friends, let us purify ourselves from everything that contaminates body and spirit, perfecting holiness out of reverence for God" (2 Corinthians 7:1). Love sweetens duties, and fear makes us guard against sin. Love is the active grace, and fear is the conserving grace. "For in Christ Jesus neither circumcision nor uncircumcision has any value. The only thing that counts is faith expressing itself through love" (Galatians 5:6). "I will make an everlasting covenant with them: I will never stop doing good to them, and I will inspire them to fear me, so that they will never turn away from me" (Jeremiah 32:40). We have good reason to walk in God's ways because we are always under his watchful eye.

We need love if we are to keep God in our hearts all the time. We need fear if we are to keep God in our minds all the time. Both love and fear are necessary. But we will now speak about fear, which is the true inner root of all obedience and worship. "Now all has been heard; here is the conclusion of the matter: Fear God and keep his commandments, for this is the whole duty of man" (Ecclesiastes 12:13). Then our hearts will have such a settled disposition that we would not dream of grieving him. We must spare no effort in honoring God. But when we are secure and careless, we forget God and freely sin in thought and action, without any remorse. In this way we demonstrate how ungodly we are. Fear is a grace that should be used constantly. We cannot always be praising God, worshiping God, and keeping busy with acts of special communion with God, but we must fear God all the time. "Do not let your heart envy sinners, but always be zealous for the fear of the LORD" (Proverbs 23:17). "Blessed is the man who always fears the LORD, but he who hardens his heart falls into trouble" (Proverbs 28:14).

A person who has finished his own devotions in the morning is not finished with God for the rest of the day. We should be constantly thinking about God and recall that his eye is on us all day long. We must get up in the fear of God, do business in the fear of God, eat and drink in the fear of God. "These men are blemishes at your love feasts, eating with you without the slightest qualm—shepherds who feed only themselves" (Jude 12). Some graces are like our lungs, which are in constant use. Fear needs to be especially active when temptations attack us. We must reason as Joseph did: "No one is greater in this house than I am. My master has withheld nothing from me except you, because you are his wife. How then could I do such a wicked thing and sin against God?" (Genesis 39:9).

d. If we do not wish to please God, we are being ungodly. The last thing an ungodly person thinks about is pleasing God. He does not want to know about God's paths and does not attempt to walk in them. "They deliberately forget that long ago by God's word the heavens existed and the earth was formed out of water and with water" (2 Peter 3:5). They do not seek out God's ways so they may follow them. So they do not go astray in their minds, but in their hearts. "Yet they say to God, 'Leave us alone! We have no desire to know your ways'" (Job 21:14). They do not have a mind to do what they do not have a mind to know, just as those who want to sleep draw the curtains when they want to keep the light out. In contrast, a godly person is always seeking to carry out God's will. "Do not conform any longer to the pattern of this world, but be transformed by the renewing of your mind. Then you will be able to test and approve what God's will is—his good, pleasing and perfect will" (Romans 12:2). "Find out what pleases the Lord. Have nothing to do with the fruitless deeds of darkness, but rather expose them. For it is shameful even to mention what the disobedient do in secret. But everything exposed by the light becomes visible, for it is light that makes everything visible. This is why it is said: 'Wake up, O sleeper, rise from the dead, and Christ will shine on you.' Be very careful, then, how you live—not as unwise but as wise, making the most of every opportunity, because the days are evil. Therefore do not be foolish, but understand what the Lord's will is" (Ephesians 5:10-17). Paul put into practice what he knew and still sought to know the Lord better, so that he might be even more useful to him. What should I be doing better?

3. Third, God must be acknowledged as the supreme truth and authority. So if we are unmoved by his promises, threats, counsels, as they are the words of the great God, and if we do not worship him reverently and subject our hearts and lives to his laws, we are being ungodly.

a. We must receive the counsels of his Word with reverence, for that is to receive it as "the word of God" (1 Thessalonians 2:13). Pagans received the oracles of their gods and were greatly moved. But we can drowsily hear of the great things of salvation, heaven, the death of Christ, and the covenant of grace and be no more moved than if it were a dream.

b. We must reverently worship God. God is said to be "awesome" in his "sanctuary" (Psalm 68:35). We do not approach God as the Supreme Majesty when we come to him forgetting that he is awesome. God is awesome where he is also most comforting. "If you do not carefully follow all the words of this law, which are written in this book, and do not revere this glorious and awesome name—the LORD your God . . ." (Deuteronomy 28:58). To have God for our God is the basis of all our comfort and hope, and he has a glorious and fearful name. In Malachi 1:14 the Lord uses two arguments about why we should worship him reverently. One is because he is a great King and Lord of hosts, and the other is because his name is to be feared among the nations. So beware of serving God in a perfunctory manner or you will be dishonoring him exceedingly even when you come to give him honor.

c. We must be willing to subject our hearts and lives to God's laws. We must subject our *hearts*. God's authority is not undermined so much as when there is only "a form of godliness" (2 Timothy 3:5) in our worship. This is an example of great ungodliness because you are robbing God of his dominion over your conscience. Hypocrisy is blatant blasphemy. "I know the slander of those who say they are Jews and are not" (Revelation 2:9). Our *lives* must also be subject to God's laws. People hate God as a lawgiver but love him when he gives them blessings. Our lives must conform to God's laws, for God wants to be honored in our behavior as well as having his throne set up in our consciences. It is the glory of a commander to be obeyed. "I myself am a man under authority, with soldiers under me. I tell this one, 'Go,' and he goes; and that one, 'Come,' and he comes. I say to my servant, 'Do this,' and he does it" (Matthew 8:9). God looks for you to reverence him in this kind of way.

4. Fourth, God wishes to be honored as the highest end. So if in all our actions, natural, moral, and spiritual, we do not aim to glorify God, we are guilty of godlessness. In our natural acts, and in matters of the least consequence, we must have a supernatural aim. "So whether you eat or drink or whatever you do, do all for the glory of God" (1 Corinthians 10:31). If I eat a meal, I must aim to glorify God in it. In spiritual acts of prayer, praise, and worship, we must always be aiming to glorify God. All the motivations of the soul look in God's direction. This is the difference between holiness and godliness. Holiness implies a conformity to the law, and godliness implies that the soul's aim is to glorify God. These two things are distinguished from each other. "You ought to lead holy and godly lives" (2 Peter 3:11). God has given his creatures many things. The only thing he has kept for himself is his glory. Therefore he does not think well of anyone who tries to rob him of that.

I have shown you several kinds of ungodliness. The worst kind of godlessness is when we act with contempt toward God's providence and disobey his laws. So if we do not want to be in the ranks of the ungodly we must beware of all these sins.

Application 1. How else will you look God in the face on the day of judgment? "The wicked will not stand in the judgment" (Psalm 1:5). So they will not be able to plead their cause. The day of judgment has been appointed "to judge everyone, and to convict all the ungodly of all the ungodly acts they have done in the ungodly way, and of all the harsh words ungodly sinners have spoken against him" (Jude 15). It is the day on which God, who is at present withdrawn within the curtains of heaven, will come and show himself, to the terror of all ungodly people.

Application 2. Great judgments were inflicted on the ungodly in this world. "He did not spare the ancient world when he brought the flood on its ungodly people" (2 Peter 2:5). "If it is hard for the righteous to be saved, what will become of the ungodly and the sinner?" (1 Peter 4:18). Because the Lord is jealous for his honor, no one will suffer more than the ungodly. "He put on vengeance and wrapped himself in zeal as in a cloak" (Isaiah 59:17). The cloak is a person's outer garment, the most easily seen. There is nothing so visible in God's providence as his jealousy for his honor.

Application 3. The main aim of the Gospel is to stop people's being ungodly. The Gospel shows us how we can enjoy God without dishonoring him. This is called the "mystery of godliness" (1 Timothy 3:16) and "godly teaching" (1 Timothy 6:3). In the days of the Gospel we have the means to know God and respect him and to have clearer ideas about his excellency and glory.

Application 4. Ungodliness is the root of all wrongdoing. Abraham was fearful in Gerar. Why? "There is surely no fear of God in this place" (Genesis 20:11). Godliness is the great bulwark of laws and all honest discipline. The first part of the Ten Commandments provides for the reverence of God. It is the foundation on which the second part of the Ten Commandments is built, which deals with respect for our neighbor. So we should purge the heart from the causes of ungodliness. We should suppress all ungodly thoughts as soon as they arise. We should put to death evil affections. We should keep God's instructions in our minds at all times. You should "train yourself to be godly" (1 Timothy 4:7). We should delight to give to God the honor he deserves. We should love him, delight in him, and fear him. We should often worship him and do everything with the aim of glorifying him.

Note 5. . . . **who change the grace of God into a license for immorality.** The Gospel and the grace of God in themselves are not able to be used for worldly purposes. But the apostle says that they can be changed and abused in this way. If the Gospel is used for evil purposes, it has first of all to be twisted. I will prove this point with three arguments.

1. From the constitution of the Gospel. It does not permit us to sin but gives us freedom to serve God. This is its great purpose. Christ did not come to reconcile God and our sins but to reconcile God and us. He came to reconcile us and to destroy our sins. He did not come to free us from the law but to free us from sin and from serving the devil. "He who does what is sinful is of the devil, because the devil has been sinning from the beginning. The reason the Son of God appeared was to destroy the devil's work" (1 John 3:8). Christ did not come to make the law less strict or sin less odious. Perfection of the law was more clearly seen after Christ came: "Be perfect, therefore, as your heavenly Father is perfect" (Matthew 5:48). Sin was never as odious as it is since grace has arrived in Christ so abundantly. Those who sinned when they were under the law did not sin against such love and kindness that we have now in the gospel era. "For if the message spoken by angels was binding, and every violation and disobedience received its just punishment, how shall we escape if we ignore

such a great salvation? This salvation, which was first announced by the Lord, was confirmed to us by those who heard him" (Hebrews 2:2-3). Christ's coming could not make us less holy or dispense with our need for holiness, for then he would have come in order to deface God's image and make us less like God. Freedom from wrath and hell is a privilege, but freedom from duty and obedience is no privilege. In the Gospel there is pardon for failings, but this does not encourage us to sin more, but to carry out our duty toward God. The great purpose of the Gospel is to make us more like God and to free us from the slavery of the devil, that we may be better servants and subjects of God.

2. There are numerous arguments that speak against this perversion of our freedom in Christ and subsequent delight in evil desires. The Spirit of God foresaw how our corrupt nature would tempt us to abuse our privileges for an evil purpose. Indeed, many had already attempted this in the apostles' day, such as the sect of the Nicolaitans, the school of Simon, and after them the Gnostics and Basilicans, who under the banner of evangelical freedom gave themselves up to lawless and brutish practices. There are numerous warnings against this. "What shall we say, then? Shall we go on sinning so that grace may increase?" (Romans 6:1). It is as if the apostle Paul was saying, "You will not lack corrupt teachers. Your hearts will incline toward this kind of evil. But you must reject all this with indignation." "You, my brothers, were called to be free. But do not use your freedom to indulge the sinful nature; rather, serve one another in love" (Galatians 5:13). Christ has done his part in purchasing glorious privileges for you. So take heed that you do not abuse them, which your base hearts are always prone to do. "Live as free men, but do not use your freedom as a cover-up for evil; live as servants of God" (1 Peter 2:16).

3. In the Gospel itself there are quite contrary inferences and conclusions than those that flesh and blood would draw from the Gospel. Three instances of the latter are looseness, laziness, and licentiousness. You will see that the Word contains things that are opposed to a worldly way of thinking.

First, looseness. People have been more loose and careless because grace has abounded in the discoveries of the Gospel. But the apostle Paul points out that such thinking is most abhorrent to gospel principles. "Shall we go on sinning, so that grace may abound? By no means!" (Romans 6:1) Do not cherish such an unworthy thought. The Gospel teaches quite the opposite. "For the grace of God that brings salvation has appeared to all men. It teaches us to say 'No' to ungodliness and worldly passions, and to live self-controlled, upright and godly lives in this present age" (Titus 2:11-12). "Since we have these promises, dear friends, let us purify ourselves from everything that contaminates body and spirit, perfecting holiness out of reverence for God" (2 Corinthians 7:1). A bee gathers honey from where a spider sucks poison.

Second, laziness. People are apt to take their ease and say that Christ must do it all, and so exclude using all the means of grace and any personal effort. This is a foul abuse, for Scripture infers that creatures should engage in spiritual work since God has done so much for them. "Continue to work out your salvation with fear and trembling, for it is God who works in you to will and to act according to his good purpose" (Philippians 2:12-13). We must wait on God more humbly as we use his ordinances since everything depends on God's helping us.

Third, licentiousness. People have used their freedom in Christ in such a perverse way that they have refused to obey the civil authorities. But the Word presents our freedom in Christ as the basis for our responsibilities. We are therefore even more keen to carry out all our duties, both to other people and to Christ. It is in this sense that the apostle Paul says, "For he who was a slave when he was called by the Lord is the Lord's freedman" (1 Corinthians 7:22). Peter adds, "Live as free men, but do not use your freedom as a cover-up for evil" (1 Peter 2:16). Christianity enlarges our consciences. As Salvain said, "*In maxima libertate minima licentia*"; we have a great deal of liberty through Christ, and yet we also have the strongest possible bond of service.

Application 1. This informs us, first, that carnal people are not adept at working out the consequences of the Gospel correctly. From the Gospel itself they say there is freedom to sin. There is no more perverse conclusion to draw from the Gospel. It is worth noticing what arguments are used in Scripture about this. Compare 1 Corinthians 7:29 with 1 Corinthians 15:32. "What I mean, brothers, is that the time is short. From now on those who have wives should live as if they had none." "If I fought wild beasts in Ephesus for merely human reasons, what have I gained? If the dead are not raised, 'Let us eat and drink, for tomorrow we die.'" The principle in both places is that the time is short. The apostle in the former instance concludes that we should be strict and temperate and that we should mortify our bodies. But the dissolute epicure argues in a totally different way. He says, "Let us eat and drink, for tomorrow we die." He draws quite a different conclusion from the same principle.

Application 2. This acts as a warning to us. When you come across such base inferences from evangelical principles, do not blame the Gospel or the ministry or the dispensation of the Gospel.

First, do not blame the Gospel. We must resist thinking that the Gospel is not clear enough and faithful enough. Such thoughts may haunt us when we see gross errors creeping in under the cover of Scripture. We are tempted to think that God should speak more clearly. But vain people stumble over God's plainest ways. Parables, which are the most vivid way to present ideas, hardened the Pharisees. "He told them, 'The secret of the kingdom of God has been given to you. But to those on the outside everything is said in parables so that, "they may be ever seeing but never perceiving, and ever hearing but never understanding; otherwise they might turn and be forgiven!"'" (Mark 4:11-12). If people ruin themselves by their own false logic, we should not blame God. People who are determined to fall will not lack a stumbling-stone.

Second, do not blame the ministry and dispensation of the Gospel if some people abuse free grace and some others cannot bear to hear it preached. The children should not go without bread just because dogs also eat it. Will hungry consciences lose their portion just because other people abuse God? No! If worldly people use these truths for their own evil ends, we cannot help it. We are not in the place of God. We can only teach the doctrine. We cannot give wicked people the gracious hearts they need so they will receive God's teaching.

Note 6. **The grace of our God.** Our next point is that grace itself cannot be twisted so that those kinds of conclusions are valid. Yet wicked people love to abuse the Gospel so that it countenances their own sins. You see from this that the abuse of the teaching of the Gospel was very ancient. Olden times were no better than today. "Do not say, 'Why were the old days better than these?'" (Ecclesiastes 7:10). In the apostles' days vile hearts abused good teaching. Indeed, out of all errors these seem to come most naturally to us. We greedily drink in the poison of carnal liberty.

Note 7. **The grace of our God.** The point to note here is the word **our**. Jude mentions their interest in God in order to encourage them to oppose error more strongly. Note that our interest in God's cause makes us zealous for the truths and glory of God. This point has two branches.

1. Interest in God begets a zeal for God. A good man is disturbed to see anyone wronged. It matters even more to him if his own family members are being upset. And it matters most of all to him if God is under attack. Can a person profess to love God and not side with God against all evil attacks on God's name? Friends have everything in common—common love and common hatred. It is the same in our spiritual friendship with God. "For zeal for your house consumes me, and the insults of those who insult you fall on me" (Psalm 69:9). When we entered into our covenant relationship with God, we made an offensive and a defensive pact with him. We count his friends our friends, his enemies our enemies; we hate what he hates, and we love what he loves. So we cannot remain silent when God's name is attacked without breaking our divine covenant. It is impossible for us to be friends with those who abuse his name.

2. The next branch is that the zeal of those who have an interest in God is the best kind of zeal. It is the best partly because it is the hottest. People

who argue over a mere opinion are not as earnest as those who contend out of affection. A man may tell someone off if he sees a stranger being abused. But if a member of his family is being attacked, he will personally leap to that person's defense. The person who loves God is prepared to sacrifice all his own interests in serving God.

Note 8. **Jesus Christ our only Sovereign and Lord.** The points that could be drawn from here are many, but I will just mention a few.

1. Jesus Christ is **Sovereign and Lord**, *despotes kai kurios*, "King of the nations" (Jeremiah 10:7), "King of the ages" (Revelation 15:3), or, as the apostle Paul states, "head over everything for the church" (Ephesians 1:22). Christ is over all things; he is supreme and absolute. He is the church's head, from whom believers receive all kind of provision.

2. Observe again that Christ is both **Lord** and **Jesus.** He came to rule and to save. I shall handle these two titles together and then separately.

a. These titles are mentioned together in certain places. "God has made this Jesus, whom you crucified, both Lord and Christ" (Acts 2:36). Christ who is the great Lord is also Jesus. He has the greatest power and the greatest mercy. He is mighty but is also a Savior. This is partly to show how we should receive him. We should not only come to him for ease but should take his yoke upon us. "Come to me, all you who are weary and burdened, and I will give you rest. Take my yoke upon you and learn from me, for I am gentle and humble in heart, and you will find rest for your souls. For my yoke is easy and my burden is light" (Matthew 11:28-29).

b. I will now take these two titles separately. Jesus is **Lord.** Since he is God, he has the same glory as the Father. As mediator he has a dominion arising from this office. He is the head of all creatures and the King of the church and on the last day will judge everyone. But he is chiefly Lord because of his heritage in the church. He is Lord over his own people, who are given to him for a possession by God the Father. "Ask of me, and I will make the nations your inheritance, the ends of the earth your possession" (Psalm 2:8). "The church . . . he bought with his own blood" (Acts 20:28). Jesus as Lord has brought the church into a marriage covenant with him. "Husbands, love your wives, just as Christ loved the church and gave himself up for her to make her holy, cleansing her by the washing with water through the word, and to present her to himself as a radiant church, without stain or wrinkle or any other blemish, but holy and blameless" (Ephesians 5:25-27).

Jesus means "Savior." Christ is a Saviour positively as well as privately. He gives us spiritual blessings as well as freedom from misery. "For God did not send his Son into the world to condemn the world, but to save the world through him" (John 3:17). Also, he is a Saviour not only by way of deliverance but by way of prevention. He does not only break the snare but keeps our feet from falling. He is like a shepherd leading the flock as well as a doctor healing our diseases. God is to be satisfied, and Satan has to be overcome. So Jesus rescues us out of the hands of Satan and redeems us out of the hands of God's justice. To rescue a condemned criminal and to take him by force out of the executioner's hands is not enough. The judge must also be satisfied and grant a pardon or the man is not safe. Christ "has rescued us from the dominion of darkness" (Colossians 1:13), and in him the Father is "well pleased" (Matthew 3:17).

Note 9. Observe from these words that the Son of God was **Christ** that he might be **Lord** and **Jesus**. He was anointed by the Father that he might accomplish our salvation.

This anointing signifies the nature of Christ's office. Under the Old Testament three kinds of people were anointed—kings, priests, and prophets. All these relations Christ sustains for the church. Men who needed saving had three problems to overcome. They were ignorant about God, distant from God, and did not have the ability to turn toward God. Christ suited these needs exactly. As a prophet he showed us our misery, as priest he provided the remedy we needed, and as king he brought this remedy to us. The Scriptures emphasize how Christ has brought us these benefits. "I am the way and the truth and the life" (John 14:6). "It is because of him that you are in Christ Jesus, who has become for us wisdom from God—that is, our righteousness, holiness and redemption" (1 Corinthians 1:30). We are ignorant, foolish creatures, and therefore Christ is made our wisdom as a prophet; we are guilty creatures, and therefore Christ is made our righteousness as a priest; we are sinful creatures, and therefore Christ is made our sanctification as a king. We are miserable creatures, liable to death and hell, and so Christ is made our redemption as a king.

Application 1. From this we learn that Christ is the proper object of faith. Faith is built on God. "Through him you believe in God, who raised him from the dead and glorified him, and so your faith and hope are in God" (1 Peter 1:21). Christ is God, and so his merit was enough to redeem the church, which is therefore said to be "bought with his own blood" (Acts 20:28). This makes Christ able to sanctify us and purge us, for his blood was offered through the eternal Spirit. "How much more, then, will the blood of Christ, who through the eternal Spirit offered himself unblemished to God, cleanse our consciences from acts that lead to death, so that we may serve the living God!" (Hebrews 9:14).

Application 2. Since Christ was God by nature, let us observe Christ's love in becoming man. What did Christ do when he took our nature? How wonderful it is to see the great God in the form of a servant, even hanging on a cross! "Beyond all question, the mystery of godliness is great: He appeared in a body, was vindicated by the Spirit, was seen by angels, was preached among the nations, was believed on in the world, was taken up in glory" (1 Timothy 3:16).

Note 10. I come now to the word implying guilt, *arnoumenoi*, **deny.** Note that it is a horrible impiety to deny the Lord Jesus. When Jude wanted to make these seducers odious, he revealed this characteristic. Christ may be denied in many ways. I shall refer to these under two headings—in opinion, and in practice.

1. In opinion. Christ is denied when men deny his nature or his office. His nature, whether his deity or his humanity, has been denied many times, as by those ancient and wicked heretics Ebion and Cerinthus. This is why John starts his Gospel, the last one to be written, with a description of Christ's Godhead and for this reason is so zealous against these heresies in his letters, as are Jude and Peter. Ebion, Cerinthus, Carpocrates, and others held that Christ was born as other people are, by the help of man. Manes held the Son of God to be a part of his Father's substance. Saturnius, Basilides, Cordion, and others denied the humanity of Christ, saying he only appeared in the form of a man.

2. Christ is also denied in practice. This happens through apostasy and a total rebellion against him. "Whoever disowns me before men, I will disown him before my Father in heaven" (Matthew 10:33). Nobody sins like apostates do, for they, as it were, after a trial and through conscious decisions acknowledge the devil as the better master. They first reject Satan and come to Christ, but then they turn away from Christ back into the arms of Satan. In this way they are, as it were, telling the world who is the better master. Therefore, "It would have been better for them not to have known the way of righteousness, than to have known it and then to turn their backs on the sacred commandment that was passed on to them" (2 Peter 2:21).

Christ is also denied when we do not bear witness to him in evil times, for not to profess is to deny. "If anyone is ashamed of me and my words in this adulterous and sinful generation, the Son of Man will be ashamed of him when he comes in his Father's glory with the holy angels" (Mark 8:38). Some are ashamed for fear of being disgraced, as well as through fear of danger.

People also deny Christ when they profess to be his followers but live lives that are unworthy of Christ. Actions are the best images of our thoughts. So evil behavior indicates that people are not genuine followers of Christ. "They claim to know God, but by their actions they deny him" (Titus 1:16).

Verse 5

Commentary on Verse 5

Though you already know all this, I want to remind you that the Lord delivered his people out of Egypt, but later destroyed those who did not believe.

We have finished with the preface. I come now to the apostle's examples by which he proves the danger of defection from the faith. The first is taken from the grumbling Israelites, the second from the apostate angels (verse 6), and the third from the beastly Sodomites (verse 7).

This verse consists of a preface and the first example of God's judgment, which came on the unbelieving Israelites. In the preface you should observe Jude's purpose, **I want to remind you**, and his insinuation, **though you already know all this**.

In this insinuation, **though you already know all this**, the word **already** ("once," KJV) needs to be explained. Jude does not mean they had previously known this but had forgotten. Nor does it mean once in the sense of "I will once put in you in remembrance." It means once in the sense "once and for all." That is, "you have certainly and irrecoverably received this as a truth."

I now move on to the first example Jude gives. **That the Lord delivered his people out of Egypt, but later destroyed those who did not believe**. **His people**, *laon*, is used in an honorable way here. **His people** are God's special people. They are the holy and elect nation who had been given the law and the covenants of promise. These people, after they were **delivered . . . out of Egypt**, were **later destroyed**. There is no point in standing on our privileges without continuing faith. See Numbers 14:37 and 1 Corinthians 10:1-5 to read about Israel's destruction. Libertine Christians are as bad as obstinate Jews. That is the drift of Jude's argument.

Notes on Verse 5

Note 1. I will begin with some general observations so you may see how apt these examples are for the apostle's purpose. Observe first that God's ancient judgments were ordained to be our warnings and examples. The Bible is a book of precedents, in which the Lord gives the world a record of his providence. "These things happened to them as examples and were written down as warnings for us, on whom the fulfillment of the ages has come" (1 Corinthians 10:11). If God was strict, holy, and just in the Old and New Testaments, then he is also strict, holy, and just now. He who struck Ananias and Sapphira dead because they lied, he who made Zechariah dumb because of his unbelief, he who kept Moses out of the Promised Land because of a few unadvised words, he who turned Lot's wife into a pillar of salt for looking back is still the same God. He has not altered a jot.

Application. So, let us take every example we find in the Word as a warning. It is excellent when we read the Scriptures with a spirit of application.

Also, when wicked men flourish, we should not be dismayed. How has God judged sinners? What do the Scriptures say? "When I tried to understand all this, it was oppressive to me till I entered the sanctuary of God; then I understood their final destiny" (Psalm 73:16-17).

Note 2. The thing that I observe in these instances is the impartiality of divine justice, for in all these examples there are some circumstances in which others would expect an exemption from wrath. The Israelites were God's own people, the angels were God's own courtiers in heaven; but in all instances you may observe that the judgments fell on multitudes and societies, collective bodies. *All* the grumbling Israelites and *all* the apostate angels received God's judgment.

No outward privilege can help us on the day of wrath. God did not even spare his angels. "For . . . God did not spare angels when they sinned, but sent them to hell, putting them into gloomy dungeons to be held for judgment" (2 Peter 2:4). Nor did God spare the people of Israel.

Nobody is allowed to sin, and so none are exempt from punishment. The law includes everyone—the son, the servant, he who sits on the throne, and those who grind at the mill. No one has a license from heaven to sin.

Wicked people do not spare God, and so God does not spare them. They abuse his justice and his mercy. They do not spare his glory or his laws. Just as they are impartial in sinning, so God is impartial in punishing.

Note 3. **I want to remind you.** A major role for a minister is to remind people. This kind of remembrance takes place in two ways.

1. It comes from the people to God, to remind God about the needs of his people. So it says in Isaiah 62:6 (KJV), "Ye that make mention of the Lord." Christ is the church's advocate, but we are the church's solicitors, to represent the sad condition of the church to God.

2. It also comes from God to the people. In this way we are reminded

about God's being, the riches of his grace, the necessities of obedience, the preciousness of our souls, and the many dangers that lie on the way to heaven. A great deal of a minister's time is to be spent in reminding people about these things. "If you point these things out to the brothers, you will be a good minister of Christ Jesus, brought up in the truths of the faith and of the good teaching that you have followed" (1 Timothy 4:6). And Paul, speaking of his apostleship, says, "I have written to you quite boldly on some points, as if to remind you of them again, because of the grace God gave me to be a minister of Christ Jesus to the Gentiles with the priestly duty of proclaiming the gospel of God" (Romans 15:15-16). "Keep reminding them of these things" (2 Timothy 2:14). "Remind the people to be subject to rulers and authorities" (Titus 3:1). "So I will always remind you of these things, even though you know them and are firmly established in the truth you now have. I think it is right to refresh your memory as long as I live in the tent of this body" (2 Peter 1:12-13). "Dear friends, this is now my second letter to you. I have written both of them as reminders to stimulate you to wholesome thinking" (2 Peter 3:1). Two psalms bear the title "A Psalm of David to bring to remembrance" (Psalms 38 and 70, KJV). The whole purpose of the sacraments is to put us in remembrance of Christ. "When he had given thanks, he broke it and said, 'This is my body, which is for you; do this in remembrance of me'" (1 Corinthians 11:24). One of the main purposes of the Spirit is to remind us of Christ's teaching. "But the Counselor, the Holy Spirit, whom the Father will send in my name, will teach you all things and will remind you of everything I have said to you" (John 14:26).

Note 4. **You already know all this.** It is the great duty of every Christian to be acquainted with the Scriptures. The apostle presumes that this is the case with the Christians to whom he is writing. This is necessary for us also, so that we may know the solid grounds of our own comfort. Everyone should have as his watchword, "You diligently study the Scriptures because you think that by them you possess eternal life" (John 5:39). Particular Scriptures are a great help in times of temptation. "It is written" is Christ's own argument against Satan (see Matthew 4:1-11). There are no Christians as weak as those who are "not acquainted with the teaching about righteousness" (Hebrews 5:13). In our speaking to other people, we must follow the apostle's instructions: "Let the word of Christ dwell in you richly as you teach and admonish one another with all wisdom, and as you sing psalms, hymns and spiritual songs with gratitude in your hearts to God" (Colossians 3:16). Only full vessels overflow. "For I am full of words, and the spirit within me compels me" (Job 32:18). Ignorant Christians are barren and have no life in their speaking. Christians must not just be "complete in knowledge" so they can reach heaven, but so they can "instruct one another" (Romans 15:14).

So then, do not leave this duty to others, as though it were only appropriate for scholars and people who have a public calling. This work should be carried out by everyone who has a soul to be saved. As the many aids we have call us to study more and more, so the errors from false teaching seem to increase more and more. All error comes from using the Scriptures in a wrong way. "Jesus replied, 'You are in error because you do not know the Scriptures or the power of God'" (Matthew 22:29). In the dark a person is liable to lose his way.

To cure this mischief, let me press you to do the following three things.

1. Read the Scriptures in your families. Start doing this among the other times of your worship at home. Your children should be trained up in this way. "From infancy you have known the holy Scriptures, which are able to make you wise for salvation through faith in Christ Jesus" (2 Timothy 3:15). This is also a good practice for you to engage in on your own. None of you are above doing this. The prophets "searched intently and with the greatest care, trying to find out the time and circumstances to which the Spirit of God in them was pointing when he predicted the sufferings of Christ and the glories that would follow" (1 Peter 1:10-11).

2. Read the Scriptures, and make sure you understand what you are reading (see Acts 8:30). The Scriptures are not to be read for delight alone but for spiritual profit and use.

3. In cases of difficulty use all the holy means at your disposal. Pray to God, as the Spirit is the best interpreter. Pray before you read, and pray after you have read. Use the helps God has given, including the commentaries. But above all, "do not treat prophecies with contempt" (1 Thessalonians 5:20). Consult the officers and guides of the church (see Ephesians 4:11-14; Malachi 2:7).

Note 5. **That the Lord delivered his people out of Egypt, but later destroyed those who did not believe.** Observe from this that after great mercies, there follow great judgments, if great sins come in between. After the people of Israel were rescued from Egypt, they were destroyed because of their unbelief. It often happens that many people are preserved, but then a greater calamity falls on them, as a greater judgment from God. "If you forsake the LORD and serve foreign gods, he will turn and bring disaster on you and make an end of you, after he has been good to you" (Joshua 24:20). "Yet they rebelled and grieved his Holy Spirit. So he turned and became their enemy and he himself fought against them" (Isaiah 63:10). There is no hatred like that which springs from corrupted love. Disappointed love, abused love, becomes outrageous. When Amnon hated Tamar, it is said, "Amnon hated her with intense hatred. In fact, he hated her more than he had loved her" (2 Samuel 13:15). There are no evils like those that come after mercy. There are no sins as great as those that are committed against mercies. There is not only filthiness in them but unkindness. "When our fathers were in Egypt, they gave no thought to your miracles; they did not remember your many kindnesses, and they rebelled by the sea, the Red Sea" (Psalm 106:7). Notice that it says, "the sea, the Red Sea," emphasizing that in the very place where they had seen the mercies of the Lord and had experienced his glorious deliverance, they rebelled against God.

Application 1. This teaching warns us that there may be danger after deliverance. There are strange changes in providence. "Each man's life is but a breath" (Psalm 39:5). When you are at your best, as when the sun is at its highest, a decline may follow.

Application 2. This is a warning to those who enjoy mercies not to sin anymore in case a worse sin befalls them (see John 5:14). There are sins we should especially beware of, particularly those that reveal our ingratitude after we have received mercies. We are apt to forget the vows we made when we were in misery. Jacob vowed in Genesis 28:22, "This stone that I have set up as a pillar will be God's house, and of all that you give me I will give you a tenth." But Jacob forgets this vow and what happens? His family goes through horrible experiences. Dinah is raped, Reuben goes into his father's bed, a murder is committed on the Shechemites under the guise of religion—and then Jacob remembers his vow. We promise much when we want deliverance, but when we have it, God is neglected. But God will not put up with this. By sad and disastrous accidents God reminds us of our old promises.

Note 6. Our next observation is taken from the cause of their destruction, intimated in those words, **those who did not believe**. The people of Israel committed many sins in the desert—grumbling, fornication, rebellion. But the apostle puts them all under this heading: **those who did not believe**. Unbelief was the root of all their misfortunes. "The LORD said to Moses, 'How long will these people treat me with contempt? How long will they refuse to believe in me, in spite of all the miraculous signs I have performed among them?'" (Numbers 14:11). From this observe that unbelief brings destruction or is the cause of all the evil that we do or suffer.

In dealing with this point, I shall touch on, first, the heinousness of unbelief, second, the nature of unbelief, and, third, the cure of unbelief.

1. I start with the heinousness of unbelief.

a. No sin dishonors God as much as unbelief. It calls into question his mercy, power, justice, and especially his truth. "Anyone who does not believe God has made him out to be a liar" (1 John 5:10). To say that someone is a liar is to say he is unfit to keep company with others. This is a special injury to God, who stands more on his word than on any other part of his name. "You have exalted above all things your name and your word" (Psalm 138:2). Because unbelief accuses God, limits him to secondary causes, and denies him his glory, it is heinous and hateful to God.

b. Unbelief is a sin that God has declared he is most displeased with. Search the annals, survey all the monuments of time, and see if God ever spared an unbeliever. Hence the apostle says that in the desert the Israelites were destroyed because of their unbelief. "They were broken off because of unbelief" (Romans 11:20). Christ never rebuked his disciples so much for anything as for their unbelief. "How foolish you are, and how slow of heart to believe" (Luke 24:25). "You of little faith, why are you so afraid?" (Matthew 8:26). Christ rebuked them before he rebuked the wind. The storm started first in their own hearts.

c. Unbelief is the mother of all sin. The very first sin was the fruit of unbelief. We easily observe a faltering of assent on that occasion (see Genesis 3:1-6). Unbelief is the basis of all hardness of heart and apostasy. "See to it, brothers, that none of you has a sinful, unbelieving heart that turns away from the living God. But encourage one another daily, as long as it is called Today, so that none of you may be hardened by sin's deceitfulness" (Hebrews 3:12-13). The person who does not believe the promises of the Word will not be ready to do any good. All our neglect and coldness in holy duties comes from the weakness of our faith. There is decay at the root. Many people are ashamed of adultery, theft, and murder, but not of unbelief, which is the mother of all these.

d. In the end, unbelief is clear evidence of reprobation. "You do not believe because you are not my sheep" (John 10:26). "When the Gentiles heard this, they were glad and honored the word of the Lord; and all who were appointed for eternal life believed" (Acts 13:48). Unbelief is God's prison, where he keeps the reprobate world. "For God has bound all men over to disobedience so that he may have mercy on them all" (Romans 11:32).

e. Unbelief is a sin that deprives us of much good and of the comforts of providence. Nothing bars and shuts out God's work of comfort in us like this sin of unbelief. "He could not do any miracles there, except lay his hands on a few sick people and heal them. And he was amazed at their lack of faith" (Mark 6:5-6). "Then Jesus said, 'Did I not tell you that if you believed, you would see the glory of God?'" (John 11:40). This is also true of God's ordinances. "For we have also had the gospel preached to us, just as they did; but the message they heard was of no value to them, because those who heard did not combine it with faith" (Hebrews 4:2). This is also true as far as prayer is concerned. "But when he asks, he must believe and not doubt, because he who doubts is like a wave of the sea, blown and tossed by the wind. That man should not think he will receive anything from the Lord; he is a double-minded man, unstable in all he does" (James 1:6-8).

Unbelief bars heaven's gates. It excluded Adam from paradise, the Israelites from Canaan, and us from the kingdom of heaven. "And with whom was he angry for forty years? Was it not with those who sinned, whose bodies fell in the desert? And to whom did God swear that they would never enter his rest if not to those who disobeyed? So we see that they were not able to enter, because of their unbelief" (Hebrews 3:17-19). So much for the heinousness of unbelief, which shows us why God destroyed those in the desert who did not believe.

2. Now I will move on to the nature of unbelief. There are two kinds of unbelief, negative and positive.

a. Negative unbelief is found in those to whom the sound of the Gospel never came or to whom God has denied the means whereby faith might take root in them. Their lack of means is not their sin, but it is their punishment, or at least their misery. These people are not condemned so much for lack of faith in Christ as for not obeying the law of nature and for sinning against the knowledge they received in Adam. They never received the light of the Gospel in Adam; neither had Adam the knowledge of this revealed to him, except by special grace after the Fall, when the promise about the woman's seed was revealed to him. Therefore, those who have never heard about Christ are not condemned simply for not believing in him. They are condemned for their sins against the law, not for their unbelief against the Gospel. They can never be saved without Christ; yet God will not condemn them for not believing in Christ, for he never gave them the means of knowing Christ.

b. Positive unbelief is found in those who have the means to believe in Christ and yet neglect and refuse him. Positive unbelief may be total or partial.

Total unbelief is in those people who continue to be pagans after they have heard the Gospel. When the Word was preached in the early church, it met with varying degrees of success, as is seen at Antioch (Acts 13:48), at Iconium (Acts 14:1-2), and at Athens (Acts 17:34).

Positive unbelief may also be partial. It is partial when people do not fully believe in Christ or wholeheartedly embrace him. Israel, out of unbelief, despised the land (see Psalm 106:24) and did not think it was worth looking after. Similarly, people refuse the counsels of the Gospel because they prefer to indulge their worldly passions.

3. The last thing to mention about unbelief is the cure for unbelief. Only God by his mighty power can cure it. "I pray also that the eyes of your heart may be enlightened in order that you may know the hope to which he has called you, the riches of his glorious inheritance in the saints, and his incomparably great power for us who believe" (Ephesians 1:18-19). The means we must use here can be put under two headings—cautions and directions.

a. Cautions. First, beware of testing God. "But they continued to sin against him, rebelling in the desert against the Most High. They willfully put God to the test by demanding the food they craved. They spoke against God, saying, 'Can God spread a table in the desert? When he struck the rock, water gushed out, and steams flowed abundantly. But can he also give us food? Can he supply meat for his people?'" (Psalm 78:17-20). "Come down from the cross, if you are the Son of God!" (Matthew 27:40). This places on God conditions that we have made up ourselves. But God never undertook to give us meat for our worldly passions. When we prescribe what God has to do for our satisfaction, we are only laying a trap for ourselves.

Second, beware of betraying faith by distrusting present means. This frequently happens. "But if someone from the dead goes to them, they will repent" (Luke 16:30). We say or think that if we had oracles or miracles, or if God spoke to us from heaven, then we would not falter in our trust as we do now. But by doing this we impeach the Scriptures. Moses and the prophets are sufficient grounds for faith, and extraordinary means will have no effect on those who are not prepared to believe through ordinary means. Whatever dispensations God may use, we are still human. "For they did not believe in God or trust in his deliverance. Yet he gave a command to the skies above and opened the doors of the heavens" (Psalm 78:22-23).

Third, beware of ifs in principles of faith. Foundation stones, if laid loose, endanger the whole building. The devil tempted Christ and said, "If you are the Son of God . . ." (Matthew 4:3). Just before these temptations there was a plain oracle from heaven saying, "This is my Son" (Matthew 3:17). But the devil nevertheless tried to sow a seed of doubt with his "if."

Fourth, beware of sin. Doubts are the fumes of sin. Uprightness brings serenity, but unbelief makes way for sin, and sin for unbelief. Sin will weaken trust; it cannot do otherwise. Shame, horror, and doubt are the consequences of sin.

b. Directions. First, strengthen your assent to the Word of God. Assurance and comfort would follow more easily if we completely assented to the truths of the Word. There are several degrees of assent—conjecture, which is only a slight inclination of the mind to what is probable, and opinion, which is a stronger inclination to think that what is presented is true. In addition to these there is "complete understanding" (Colossians 2:2). We should never rest until we come to this.

Second, urge your hearts with the truths you assent to and let them work on your affections. See Romans 8:31, Hebrews 2:3, and Job 5:27.

Verse 6

Commentary on Verse 6

And the angels who did not keep their positions of authority but abandoned their own home—these he has kept in darkness, bound with everlasting chains for judgment on the great Day.

In this verse you have the second example of a defection from the faith. Jude mentions the apostate angels. These angels, despite the dignity and height of their nature, rebelled against God and were left to a dreadful judgment. In this instance there is an argument not *a pari* (as in the previous verse), but *a majore ad minus*—not from a like case, but from the greater to the lesser. If God did not spare such creatures who through the grace of creation were so excellent, certainly he will not spare us, whatever gospel privileges we have, if we do not walk in his ways.

From these words note, first, the sin of the angels—they **did not keep their positions of authority**; and, second, observe their punishment.

The phrases that imply their punishment fall into two categories—present and future. The first part of the present judgment is *poena damni*, their loss, implied in the clause **abandoned their own home**, in which their guilt is further intimated. Here Jude makes it to be their act, but Peter in the parallel passage says that it is God's act: "For if God did not spare angels when they sinned, but sent them to hell . . ." (2 Peter 2:4).

The second part of the angels' punishment is *poena sensûs*, their punishment of sense or pain: **these he has kept in darkness, bound with everlasting chains.** This is an allusion to the state of all malefactors or condemned people, who are kept in prison until the time of their final judgment. The evils of this prison are two. They are **bound with everlasting chains**, and they are **kept in darkness.**

After the present judgment of the angels comes their future judgment, which is implied by the words, **for judgment on the Great Day.** By **judgment** is meant the sentence of condemnation that will be passed on them in the sight of the whole world, and then the consequences, which are eternal misery and torment.

Notes on Verse 6

Note 1. I start with the phrases that imply their sin and fall. **And the angels.** The expression is plural to indicate the large number who fell. **Their positions of authority.** This may be translated either "their authority" or "their beginning" or "their first estate." If you translate it "authority," it fits in well with the apostle's aim here. The angels were often called "authorities" in Scripture because of their great power and excellent nature. "For by him [Christ] all things were created: things in heaven and on earth, visible and invisible, whether thrones or powers or rulers or authorities" (Colossians 1:16). "Thrones," "powers," "rulers," and "authorities" all imply the dignity of the angelic nature. Indeed, the devils themselves, because of the power and cunning they still have, are called "authorities." "For our struggle is not against flesh and blood, but against the rulers, against the authorities, against the powers of this dark world and against the spiritual forces of evil in the heavenly realms" (Ephesians 6:12). If you translate this word "beginning" or "first state," it more fully expresses the misery and fall of the apostate angels. They have not only left their excellency and power, but also they have moved away from the integrity and righteousness in which they were originally created.

Peter states, "God did not spare angels when they sinned" (2 Peter 2:4). And John quotes Jesus' words, "He [the devil] was a murderer from the beginning, not holding to the truth, for there is no truth in him" (John 8:44). That purity and integrity in which they were created was "truth," the perfection of any rational creature. The holiness they had could only be kept up by truth or correct thinking about God. In expanding this point I will ask:

1. What was this *arche*, **authority**, or first state?
2. What was their sin?
3. How did they come to sin?
4. The number of those who fell.
5. When they fell.

1. I confess that the Scriptures do speak somewhat sparingly about the nature or fall of angels, but we are left with some helpful hints. What then is the first state from which they departed? I answer: Their original condition was one of holiness and happiness. The Lord saw to it that every creature he made was good. How much more would this apply to angels, whom God created for his own train and company. In their innocence they were all good and happy, and contemplated and beheld God, and embraced him with delight. All that is supernatural in the good angels is the grace through which they abide in the knowledge and love of God,

whereas other angels left **their** positions of authority. It is probable that this grace was given to good angels in the very moment of their creation. They were chosen in Christ, who is the head of men and angels (see Colossians 1:16).

2. What was their sin? There is a great deal of difference among the divines about this, and they conjecture about this instead of sticking to certain proof. However, there is enough to vindicate God's justice against them. To find out what their sin was, consider the following three propositions.

First, the law that made their act to be sin was the moral law, a copy of God's holiness, his revealed will to all rational creatures. "God did not spare angels when they sinned" (2 Peter 2:4).

Second, there is pride in every sin—namely, a despising and contempt of God's commandments. To support this the fathers (Gregory, Augustine, and Damascene) usually quote Isaiah 14:12-13: "How you have fallen from heaven, O morning star, son of the dawn! You have been cast down to the earth, you who once laid low the nations! You said in your heart, 'I will ascend to heaven; I will raise my throne above the stars of God; I will sit enthroned on the mount of assembly, on the utmost heights of the sacred mountain.'" But these are only metaphorical passages concerning the king of Babylon. The evidence that is most cogent comes in 1 Timothy 3:6: "He must not be a recent convert, or he may become conceited and fall under the same judgment as the devil." That is, in case he makes himself guilty of the sin for which the devil was condemned and rejected by God, namely, the sin of pride. James says there is such a thing as devilish wisdom: "Such 'wisdom' does not come down from heaven but is earthly, unspiritual, of the devil" (James 3:15). Sin is often connected with the judgment that follows it. God threw them down from **their positions of authority**, and this was a sign that they had aspired to something above their station. This may also be deduced from the first temptation: "You will be as gods."

Third, the best way of looking at this is to see their sin as a compound sin. As there are many sins in the one act through which Adam fell—unbelief, pride, ingratitude, and disobedience—so with this act of the angels there might be many sins, though the chief sin was pride.

3. How the angels came to sin. The angels were created pure, and they had no evil desires in them. As they were in heaven, they had no object outside to draw them or allure them. As there was no evil in heaven, how could they sin?

a. I answer that it is probable that many of the angels sinned through temptation and that one great angel, now called Beelzebub, first fell and drew the others after him. Matthew 25:41 refers to "the eternal fire prepared for the devil and his angels," and in Matthew 10:25 we read, "If the

113

head of the house has been called Beelzebub, how much more the members of his household!" "It is only by Beelzebub, the prince of demons, that this fellow drives out demons" (Matthew 12:24). He was the ringleader of the unclean spirits, the devil, Satan, the great dragon, the god of this world. From this it is reasonable to conclude that he was the chief of the apostate angels, and he led a rebellion against God.

b. But the question still remains: How did the first angel fall? It is hard to conceive how sin came into the angels first. All we can say is this: Angels were created good, yet mutable and free, and some voluntarily chose not to abide in their positions of authority. The only answer Augustine gave to this question was, *Deus non sunt*—"they are not God." It is God's prerogative alone to be immutable. They could sin because they were creatures. Aquinas reasoned: God cannot sin, because his act is his rule; but all creatures, though never so pure, if not assisted by grace, may sin. "If God places no trust in his servants, if he charges his angels with error . . ." (Job 4:18). There is mutability in the angelic nature; so they can commit errors. Certainly God was not the cause of their fall, as if he had infused evil into them. It was the error of the Manichees to say that they were created evil.

4. How many angels fell? The scholastics are too rash. Some say just as many fell as stood, others that a third of them fell, misinterpreting Revelation 12:4 ("His [the red dragon's] tail swept a third of the stars out of the sky and flung them to the earth"). What is referred to here is the defection of the church. However, we are certain that many angels fell. That the number is great is deduced because the world is full of these evil spirits, and a whole legion, which is made up of some thousands, is said to possess one man (see Luke 8:30).

5. When did the angels fall? In general terms we may say that they existed very soon after creation. "The devil . . . was a murderer from the beginning" (John 8:44). "The devil has been sinning from the beginning" (1 John 3:8). Valentius and Basilides, in the generation following the apostles, erroneously said the angels were not created but were begotten of God. But they were in fact created, and they were created in time (see Colossians 1:16; Psalm 148:2). Clearly, after they were created, they sinned before man fell, for the devil, in and through the serpent, deceived Eve. "Eve was deceived by the serpent's cunning" (2 Corinthians 11:3). Therefore, the angels probably fell a short time after they were created. They did not sin as soon as they were created, or it might seem that they were naturally evil. It is probable that some time elapsed between their creation and defection, but a very little time, to show the mutability of the creature.

Application 1. Observe that such excellent creatures fell. Angels themselves were created excellent but mutable. To see such glorious stars leave their station and fall from heaven like lightning should make us poor creatures tremble and look to our own standing. "So, if you think you are standing firm, be careful that you don't fall!" (1 Corinthians 10:12). Self-confidence is the sure way to ruin. The angels were the courtiers of heaven, the glory of the creation, in the first rank of created beings, and yet they fell. Who can presume to stand when angels fell?

Application 2. They fell dreadfully, and from angels came devils, engaging in theft, lying, envy, and murder toward human beings. The best things, when they are corrupted, become the worst, just as no vinegar is so tart as that which is made from the sweetest wine. When people sin against the light and against grace, they become cruel. "If they have escaped the corruption of the world by knowing our Lord and Savior Jesus Christ and are again entangled in it and overcome, they are worse off at the end than they were at the beginning" (2 Peter 2:20). What malice these evil angels have now against God and man! They go around seeking someone to devour. There are none so bad as apostates.

Application 3. Learn from the sin in general through which they fell. It was pride. See the danger of this sin; it always goes before a fall. The angels lost their holiness out of a desire to be great; they would be over everything or over nothing at all. It is always dangerous when people prefer to be great rather than to be good. So look on pride as the sure forerunner of a fall.

Application 4. Notice that the first sin ever committed was punishment in itself. **The angels . . . did not keep their positions of authority**. The sin is expressed in such a way as to imply their loss. Duty has its reward and sin its punishment. Never think that you will ever gain anything from offending God. You only defile and debase and degrade yourselves from your own excellency when you sin.

Note 2. **But abandoned their own home**. The apostate angels, after they sinned and fell, left the place of happiness and glory they had previously enjoyed. "And there was war in heaven. Michael and his angels fought against the dragon, and the dragon and his angels fought back. But he was not strong enough, and they lost their place in heaven. The great dragon was hurled down—that ancient serpent called the devil or Satan, who leads the whole world astray. He was hurled to the earth, and his angels with him" (Revelation 12:7-9). That Scripture, I admit, is mystical and speaks about the overcoming of Satan in this present world and casting him out of both the church, "heaven," and the world, "earth." But this is also a clear allusion to Satan's first fall from heaven. I offer you the following propositions concerning the fall of the angels.

1. The place of their innocence was heaven, around God's throne, where the good angels continually stand before him beholding his face (see

Daniel 7:10). In such a blessed place and in such blessed company was their *oiketerion*, habitation or abode, **their own home**.

2. In this place they were to enjoy God and honor him. Their happiness was to enjoy God, their duty to glorify him. There they beheld his face (see Matthew 18:10), for the vision and sight of God is the happiness of rational creatures, and therefore our happy state is expressed as, "then we shall see face to face" (1 Corinthians 13:12). David says there is "eternal pleasure" at God's "right hand" (Psalm 16:11). In heaven, then, God manifested himself to them. There they were to applaud his counsels, receive his commands, love him with the most perfect embraces of their will, fulfill his commandments, and listen to his voice.

3. From this place they are now driven into the lower part of the world, which is a place more suited to sin and misery. "God did not spare angels when they sinned, but sent them to hell, putting them in gloomy dungeons to be held for judgment" (2 Peter 2:4). This expression denotes the dreadfulness of their fall from so glorious a mansion to such a place of misery. For wherever they are, they carry their own hell with them, though through God's permission they are yet allowed to remain in the air or on earth.

4. Leaving heaven, they left all the happiness and glory they had enjoyed there—namely, the light they had in their understanding as they beheld God, the power in their wills to love and serve him. In place of all this they were filled with darkness and malice and became the irreconcilable enemies of God and man. As for their light, their gracious knowledge is quite extinct, their natural knowledge eclipsed, and their experience is not enough to engage their heart with God. As for their integrity and holiness, instead of a will to love and serve God, they have nothing but obstinate purposes to do evil and to hinder God's glory and the good of men. "Your enemy the devil prowls around like a roaring lion looking for someone to devour" (1 Peter 5:8).

Application 1. God has given proper places where creatures will perform their duty and enjoy their happiness. As the angels had heaven, which was *idoion oiketepion*, **their own home**, their proper place, so Adam had paradise, and the saints have the church. It is misery enough to be thrown out of the place where God had made himself known. People who are cast out of the church are handed over to Satan. "Hand this man over to Satan" (1 Corinthians 5:5). In the church Christ rules; in the world Satan rules. It is dangerous to leave your own place and to be cast out of the congregation of the faithful, where God dwells and is glorified.

Application 2. Sin deprives us of God's presence. This is the wall of separation between us and God. "But your iniquities have separated you from your God; your sins have hidden his face from you, so that he will not hear" (Isaiah 59:2). Sin not only causes God to stand apart from us, but it has a strange effect on us and makes us shy of God's presence. So when you are tempted to sin, think, "God could not endure the sight of angels once they were defiled with sin. If I give in to this temptation, I will dishonor God. It will either make the Spirit leave me, or it will make me leave the throne of grace." Guilty souls cannot stand in God's presence, and God will not tolerate the presence of guilty sinners. Peter said to Jesus, "Go away from me, Lord; I am a sinful man!" (Luke 5:8). And God said, "Depart from me, you who are cursed, into the eternal fire prepared for the devil and his angels" (Matthew 25:41).

Application 3. Observe also that Jude says that it was *their* (the angels' act), but Peter says it was *God's* act. Jude says, **the angels . . . abandoned their own home**. Peter says, "God did not spare angels when they sinned, but sent them to hell" (2 Peter 2:4). Our ruin is caused by the use of our free will. God does not punish us willingly, and he takes no delight in our destruction. We sin and so freely depart from our own happiness. We leave and then God throws us out.

Application 4. God throws Satan out of heaven. Do you imitate your heavenly Father? Do you throw Satan out of your heart? Who would entertain the one God has cast out of heaven? So do not allow him any foothold in your heart (see Ephesians 4:27). Satan's great aim, now that he cannot get into heaven himself, is to live in the hearts of men.

Application 5. From the word *oiketerion*, **their own home**, observe that the true dwelling-place and rest is heaven. It was the habitation of the angels and the rest of the saints. Oh, how you should long for your home. Let your heart and your hopes be there. Enter into your eternal inheritance by degrees. The angels left their home. You should always be traveling toward it. Let your hearts be in heaven. "Since, then, you have been raised with Christ, set your hearts on things above, where Christ is seated at the right hand of God" (Colossians 3:1). "But our citizenship is in heaven" (Philippians 3:20). Good angels still exist, and they are blessed companions. "You have come to thousands upon thousands of angels in joyful assembly" (Hebrews 12:22).

Note 3. **These he has kept in darkness, bound with everlasting chains**. I will start with the **everlasting chains**. There are two things to mention here: first, that the angels are kept in **chains**, and, second, that these chains are **everlasting**.

1. The angels are kept in **chains**. But what chain can hold angels? Can spirits be bound with iron?

a. I answer: These are spiritual chains, suited to the spiritual nature of angels. Spiritual chains are things like guilty consciences. Their consciences remind wicked angels that they are condemned to damnation because of their sin. This is a sure chain, for it is a chain of judgment that cannot be shaken off. It is bound and tied to them and to us by God's hand of justice. The condition of a guilty sinner is often compared to that of a prisoner. "I, the LORD, have called you in righteousness; I will take hold of your hand. I will keep you and will make you to be a covenant for the people and a light for the Gentiles, to open eyes that are blind, to free captives from prison and to release from the dungeon those who sit in darkness" (Isaiah 42:6-7). "This is what the LORD says: 'In the time of my favor I will answer you, and in the day of salvation I will help you; I will keep you and will make you to be a covenant for the people, to restore the land and to reassign its desolate inheritances, to say to the captives, "Come out," and to those in darkness, "Be free!" They will feed beside the roads and find pasture on every barren hill'" (Isaiah 49:8-9). "The Spirit of the Sovereign LORD is on me, because the LORD has anointed me to preach good news to the poor. He has sent me to bind up the brokenhearted, to proclaim freedom for the captives and release for the prisoners" (Isaiah 61:1).

Sin is also often compared to a prison in which we are enclosed. "God has bound all men over to disobedience, so that he may have mercy on them all" (Romans 11:32). "But the Scripture declares that the whole world is a prisoner of sin" (Galatians 3:22). Guilt is compared with the chains that are put on us by God the Judge. "The evil deeds of a wicked man ensnare him; the cords of his sin hold him fast" (Proverbs 5:22). "My sins have been bound into a yoke; by his hands they were woven together" (Lamentations 1:14).

b. These chains that bind angels are the chains of God's eternal decrees. As there is a golden chain, the chain of salvation, that continues from link to link until the purposes of eternal grace end in the possession of eternal glory, so there is an iron chain of reprobation that begins in God's own voluntary passing them by, continues in men's voluntary apostasy, and ends in their just damnation. "The man he imprisons cannot be released" (Job 12:14).

2. These chains are **everlasting** chains because the wicked angels stand guilty forever, without hope of recovery or redemption. All natural persons are in chains, but there is hope for many of these prisoners. But the chains on the evil angels are forever and ever. The chains that now keep them and hold them in their lost state will hereafter continue as part of their final punishment, when much of the freedom they presently have will be abridged. From this we observe these practical inferences.

a. Sins are, as it were, bonds and chains. Wicked people are in bondage both here and hereafter. Now they are in snares, and then they will be in chains. Here they are taken captive by Satan in his snares (see 2 Timothy 2:26), and hereafter they are bound with him in chains. Sin itself is a bondage, and hell a prison. Were there nothing in sin but the present slavery, that would be enough to ward us off from sin. But alas, this is not all there is, as there are not only snares but chains. The good angels have freedom to serve God, while the evil angels are imprisoned by their own obstinacy and wickedness. Remember this when you are convicted by a sin that you cannot leave, and take great care that it does not become a chain of everlasting darkness.

b. These chains can never be broken. The angels cannot break them themselves, and Christ will not, for their day of grace is past. Our chains too would be eternal if Christ did not break them and open the prison door to the captives (see Isaiah 61:1). We have an advantage over the angels, for a year of freedom has been proclaimed to us. Christ himself was bound with our chains. He was put in prison so that we might go free. People who reject the mercy Christ offers can never free themselves from the hands of justice but forever remain under the power and wrath of the living God. "It is a dreadful thing to fall into the hands of the living God" (Hebrews 10:31).

Note 3. **Kept in darkness.** We now come to the second part of the punishment of pain, taken from the other inconvenience of a prison, *hupo zophov*, **kept in darkness**, an allusion to criminals who are thrown into dungeons, where, in addition to being bound in heavy chains, the very darkness of the places increases their misery. Light is pleasant, as it gives us the sight of what is lovely in the world; and when we are deprived of this, the mind, like a mill deprived of grain, begins to work on itself. I will now expand on the proposition that the angels are **kept in darkness**.

1. *Darkness* in Scripture represents three things: first, ignorance; second, sin; and, third, misery. Light represents the opposite qualities— knowledge, holiness, and happiness. Because light discovers all things, it stands for knowledge; because of all bodily qualities it is more pure, it stands for holiness; and because it is wonderfully pleasing and delightful to our senses, it stands for glory. In the same way darkness, which is nothing but the absence of light, stands for ignorance (see John 3:19), sin (see 1 Peter 2:9), and misery (Matthew 6:23). Ignorance makes us stumble over sin, and through sin we fall into the pit of everlasting darkness.

a. Darkness is the devil's punishment, the highest misery for the highest rank of reasonable creatures. Oh, why should we love what is the misery of the fallen angels? Our Saviour speaks about those who prefer darkness to light (see John 3:19). Such people prefer error to truth, evil desires rather than Christ, and ignorance rather than knowledge. It is one of the saddest facts about the fall of humankind that we are in love with our own misery. We should hate sin, but we actually hate the light that exposes sin. Ignorant people love a foolish ministry, and God's faithful witnesses are a torment to them (see Revelation 11:10). Blind people are all for blind guides.

b. Light that gives us no comfort is but darkness. Satan has some knowledge left, but no comfort. "You believe that there is one God.

Good! Even the demons believe that—and shudder" (James 2:19). The more aware they are of God's being and glory, the greater is the horror that these spirits experience. It is very miserable when we have only enough light to awaken our consciences and enough knowledge to be self-condemned. We will be punished if we know God but do not enjoy him. So do not rest until you can see God with a light that brings you comforting enjoyment of him. "For with you is the fountain of life; in your light we see light" (Psalm 36:9). There is light in God's light, but all other light is darkness.

c. Notice the difference between God and Satan. "God is light; in him there is no darkness at all" (1 John 1:5). Satan is darkness. God lives in light, but Satan is kept in chains in darkness. The first thing that God made in the world was light, and the Spirit's first gift to the human soul is illumination. But Satan's aim and work is to bring in darkness. "The god of this age has blinded the minds of unbelievers, so that they cannot see the light of the gospel of the glory of Christ, who is the image of God" (2 Corinthians 4:4). Ignorance is the foundation of Satan's kingdom. So then, the more darkness there is, the more Satan is pleased. A child of God is a child of light, and what has he to do with the works of darkness? (See Ephesians 5:11.) There should be a complete antipathy between you and sin, just as there is between God and Satan.

d. The world, when compared with heaven, is a dark place. It is the place to which the devils are thrown down, and they are held under darkness. It is an obscure corner of the creation, a place fit for our trial but not for our reward. Looked at with spiritual eyes, it is but a great and vast dungeon where we cannot have a clear sight of God. It is Satan's walk, a place of danger and defilement. It is all we can do to keep ourselves pure and faultless from all this (see James 1:27; 2 Peter 2:20). The inheritance that is given to the saints is given to them "in the kingdom of light" (Colossians 1:12). Let us look for that and long for that, for "God . . . lives in unapproachable light" (1 Timothy 6:15-16).

Note 4. **For judgment on the great Day**. On judgment day the punishment of the devils will be greater than it is now. The devils' punishment is great now, but it will be far greater in the future. "Have you come here to torture us before the appointed time?" (Matthew 8:29). A time will come when God's wrath with them will be increased, and this time is the day of judgment, the great day of the Lord, when the devils will be brought before the tribunal of Christ and his saints. The good angels will come as Christ's companions, and the evil angels as his prisoners. "When the Son of Man comes in his glory, and all the angels with him, he will sit on his throne in heavenly glory" (Matthew 25:31). "This will happen when the Lord Jesus is revealed from heaven in blazing fire with his powerful angels" (2 Thessalonians 1:7). "Do you not know that we will judge angels?" (1 Corinthians 6:3). On that day the devils' pride will be thwarted, and Christ's glory and that of the good angels and the saints will be seen. After that the devils will be consigned to horrible torments. Hell is their estate and portion. "Depart from me, you who are cursed, into the eternal fire prepared for the devil and his angels" (Matthew 25:41).

1. The judgment of the wicked is not yet complete. On that great day it will increase. In this life we are adding sin to sin, and in the next life God will be adding torment to torment. Oh, what a sad train of judgments follows a sinner!

2. Origen was too charitable on this subject. He taught that there would be a flaming river through which all creatures have to pass and so be purged and then, at last, saved. This even included the devils. But the reality is that not all men will be saved, and the devils are kept for a more severe judgment.

3. Angels will be judged. No one will be exempt. On **the great Day** you will see those glorious creatures bound with chains of darkness. And like the evil angels, the kings and captains of this world will be brought in trembling before the Lamb's throne. "Then the kings of the earth, the princes, the generals, the rich, the mighty, and every slave and every free man hid in caves and among the rocks of the mountains" (Revelation 6:15). The great as well as the small will appear before that great tribunal. "And I saw the dead, great and small, standing before the throne, and books were opened" (Revelation 20:12).

4. The wicked angels will be plunged into the depths of hell, while saints enter into their Master's glory. God loves a returning sinner more than an apostate angel.

Note 5. **The great Day.** There is one more point to note before I leave this verse. That judgment day will be a *great Day*. This is so in many ways.

1. First, it will be a **great Day** because of the consummate act of Christ's regal office. Of all offices, Christ's kingly office is the most eminent. This kingly office will shine in its most brilliant luster on that **great Day**. Therefore, judgment day is called the day of the Lord. "But the day of the Lord will come like a thief" (2 Peter 3:10). It will be the day on which Christ will show himself to be the Lord.

a. On **the great Day** Christ will reward his friends. Those who have been faithful to Christ's interests may be frowned on by the world, but they will not regret anything on the day of Christ's royalty. "Then the King will say . . ." (Matthew 25:34). The apostle Peter was concerned about what he would lose and complained to Christ, "We have left everything to follow you! What then will there be for us?" (Matthew 19:27). What had Peter forsaken? A net, a cottage, a fishing boat. We are apt to think a great deal about what we part with for Christ's sake. If we suffer but a harsh word, a small inconvenience, a frown, we later say, "What will we have to compensate for all this?" But we do not need to look for any other paymaster than Christ. He will not be slow to reward us when payment day comes. "I tell you the truth, at the renewal of all things, when the Son of Man sits on his glorious throne, you who have followed me will also sit on twelve thrones, judging the twelve tribes of Israel" (Matthew 19:28). The day of judgment will be a great day of regeneration. Then there will be new heavens, a new earth, new bodies, new souls—everything will be new! Christ will ensure that we are not the losers on **the great Day**.

b. On **the great Day** Christ will have total victory over his enemies. "By myself I have sworn, my mouth has uttered in all integrity a word that will not be revoked: Before me every knee will bow; by me every tongue will swear" (Isaiah 45:23). This refers to Christ's sovereignty and total victory over his enemies. This Scripture is alluded to twice in the New Testament, and in both instances it is applied to Christ. In Philippians 2:10 the apostle says, "that at the name of Jesus every knee should bow." The same Scripture is cited by the apostle Paul again, in Romans 14:11: "For we will all stand before God's judgment seat. It is written: '"As surely as I live," says the Lord, "Every knee will bow before me; every tongue will confess to God."'" So the bowing of knees or stooping of enemies is not completed until then. Christ now often overrules the counsels and schemes of his enemies and brings destruction on them. But there is no trembling now as there will be on **the great Day**.

2. The day of judgment is a **great Day** because great things will happen on that day. We see this as we consider, first, the preparations for that day; second, the day itself; and, third, the consequences of the day.

a. There are two preparations for Christ's coming mentioned in Scripture: first, the archangel's trumpet and, second, the sign of the Son of man.

First, there is that great noise and terror of the voice of the Lord, heralded by some special angels through whom the world is, as it were, summoned to appear before Christ's tribunal. "For the Lord himself will come down from heaven, with a loud command, with the voice of the archangel and with the trumpet call of God, and the dead in Christ will rise first" (1 Thessalonians 4:16). "And he will send his angels with a loud trumpet call, and they will gather his elect from the four winds, from one end of the heavens to the other" (Matthew 24:31).

Second, the sign of "the Son of Man" (Matthew 24:30). We cannot say for certain what this is until we experience it. Some think it will be a strange star, similar to the one that appeared at Christ's first coming, which led the wise men to him. Others think this will be the sign of the cross, which would be seen by the world as Christ's badge. For the great theme of the Gospel is Christ crucified; it is called the word of the cross. Some think this will appear in the heavens, as it did to Constantine when he went to fight against Maxentius after seeing the words, *en touro nikeseis*—"by this you will overcome." Eusebius described that vision as the figure X, the first letter of Christ's name in Greek. So, many of the ancient commentators thought the cross was Christ's ensign and royal banner, which he will display in the heavens, just as kings do when they make their triumphant approach, having their banners carried before them. But I cannot be as dogmatic as that.

b. Let us consider the day itself and the great things that will occur on that day. It is a day when all mankind will be gathered together. On that day Adam will see all his descendants at a single glance. But it is especially a day for the collecting together of the saints, who are at present scattered in various countries, towns, and houses, wherever God has any work and service for them to carry out. On the great day of judgment they will all come together in one assembly. But the wicked will be herded together like bundles of straw and sticks that set one another alight (see Matthew 13:40-42).

On the great day of judgment Christ will be admired by his followers: ". . . on the day he comes to be glorified in his holy people and to be marveled at among all those who have believed" (2 Thessalonians 1:10). The angels will stand wondering what Christ is about to do with the creatures who have just crept out of the dust. All of the good angels will shine like the sun. What a glorious day that will be when there will be a constellation of so many suns! They will share with Christ in the glory of his kingdom as they are associated with him in judging the world. "The upright will rule over them in the morning" (Psalm 49:14). People who are at present scorned and persecuted will on the morning of the resurrection, when they wake up to meet Christ, have dominion of the world. The elect will be acquitted before the ungodly are condemned, so that they may join Christ in judging the world. "Do you not know that the saints will judge the world?" (1 Corinthians 6:2).

c. There are three consequences of that day. First, the sending of the people who are judged into their everlasting state; second, the giving up of the kingdom to the Father; and, third, the burning of the world.

First, the people who are judged will be sent to their everlasting state—the elect to glory, and the wicked to torments. "Come, you who are blessed by my Father; take your inheritance, the kingdom prepared for you since the creation of the world" (Matthew 25:34). That is, "You have been too long absent from me. Come, receive the fruit of your faith and hope." But we read in Matthew 25:41, "Depart from me, you who are cursed, into the eternal fire prepared for the devil and his angels." They will be banished from Christ's presence with a terrible ban that cannot be reversed. On earth God's sentences were often repealed when the nation repented (see Jeremiah 18:8). So although he never changes his decree, he does often change his sentence. But the day of patience will on that day be over, and this sentence cannot be changed.

The second consequence that will take place on that day is that the kingdom will be given over to the Father. "Then the end will come, when he hands over the kingdom to God the Father after he has destroyed all dominion, authority and power. For he must reign until he has put all his enemies under his feet. The last enemy to be destroyed is death. For he 'has put everything under his feet.' Now when it says that 'everything' has been put under him, it is clear that this does not include God himself, who put everything under Christ. When he has done this, then the Son himself will be made subject to him who put everything under him, so that God may be all in all" (1 Corinthians 15:24-28). The word *kingdom* stands for royal authority or the subjects who are governed, as we sometimes call the people the kingdom of England or the kingdom of France. Christ is head of the earth, and in heaven we subsist not only by virtue of his everlasting merit but because of his everlasting influence, for he is life. "I am the way and the truth and the life" (John 14:6). Oh, what a great and glorious day this will be, when we see Christ and all his little ones following him, and the great Shepherd of the sheep going into his everlasting folds.

The third consequence of this great day is the world being burned. This is clearly set out by Peter:

> *Dear friends, this is now my second letter to you. I have written both of them as reminders to stimulate you to wholesome thinking. I want you to recall the words spoken in the past by the holy prophets and the command given by our Lord and Savior through your apostles. First of all, you must understand that in the last days scoffers will come, scoffing and following their own evil desires. They will say, "Where is this 'coming' he promised? Ever since our fathers died, everything goes on as it has since the beginning of creation." But they deliberately forget that long ago by God's word the heavens existed and the earth was formed out of water and with water. By water also the world of that time was deluged and destroyed. By the same word the present heavens and earth are reserved for fire, being kept for the day of judgment and destruction of ungodly men. But do not forget this one thing, dear friends: With the Lord a day is like a thousand years, and a thousand years are like a day. The Lord is not slow in keeping his promise, as some understand slowness. He is patient with you, not wanting anyone to perish, but everyone to come to repentance. But the day of the Lord will come like a thief. The heavens will disappear with a roar; the elements will be destroyed by fire, and the earth and everything in it will be laid bare. Since everything will be destroyed in this way, what kind of people ought you to be?*

You ought to live holy and godly lives as you look forward to the day of God and speed its coming. That day will bring about the destruction of the heavens by fire, and the elements will melt in the heat. But in keeping with his promise we are looking forward to a new heaven and a new earth, the home of righteousness. So then, dear friends, since you are looking forward to this, make every effort to be found spotless, blameless and at peace with him. Bear in mind that our Lord's patience means salvation, just as our dear brother Paul also wrote you with the wisdom that God gave him. He writes the same way in all his letters, speaking in them of these matters. His letters contain some things that are hard to understand, which ignorant and unstable people distort, as they do the other Scriptures, to their own destruction. Therefore, dear friends, since you already know this, be on your guard so that you may not be carried away by the error of lawless men and fall from your secure position. But grow in the grace and knowledge of our Lord and Savior Jesus Christ. To him be glory both now and forever! Amen. (2 Peter 3:1-18)

This passage is to be taken literally, for the fire it speaks about should be compared with the flood of water in Noah's day, which was a real judgment.

From all of this you can see how the day of judgment will be a **great Day**. Now we have to apply this to ourselves. If it is going to be a **great day**, let us take it seriously. This is the greatest day that we will ever see, and so we will be more affected by this day than by anything else. We think so infrequently about this coming day that it hardly has any influence on us. O Christians, look for it more diligently, long for it more diligently, and provide for it more diligently.

Application 1. Look for this great day. "And we eagerly await a Savior from there [heaven], the Lord Jesus Christ, who, by the power that enables him to bring everything under his control, will transform our lowly bodies so that they will be like his glorious body" (Philippians 3:20-21). "We wait for the blessed hope—the glorious appearing of our great God and Savior, Jesus Christ" (Titus 2:13). Every time you look up at the clouds, remember you have a Saviour who in time will come from there and call the world to account. Faith should always be ready to meet him, as if he were on his way. It was said that a virgin would conceive. Did this not happen? It was said that God would bring his son out of Egypt. Did this not happen? It was predicted that he would ride into Jerusalem on the foal of a donkey. Did this not happen? Surely the God who has been faithful all along will not fail us in the future.

Application 2. The faithful love his appearing; see 2 Timothy 4:8. This is the great day that they long to see, when they will meet with their beloved and see him in all his glory and royalty. They have heard a great deal of Christ and tasted much of Christ, and they love him much, but they have not yet seen him. They know him through spiritual experience but have never seen him. Christ is going to come again to complete what he began. He first came to redeem our souls and then to save our bodies from corruption. So lift up your heads, for the day of "redemption is drawing near" (see Luke 21:28). Christ is coming to break the chains of death. To speak about this day with horror is wrong for anyone who is looking forward to such great privileges.

Application 3. Provide for that day. It is called "the . . . glorious day of the Lord" (Acts 2:20). We should devote our lives in preparing for it. But how can we do this? I answer: By making peace with God in and through Jesus Christ. We do this by abiding in Christ, by having frequent communion with Christ at the throne of grace, by loving the brethren, and by showing kindness to the poor. We must be faithful in attending the ordinances Christ has left his church, as they are a pledge of his return. Above everything else, these ordinances must be kept pure and not corrupted.

Verse 7

Commentary on Verse 7

In a similar way, Sodom and Gomorrah and the surrounding towns gave themselves up to sexual immorality and perversion. They serve as an example of those who suffer the punishment of eternal fire.
This verse has the third example of the danger of defecting from the faith, and it ties in with the previous two examples. The angels had the blessings of heaven, the Israelites had the blessing of the church, and Sodom had the blessing of the world. But when the angels committed apostasy they lost heaven, when the Israelites grumbled they were shut out of Canaan, and the Sodomites, along with their fruitful soil and pleasant land, were destroyed. You see, heavenly mercies, church mercies, and mercies of this world are all forfeited when people refuse God's grace. This last instance is stated as the first part of a similitude, which is further explained in the next verse. I will now explain three things about verse 7.

1. The places or people judged. **In a similar way, Sodom and Gomorrah and the surrounding towns.** The two cities mentioned here, **Sodom and Gomorrah,** are also mentioned in Genesis 19:24, because they were the principal cities. In Hosea 11:8 two other cities are mentioned, Admah and Zeboiim. But in Deuteronomy 29:23 all four cities are mentioned: "The whole land will be a burning waste of salt and sulphur—nothing planted, nothing sprouting, no vegetation growing on it. It will be like the destruction of Sodom and Gomorrah, Admah and Zeboiim, which the Lord overthrew in fierce anger." The cities are mentioned rather than the people who lived in the cities, to denote the destruction of the places as well as of the people who lived there.

2. Their sin is specified: **gave themselves up to sexual immorality and perversion.** They are accused of committing two great sins.

a. The first is, they **gave themselves up to sexual immorality,** *ekporneusasai.* This signifies their excess and their vehement addiction to unclean practices.

b. Their second sin is **perversion,** literally, "going away after different flesh." This is a modest and covert expression, implying their monstrous and unlawful lusts, contrary to the course and institution of nature—that is, sodomy. The apostle Paul expresses it in this way: "The men also abandoned natural relations with women and were inflamed with lust for one another. Men committed indecent acts with other men, and received in themselves the due penalty for their perversion" (Romans 1:27). Jude calls this, literally, "strange flesh" or "other flesh," *sarkos heteras,* because it was other than nature had appointed, or because it is impossible that man and man in that execrable act should become one flesh as man and woman do.

c. Their judgment is stated: **those who suffer the punishment of eternal fire**. Sodom and the cities near it were consumed with fire and brimstone from heaven, which, though terrible, was but a temporal fire. So in what sense does the apostle call this an **eternal fire**? Some say this simply means utter destruction and try and prove this by quoting the parallel verse in 2 Peter: "he condemned the cities of Sodom and Gomorrah by burning them to ashes" (2:6); that is, God utterly destroyed them. But I do not understand why we need to be so cautious, as the Sodomites are generally represented as men under everlasting judgment.

3. Here is the end and aim of the judgment. **They serve as an example**. That is, by their experience they instruct the world to keep God's law. Therefore everywhere in the prophetic warnings of the Word is this instance alluded to.

I have explained the meaning of the words in this verse, but how shall we link them to the apostle's purpose? The answer is that they suit his purpose very well. There is a parallel to be drawn from this example and Jude's purpose in writing. The Sodomites went after strange flesh, and the apostates Jude warns us about followed strange opinions. These errors inclined them toward sensuality; so this example is even more suited to the apostle's purpose in writing. The school of Simon, the Nicolaitans, and the Gnostics defiled themselves with abominable lust, as the Sodomites did. Therefore Jude warns that they will be destroyed as Sodom was, yes, with eternal fire, of which the fire on Sodom is a type. This will be especially the case with these apostates since they had been once enlightened with some knowledge of the truth, which the Sodomites were not.

Notes on Verse 7

Note 1. **Sodom and Gomorrah**. Cities and countries suffer for the evil of their inhabitants, and thus Sodom and Gomorrah and the surrounding cities were consumed with fire and brimstone and turned into a dead lake. Original sin brought with it an original curse. Adam's fall brought a curse on the whole earth. "To Adam he [God] said, 'Because you listened to your wife and ate from the tree about which I commanded you, "You must not eat of it," cursed is the ground because of you; through painful toil you will eat of it all the days of your life. It will produce thorns and thistles for you'" (Genesis 3:17-18). Actual sins bring an actual curse: "He turned rivers into a desert, flowing springs into thirsty ground, and fruitful land into a salt waste, because of the wickedness of those who lived there" (Psalm 107:33-34). The earth, which was intended to be a monument of God's glory, is now to a large extent a monument of God's displeasure and our rebellion. It can be observed, on the other hand, that the glorious times of the Gospel are expressed by the restoration of the creatures.

He will also send you rain for the seed you sow in the ground, and the food that comes from the land will be rich and plentiful. In that day your cattle will graze in broad meadows. The oxen and donkeys that work the soil will eat fodder and mash, spread out with fork and shovel. In the day of great slaughter, when the towers fall, streams of water will flow on every high mountain and every lofty hill. The moon will shine like the sun, and the sunlight will be seven times brighter, like the light of seven full days, when the LORD binds up the bruises of his people and heals the wounds he inflicted. (Isaiah 30:23-26)

The wolf will live with the lamb, the leopard will lie down with the goat, the calf and the lion and the yearling together; and a little child will lead them. The cow will feed with the bear, their young will lie down together, and the lion will eat straw like the ox. The infant will play near the hole of the cobra, and the young child put his hand into the viper's nest. (Isaiah 11:6-8)

As the condition of the servant depends on the master, so does the state of the creature depend on our conformity or disobedience to God.

Note 2. Those cities were utterly destroyed; see Isaiah 13:19; Jeremiah 49:18; 50:40; Zephaniah 2:9; 2 Peter 2:6. From this we learn that in judgments wicked people will be utterly destroyed. The synagogue of Satan will be utterly destroyed, but not the city of God. In their saddest miseries there is hope for God's children; their dead stock will bud and flower again. They are "prisoners of hope" (Zechariah 9:12). But the judgment on the wicked will be different. "Not a root or a branch will be left to them" (Malachi 4:1). Their memorial is blotted out, but Zion's cannot be erased. Enemies of the church aim to rub out the memory of the church. And in many instances, to all appearances, there is nothing left, and yet out of their ruins and ashes springs up a new brood and holy seed of God.

Do not hunt with the wicked or allow your souls to enter into their secrets. Evil societies will be destroyed, root and branch.

Note 3. **And the surrounding towns.** Observe that likeness in sin will involve us in the same punishment. The inhabitants of Sodom and Gomorrah perished, as did **the surrounding towns.** God's wrath makes no distinction. "*Quos una impietas profanavit, una sententia dejicit,*" said Ambrose. "They were found in the same sin, and therefore surprised by the same judgment." "Rebels and sinners will both be broken together" (Isaiah 1:28). That is, the one as well as the other, no matter what names they go under, will be destroyed. Why? Fellowship in evil can neither excuse sin nor keep wrath away. To walk with God is praiseworthy, even if you are on your own. To walk with men in the way of sin is dangerous, even though millions do it with you.

Note 4. Note something else from **the surrounding towns.** The lesser cities imitated the greater cities. Admah and Zeboiim followed the example of Sodom and Gomorrah. If sin is condoned by the leaders, it is followed by the people who obey their commands. When "your whole head is injured, your whole heart [is] afflicted" (Isaiah 1:5).

Note 5. **Gave themselves up to sexual immorality.** From this, the first crime specified, learn that adulterous uncleanness greatly displeases God. When they were given over to fornication, they were given over to God's judgment.

1. This is a sin which not only defiles the soul but the body as well. "Flee from sexual immorality. All other sins a man commits are outside his body, but he who sins sexually sins against his own body" (1 Corinthians 6:18). Most other sins imply an injury done to others or to God or to our neighbor. This sin is a direct injury to ourselves, to our own bodies. In contrast, "each of you should learn to control his own body in a way that is holy and honorable" (1 Thessalonians 4:4). This sin is a wrong against the temple of the Holy Spirit. "Do you not know that your body is a temple of the Holy Spirit, who is in you, whom you have received from God?" (1 Corinthians 6:19). As the body is the temple of the Holy Spirit, it dishonors the body to make it a channel of lust.

2. This sin hardens the soul. The softness of all sensual pleasures hardens the heart, but this sin, being the consummate act of sensuality, does even more, ". . . because they have deserted the Lord to give themselves to prostitution, to old wine and new, which take away the understanding of my people" (Hosea 4:10-12). Sexual immorality and drunkenness are mentioned together because they usually go together, and both take away the heart, deaden the conscience, and take away the tenderness of the affections.

3. This sin greatly perverts the order of human societies. Solomon said it was worse than theft. "So is he who sleeps with another man's wife; no

one who touches her will go unpunished. Men do not despise a thief if he steals to satisfy his hunger when he is starving. Yet if he is caught, he must pay sevenfold, though it costs him all the wealth of his house. But a man who commits adultery lacks judgment; whoever does so destroys himself" (Proverbs 6:29-32). Adultery causes great confusion in families. Therefore adultery under the law was punished by death, which theft was not.

4. Adultery is a sin that is usually linked with impenitence. It wears out remorse and every spark of a good conscience. "The mouth of an adulteress is a deep pit; he who is under the LORD's wrath will fall into it" (Proverbs 22:14). "None who go to her [the adulteress] return or attain the paths of life" (Proverbs 2:19). "I find more bitter than death the woman who is a snare, whose heart is a trap and whose hands are chains. The man who pleases God will escape her, but the sinner she will ensnare" (Ecclesiastes 7:26).

Note 6. **Gave themselves up to . . . perversion.** From this other sin observe that sin never stands still. First there is uncleanness, then sexual immorality, then perversion. When a stone runs down a hill, it does not come to rest until it reaches the bottom. A sinner becomes more and more filthy, as the Sodomites did.

Note 7. **Who suffer the punishment of eternal fire.** The wicked Sodomites were not only burnt up by temporal judgment but were thrown into hell, which is here called, **eternal fire.** Hell is represented in two ways—by the worm that does not die and by the fire that is not quenched (see Mark 9:44). The allusions are to worms that feed on dead bodies and to fire that was used to burn dead bodies in previous ages. The first implies the worm of conscience, and the latter the fire of God's wrath.

1. The worm breeds in the body itself and so is a suitable representation of the gnawing of conscience.

a. First, conscience works on what is past, the recollection of former enjoyments and past pleasures. "Son, remember that in your lifetime you received your good things" (Luke 16:25). This refers to time wasted, opportunities of grace slighted, and deliberate sin.

b. Second, there is a sense of present pain.

c. Third, there is a reference to their future and their hopeless condition. Despair is one ingredient of their torment. ". . . only a fearful expectation of judgment and of raging fire that will consume the enemies of God" (Hebrews 10:27). So much for the worm.

2. The next idea is the **fire,** or the wrath of God falling on them. God has a direct hand in the sufferings of the damned. "It is a dreadful thing to fall into the hands of the living God" (Hebrews 10:31). No creature is strong enough to bear all of God's wrath. Do we think that a prayer is too long, or a sermon? What will hell be like? In the night, if we cannot sleep, we count the hours, and every minute seems tedious. Oh, what will peo-

ple do who are "tormented day and night for ever and ever" (Revelation 20:10)? This falls on all who forgot God. Oh, who would run the hazard for such small, temporal satisfactions? Indulgence in brutish lust gives brief pleasure now, but the worm never dies, and the fire will never be put out.

Note 8. **They serve as an example.** This is the final thing to note from this verse. Observe from this that Sodom's destruction is a great example to the world. Both Peter and Jude show that the purpose of God's judgments on Sodom was that they might be an example to everyone who desires to live a godly life.

You may ask: What have we to do with Sodom? Their sins were so unnatural and their judgments so unusual. First, think about their sins. I ask: are Sodom's sins absent from us today? If it is not **perversion**, it is **sexual immorality**, and if it is not **sexual immorality**, it is pride and idleness. And what about our sins of impenitence, unbelief, abuse and neglect of the Gospel, and despising the offers of grace? The worst sins against the law are not as great as the sins against the Gospel (see Matthew 11:24). We who have more light and more love sin against the God of grace.

Second, think about the judgments that fell on them. While God does not nowadays afflict a country with judgments immediately from heaven or make it completely useless as he did to Sodom, yet he is no less displeased against sin. A similar judgment may come on us.

We now come to see how this example can be applied to us. I shall consider three things here. First, the state of Sodom; second, the sins of Sodom; and third, the judgment on Sodom. The first will show you God's mercy, the second their guilt, and the third God's justice. These three often follow each other. Despite great mercies we commit great sins, and great sins bring great judgments.

Application 1. I begin with the state of Sodom.

1. Note the quality of the place. There were many good cities, of which Sodom was the principal one, in the plain of Jordan. It was full of people and had plentiful supplies of corn, wine, oil, and all earthly goods. "Lot looked up and saw that the whole plain of the Jordan was well watered, like the garden of the Lord, like the land of Egypt, toward Zoar. (This was before the LORD destroyed Sodom and Gomorrah.)" (Genesis 13:10). And yet later this was the place of so much wrath and complete desolation. What can the world learn from this? That we must give an account for common mercies. God chastened the servant who had one talent but did not use it (Matthew 25:14-30). The world is a place of trial, and all men have a trust committed to them.

2. Note those cities' earlier deliverance. Four kings went to war against them and captured them and carried them off before they were rescued by Abraham (Genesis 14:15-16). Deliverance from war and captivity leaves us

with a great responsibility to live godly lives. When God has once spared us, if we do not repent, we will be utterly destroyed. Deliverance, if not used in the right way, turns into a mere reprieve. We are not so much preserved as reserved for a greater misery. "Many times he delivered them, but they were bent on rebellion and they wasted away in their sin" (Psalm 106:43). If we do not amend our ways after we have been delivered, we will definitely be destroyed.

3. Note God's patience with them. For a long time Sodom slept quietly in its sins, unmolested and undisturbed. The Lord is gracious, but not senseless. As he will not always contend, so he will not always forebear.

4. Note Lot's admonition. It seems that he often reproved them, and they scorned him. "'Get out of our way,' they replied. And they said, 'This fellow came here as an alien, and now he wants to play the judge! We'll treat him worse than them.' They kept bringing pressure on Lot and moved forward to break down the door" (Genesis 19:9). Lot's soul was not only upset by their immorality, but as opportunities arose, he tried to dissuade them from their evil ways. From this you can learn that God seldom punishes without first giving a warning.

Sins are aggravated not only by the foulness of the act, but by the degrees of light against which they are committed. The people of Sodom sinned very badly in their actions, but they could not sin against so much light as we do. Therefore it will easier for them on judgment day than for us.

Application 2. Now we come to look at the sins of Sodom. "Now this was the sin of your sister Sodom: She and her daughters were arrogant, overfed and unconcerned; they did not help the poor and needy. They were haughty and did detestable things before me. Therefore I did away with them as you have seen" (Ezekiel 16:49). Add to this the sins mentioned by Jude and their evil roll is complete. I will look at, first, their sins and, second, the aggravations.

1. First, I turn to their sins.

a. Pride. It is hard to enjoy plenty and not grow haughty. Prosperous winds soon fill the sails, but, blowing too strongly, they overturn the boat. How few are able to carry a full cup without spilling it. How few people can manage plenty without becoming proud. People become rich and then high-minded, and that leads to their ruin.

b. Idleness. An easy, careless life is a dangerous path to tread. God sent everyone into the world to be active. Standing pools putrefy. So idle people settle into vile and degenerate lusts.

2. Now I come to consider the aggravations of their sins.

a. Shamelessness. "The look on their faces testifies against them; they parade their sin like Sodom; they do not hide it. Woe to them! They have brought disaster upon themselves" (Isaiah 3:9). When a people are shameless, they are past hope. Such people dare God to punish them.

b. Contempt of reproof. When the person who reproves us is blamed more than the evil deed, it is a sure sign of impending ruin. Lot's sons-in-law "thought he was joking" (Genesis 19:14) when Lot told them to leave Sodom. When God's messengers are condemned, God can hold back his judgment no longer.

Application 3. I now move on to consider the judgment that befell Sodom.

1. Note the suddenness of the judgment. The sun shone in the morning as it had on any other day. "By the time Lot reached Zoar, the sun had risen over the land. Then the Lord rained down burning sulphur on Sodom and Gomorrah—from the Lord out of the heavens" (Genesis 19:23). The inhabitants of Sodom and Gomorrah were taken by surprise. God often surprises people in their security.

2. Note that the punishment was a just punishment. The sin was like the punishment. They first burned with lusts and then with fire. They burned with vile unnatural lusts, and therefore, against the ordinary course of nature, fire came down from heaven.

3. Observe God's power. God had previously drowned the world with water, and now he consumed Sodom with fire. All the elements are at his beck and call.

4. Take note of the severity of God. He rained down burning sulfur on Sodom and Gomorrah. This is a type of hell (see Isaiah 30:33; Revelation 20:15). The calamities that fall on the godly are a sign that they will be saved (see Philippians 1:28), for they purify them from sin. But the calamities that overtake the evil are types of hell and preambles to future woes.

God delights to make those who have been examples to others in sinning, examples to them in punishment.

Verse 8

Commentary on Verse 8

In the very same way, these dreamers pollute their own bodies, reject authority and slander celestial beings.

In the very same way, or "likewise," is the adverb that implies the connection between two terms that are compared. Those who went after strange flesh perished, and *in the same way* **these dreamers pollute their own bodies** and so will perish. This verse describes these people as **dreamers**. We also discover two of their sins. First, they reveal how impure they are as they **pollute their own bodies**. Second, their attitude to their superiors is expressed in two phrases: they **reject authority**, and they **slander celestial beings**. The first clause probably refers to civil authority, which is usually expressed in Scripture as *kuriotes*, or domination, as in this verse where it is translated **authority**. Slandering celestial beings, or speaking evil of dignities, likely refers to ecclesiastical people, such as apostles, pastors, teachers, and elders.

I will now explain the words in more detail. **In the very same way.** In the original, *homoios mentoi kai houtoi* can be translated as "likewise" or "notwithstanding." That is, although there are many such apparent instances of God's judgment, and those set before us are an example to us, yet they, since they are blinded by their wicked passions, are not afraid but boldly travel toward their own destruction.

These dreamers pollute. The word in the original for **dreamers** is *enupniazomenoi*, meaning "led, inspired, or acted upon as a result of dreams or deluded by dreams." Beza says it means being lulled to sleep, referring to the security in which they trust. I prefer to think that it means the error by which they were, as it were, bewitched and enchanted.

Pollute. They pollute themselves with libidinous practices. They are "those who follow the corrupt desire of the sinful nature" (2 Peter 2:10). The Gnostics gave themselves over to all kinds of incestuous pollution. The Nicolaitans believed it did not matter if you committed adultery (see Revelation 2:6, 15). How many different ways they polluted the flesh is impossible to express with any modesty.

Reject authority. The word for **reject** is *athetountes*, which means to remove a thing from its place with some scorn and indignation. So it implies their utter enmity toward civil policy and government. They "despise authority" (2 Peter 2:10). The word for **authority**, *kuriosteta*, means more than if he had written *kurious*, rulers. They did not only despise the magistrates, or men invested with power to rule over them, but they rejected the magistracy itself. They behaved toward it as if it were not a fit thing for believers to endure, since they were free in Christ.

The last part of this verse states that these people **slander celestial beings**. Some people, such as Clemens Alexandrinus, understand this to refer to angels. Then it would mean that these impure heretics devised things to mislead the angels. However, I think it implies their scorn, curses, and reproaches toward the officers of the church, who are the glory of Christ.

Throughout this verse you have a general description of our modern Ranters, Levellers, and Quakers, who through dreams are led to defile the flesh, and who despise all authority, both in the church and in the world. They speak with bitter and evil curses so that people of our day give us an all too clear picture of the people spoken of in Scripture. It is sadly fulfilled in front of our eyes.

Notes on Verse 8

Note 1. Concerning **these dreamers pollute**, note that the erroneous thoughts of wicked people are but a dream. Wicked people are dreamers. First, they are dreamers in connection with their state and condition. Every worldly person is in a state of "deep sleep" (Isaiah 29:10). They snore on their bed of ease without any sense of their dangerous condition. They are like Jonah in the ship who slept while the storm raged. They sleep, but "their destruction has not been sleeping" (2 Peter 2:3). Second, they are dreamers in the sense that their vain thoughts are aptly compared with dreams. A dream gives a false delight and deceives with a vain hope.

1. Dreams tickle our fancy. They hug a cloud, as we say, and embrace the pleasures of the world in place of true riches. Worldly people run from pleasure to pleasure as if they are in some sweet dream. "Man is a mere phantom as he goes to and fro: He bustles about, but only in vain; he heaps up wealth, not knowing who will get it" (Psalm 39:6). They imagine that they are happy and are content with their condition.

2. Dreams deceive us by giving us false hopes. The prophet Isaiah compares the dream of the enemies of the church to a dream of a night vision. "Then the hordes of all the nations that fight against Ariel, that attack her

and her fortress and besiege her, will be as it is with a dream, with a vision in the night—as when a hungry man dreams that he is eating, but he awakens, and his hunger remains; as when a thirsty man dreams that he is drinking, but he awakens faint, with his thirst unquenched. So will it be with the hordes of all the nations that fight against Mount Zion" (Isaiah 29:7-8). So it is with these dreamers—all their hopes are dashed in an instant. The foolish virgins slept (Matthew 25:1-13), and they dreamed that the door of grace would remain open to them, but they found it shut. Many flatter themselves with fair hopes until they awake in flames.

Take heed, then, of being deceived by your own dreams and the imagination of your own brain. There are no dreams as foolish as those we dream while we are awake, as Epiphanus says of the Gnostics. Waking dreams are most pernicious. There are two kinds of such dreams: first, dreams of opinion, which hug error instead of truth; and, second, dreams of hope, when we cherish presumption instead of faith.

a. Dreams of opinion. These are rife today. Idle and ungrounded notions, no matter how plausible they appear, are but the dreams of a misty, sleepy brain. To avoid these you must beware of a blind mind. People sleep in the dark, and in sleep fancy gets the better of reason. Study the Word, or else there will be no light in anything that is brought to you. Many people are perverted by mystical interpretations when people bring to the Word what is not really there.

b. Dreams of hope. People dream about external happiness in temporal enjoyments (see Psalm 49:11; Luke 12:19; Revelation 18:9). Others dream about attaining an end without using the means. They live in sin and yet hope to die comfortably and at last go to heaven, as if it were an easy thing to leap from Delilah's lap to Abraham's side. If you do not want to dream like this, examine your heart. Examination is like rubbing your eyes after sleeping. People laugh at their dreams when they are awake. When we confess our sin, we are telling our dreams to wake up, and we come to ourselves.

Note 2. **Pollute their own bodies**. From this observe that dreams of error dispose us to sinful and unclean practices. Impurity in religion is usually accompanied by impurity in body. This comes about partly by the just judgment of God, who punishes their spiritual fornication with bodily fornication. "A spirit of prostitution leads them astray; they are unfaithful to their God. They sacrifice on the mountaintops and burn offerings on the hills, under oak, poplar and terebinth, where the shade is pleasant. Therefore your daughters turn to prostitution and your daughters-in-law to adultery" (Hosea 4:12-13). It is God's way for the odiousness of the one to make them see the heinousness of the other. "Therefore God gave them over in the sinful desires of their hearts to sexual impurity for the degrading of their bodies with one another" (Romans 1:24). All sins are rooted in wrong thoughts about God. "Dear friend, do not imitate what is evil but what is good. Anyone who does what is evil has not seen God" (3 John 11). Nothing brings shame on the ways of God like the scandals of those who profess to walk in them. If you do not walk in the light as "children of light" (see Ephesians 5:8), you will be a reproach to the truth and deprive it of its testimony.

Note 3. Notice that sin is a defilement. It stains and darkens the glory of man (see Matthew 15:20). Those who glory in sin glory in their own shame. This is like a man boasting about his own dung and counting his spittle as an ornament. See Psalm 14:3. Desire to be washed, and that thoroughly (see Psalm 51:2).

Note 4. Again, notice that of all sins, the sin of uncleanness or unlawful sexual intercourse is most defiling. It defiles the whole person, but especially the body. It stains the soul with filthy thoughts, and the body it pollutes (see 1 Corinthians 6:18). All other sins concern external objects, such as wine, food, and riches. But with sexual intercourse the body itself is not only the instrument but also the object of the pollution (see Romans 1:24; 1 Thessalonians 4:3-4). This pollution saps the strength of the body. "Keep a path far from her [an adulteress], do not go near the door of her house, lest you give your best strength to others and your years to one who is cruel, lest strangers feast on your wealth and your toil enrich another man's house. At the end of your life you will groan, when your flesh and body are spent" (Proverbs 5:8-11). This kind of behavior does not recall that the body is consecrated to God (see Romans 12:1) and a temple of the Holy Spirit (see 1 Corinthians 6:19).

Note 5. **Reject authority.** Observe that errors, especially those that incline toward sensuality, make people unruly. Dreamers who defile themselves also **reject authority**. Error takes away the dread of God, and sedition the dread of the magistrate, so that people more freely defile the flesh. God has two deputies to keep a sinner in awe of him: conscience and the magistrate. False doctrine numbs the conscience, so that all authority is set aside. The rights of the magistrate are ignored, and as these dreamers' conscience does not stand in the way of their lust, so the magistrate does not stand in the way of their sin. That there were such libertines in the early church is clear from Galatians 5:13; 1 Corinthians 7:20-23; 1 Peter 2:16.

Application 1. This shows the evil of inordinate lusting. We may learn about where this comes from and where this leads to. It proceeds from the pride and obstinacy of error; people dream and are then licentious; and it helps people to ignore all their duties to God and other people. Nip this disposition in the bud. It is in all our natures (see Job 11:12). It brings about base understanding and untamed affections. We love to break through all bonds and restraints as if no one was lord over us (see Psalm 12:3-4).

Application 2. When freedom with no restraints runs riot, there will be utter confusion. According to Socrates, the ruin of the state is brought on by pernicious and evil doctrines. Tully, in his book *De Legibus*, says, "The glory of Greece declined when the people were given *malis studiis, malisque doctrinis*," that is, evil manners and evil opinions. Let us lay these things to heart.

Application 3. Understanding these things may remove the prejudice that is often cast on religion and the true ways of God. It is not truth that troubles Israel but error. "'I have not made trouble for Israel,' Elijah replied. 'But you and your father's family have. You have abandoned the LORD's commands and have followed the Baals'" (1 Kings 18:18). It is an old lie that strict religion is no friend of people with independent minds. As soon as Christianity began to spread, people protested against it as if it would harm civil power. The enemies of Christianity tried to tell rulers that their thrones and kingdoms would not be safe if Christianity was generally accepted. In this way Christ was accused (see Luke 23:2), as Paul was also (see Acts 24:5). But in each case there was no reason for them to be accused. Let the world say what it will, Christianity is a friend of the magistrates, for it commands that civic duties should be carried out as a sacred bond. "Fear the LORD and the king, my son, and do not join with the rebellious" (Proverbs 24:21). "Give to Caesar what is Caesar's, and to God what is God's" (Matthew 22:21). "Show proper respect to everyone: Love the brotherhood of believers, fear God, honor the king" (1 Peter 2:17). "Obey the king's command, I say, because you took an oath before God" (Ecclesiastes 8:2).

Christianity is also a friend of the magistrates because through its influence people's hearts become meek and they care about being faithful to God and other people. Constantine's father said, "I expect those who are faithful to God to be faithful to me." An ungodly man said: "Either wholly abandon religion, or maintain it more completely."

Note 6. Again I observe in the same clause that it is a sin to despise authority. They **reject authority**. This is the accusation these seducers are charged with. This is sinful because it is against the injunctions of the Word. "Everyone must submit himself to the governing authorities, for there is no authority except that which God has established" (Romans 13:1). "Remind the people to be subject to rulers and authorities, to be obedient, to be ready to do whatever is good" (Titus 3:1). We tend to forget our civil duties or to neglect them, as if the same authority did not lie behind the second half of the Ten Commandments as lies behind the first half of the Ten Commandments. This is a sin because civil powers are ordained by God. The general instruction of it is from God, although the particular constitution is from man. Compare Romans 13:1 with 1 Peter 2:13. Government itself is from God, but this or that particular form of government is not determined by God. This is the difference between civil and ecclesiastical government, for in ecclesiastical government the particular form is specified, and the thing itself appointed by God.

It is also a sin to **reject authority** because authority is used to preserve human societies. By nature we are sociable creatures. So then, let us obey every human ordinance for the Lord's sake. Public welfare is affected by our obedience, as is the honor of religion, both of which should be dear to one who fears God.

Note 7. The last phrase in this verse is: **slander celestial beings**. Church officers are probably meant here. Note that respect is due to people invested with church power. It is established by God and therefore should not be ignored. Ministers are to be obeyed. "Obey your leaders and submit to their authority. They keep watch over you as men who must give an account. Obey them so that their work will be a joy, not a burden, for that would be of no advantage to you" (Hebrews 13:17). They are due respect and honor. "Now we ask you, brothers, to respect those who work hard among you, who are over you in the Lord and who admonish you. Hold them in the highest regard in love because of their work" (1 Thessalonians 5:12-13). "The elders who direct the affairs of the church well are worthy of double honor, especially those whose work is preaching and teaching" (1 Timothy 5:17). You should not speak badly about them. "Do not entertain an accusation against an elder unless it is brought by two or three witnesses" (1 Timothy 5:19). While they may as people be mean and despicable, yet they are called to a high office and have the promise of a great power and presence with them. "I will give you the keys of the kingdom of heaven; whatever you bind on earth will be bound in heaven, and whatever you loose on earth will be loosed in heaven" (Matthew 16:19). "If you forgive anyone his sins, they are forgiven; if you do not forgive them, they are not forgiven" (John 20:23). Their regular proceedings are ratified in the court of heaven. We live in an age when nobody is held in more contempt than ministers, and when nothing is valued less than the authority of the church. It has become the eyesore of the times.

Verse 9

Commentary on Verse 9

But even the archangel Michael, when he was disputing with the devil about the body of Moses, did not dare to bring a slanderous accusation against him, but said, "The Lord rebuke you!"

The apostle had accused the seducers against whom he wrote of opposing the authority of magistrates and of speaking contemptuously against those lights that God had set in the church. Now he comes to aggravate their effrontery and impudence by the deportment of Michael the archangel toward the devil. In this comparison there is an argument *a majore ad minus*, from the greater to the less.

1. Note this from the people who are contending—**Michael the archangel** with **the devil**. If Michael, so excellent in nature, so high in office, acted with such modesty and awe when he contended with Satan, an impure spirit already judged by God, then what sorry creatures dare despise people invested with the dignity and high rank of magistrate?

2. There is an aggravation from the cause, **when he was disputing with the devil** *about the body of Moses*. This is a matter in which the mind of God was clearly known. How dare they speak evil of things they do not know—that is, in matters so far above their reach.

3. An aggravation is implied from the disposition of the angel: he **did not dare to bring a slanderous accusation against him**. His holiness did not allow him to deal with the devil in an indecent and injurious manner. But the people who lead others astray rashly belch out their reproaches and curses against superiors without any fear.

4. Notice how Michael spoke: **"The Lord rebuke you."** The whole judgment of the cause is referred to God. But these Gnostics took things upon themselves as if all judgments about things, people, and actions were placed in their hands, just as Quakers now take it upon themselves to curse and to pronounce dreadful judgments on God's most holy servants according to their own pleasure. The summary of all this is that if an angel who is great in power dares not to bring against the worst creatures, in the heat of an argument about a good cause, any undue language or reproach,

it is definitely a horrible impudence for people to speak contemptuously and even with curses and in a blasphemous manner about those whom God has given high office in ecclesiastical or civil matters.

This is the sum of the words. But because this Scripture is difficult, before I come to the observations, I will premise some questions.

Question 1. Where did the apostle obtain this story from? The Scriptures do not mention it.

Answer. The substance of it is in Scripture. We read that the body of Moses was secretly buried by the Lord. "He [the Lord] buried him [Moses] in Moab, in the valley opposite Beth Peor, but to this day no one knows where his grave is" (Deuteronomy 34:6). Concerning the circumstances surrounding this, Jude might have received this information by divine revelation, which is here made Scripture. It was quite normal for those who wrote the Scripture to add circumstances that were not mentioned in the passage where the story was first recorded. In Exodus we read about the opposition of the magicians to Moses, but their names are not recorded in Exodus; but they are mentioned in 2 Timothy 3:8: "Just as Jannes and Jambres opposed Moses . . ." The complete story of their opposition to Moses is in the Talmud, and in Apuleius and others' histories we read that these were famous magicians. In a similar way we read of Joseph in Psalm 105:18, "They bruised his feet with shackles, his neck was put in irons." But this detail is not mentioned in the story in Genesis. In a similar way we are told in Hebrews 12:21, "The sight [Mt. Sinai] was so terrifying that Moses said, 'I am trembling with fear.'" These things might have been received by tradition or by divine inspiration, or they may have been extant in some known book or record then in use. Origen quotes a book, *About the Assumption of Moses*, for this part of the story, some parts of which are in Jewish books to this day.

Question 2. Is this a real history or an allusion?

Answer. There are three opinions about this.

1. One is that it is a figurative expression of God's care for his church. Those who hold this view understand by the words **the body of Moses** either the whole body of the Levitical worship or else the community of Israel, represented in Joshua the high priest. "Then he showed me Joshua the high priest standing before the angel of the LORD, and Satan standing at his right side to accuse him. The LORD said to Satan, 'The LORD rebuke you, Satan! The LORD, who has chosen Jerusalem, rebuke you! Is not this man a burning stick snatched from the fire?'" (Zechariah 3:1-2). In Joshua the newly restored Levitical worship is represented, and the angel of the Lord before whom he stood is Christ, the judge, advocate and defender of the church. And "the LORD," that is, the Lord Christ, previously called "the angel," presents the efficacy of his mediation against this malicious opposition of Satan. So some people accommodate this text in Jude to fit

the sense of the quotation in Zechariah. The main reason for doing this is the form of words used in Zechariah: "The LORD rebuke you, Satan!"

It is possible to argue in this way, but such an argument does not rest on a firm basis. Junius, who first advanced this interpretation, now seems to distrust it. The argument lacks force, for the same form of words might have been used on different occasions. My reasons against this interpretation are that these expressions are a type and a vision. To make a type of a type, especially in the New Testament, which usually explains the difficulties of the Old Testament, seems to be irrational. And though by **Michael** Christ may be meant, to change from "Joshua" to **Moses** is much too forced.

2. Other people think this is not historical but a fable or parable from the Talmud. They think that Jude, in quoting it, does not prove that the story is true but only uses it to instruct them, for they loved these kinds of fables. The fathers often made use of their own stories and fictions concerning gods to argue against the ungodly, and so, it is said, that type of argument is used here. But against this interpretation it must be said that the argument in this verse is used by way of a straightforward assertion, not as an argument *ad hominem*. Peter on a similar occasion says, "yet even angels, although they are stronger and more powerful, do not bring slanderous accusations against such beings in the presence of the Lord" (2 Peter 2:11). I say that he does not state this as if it were a Jewish fable, but as a real argument taken from the nature of the holy angels.

3. A third opinion is that it is real history—that is, that the devil was keen to discover the whereabouts of Moses' grave and to take his body, and Michael resisted his attempts to do this. Michael was a leading angel, and the devil's attempts were made fruitless by his holy and modest address to God, **"The Lord rebuke you!"**

Question 3. The next question is, who is meant by **the archangel Michael**?

Answer. **Michael** is the name of his person and **archangel** of his office. "Michael" means "strong God," or "like the strong God," and therefore some apply it to Jesus Christ, who in many places in Scripture is set out as the head of the angels (see Genesis 48:16; Exodus 3:2; Daniel 10:13; 12:1). In the Daniel passages Jesus Christ seems to be intended by Michael, as he is the Prince of Israel. But it is not absolutely necessary to interpret those verses as referring to Christ; much less is he intended here, as it would be beneath his dignity to contend with the devil. While Christ did contend with the devil during his humiliation (Matthew 4), he would not have done so before then. Besides, the phrase **did not dare to bring** is not applicable to Jesus Christ; and besides, Christ and the archangel are in Scripture distinguished from each other. Indeed, Peter applies this to angels in general: "yet even angels, although they are stronger and more powerful, do not bring slanderous accusations against such beings in the presence of the Lord" (2 Peter 2:11).

But, you might object, how can any creature be called **Michael**, which means equal to God in power and strength? Taken comparatively, it may be applied to the highest in dignity among the creatures, the highest angel, just as there is a Beelzebub or chief devil. Matthew 25:41 says, "the devil and his angels." So in heaven, there may be a **Michael**, the leader of the blessed angels.

Question 4. Why should the devil so earnestly dispute about the body of Moses?

Answer. The rabbis, among their other fables, interpret this as the desire that the devil had to destroy Moses through death, as there was nobody like Moses who saw God face to face. Therefore he raged against Moses and tried to destroy him. The psalmist had this idea in mind when he wrote, "The wicked lie in wait for the righteous, seeking their very lives" (Psalm 37:32). Some Christians say this striving was before Moses' burial, but others say it was after Moses' burial. Junius thought this applied to Moses' body before it was buried, so that his body would not remain out of sight, so Satan could perhaps vent his fury on it and abuse it. But this is not a profitable line of interpretation. It is more probable that God suddenly disposed of the body in some secret burial place. Some say that after this burial the devil tried to take it up again, and so there arose this contention between him and Michael. But why should the devil contend so much about the buried body of Moses?

To answer this we must consider what God's purpose was in concealing Moses' burial. Possibly this might be done in case the people of Israel should overzealously give honor to the dead body of such a famous and excellent prophet, which would then become a snare to the people. Possibly there might be something typical in this—the dead body of Moses being buried in an unknown place, in case they should take it up and carry it into the land of Canaan to signify the abolition of the legal ordinances under the Gospel. The devil might be supposed to contend for the body of Moses partly out of obstinate curiosity, whereby sinful creatures are strongly inclined to desire forbidden things. The devil might do this partly to defeat the purposes of God, but chiefly to use the dead Moses to set up himself in the hearts of the living, seeking thereby to get them to worship the patriarch's relics or remains.

Having dealt with these questions, the explanation of the words is easy.

The archangel Michael. That is, some principal angel deputed to this service and ministry.

When he was disputing with the devil, *diabolo diakrinomenos.* The word **disputing** means an altercation or contention in words.

About the body of Moses, about the knowledge of his place of burial.

Did not dare to bring a slanderous accusation, *krisin epenegkein blasphemias*, "the judgment of blasphemy" or such unworthy language as the heat of contention is liable to provoke and extort from us.

But said, "The Lord rebuke you!" This is a modest form of speech referring the matter to God's cognizance, or perhaps a prayer that the Lord would check this malicious opposition.

Notes on Verse 9

Note 1. Note that to make their slander appear even more virulent, Jude compares it with the modesty of an archangel. From this note that pride and contempt in those of low degree is less tolerable than in those whom God has advanced to a higher rank and sphere. This is partly because such people have less temptation to be proud; and when a sin is committed without temptation, it indicates that the heart is strongly inclined that way, just as it takes no force to make a ball roll downhill. With a lowly condition there should be a lowly mind. "Better to be lowly in spirit among the oppressed than to share plunder with the proud" (Proverbs 16:19). As the modesty of the archangel was a rebuke to the pride of the Gnostics, so should those who have been greatly honored shame the proud lowly with their comely plainness. It is shameful for lowly people to be puffed up and full of pomp as they quote Greek and Latin sentences, as if all this learning was their own thoughts. The apostle Paul condemned the Corinthians for their pompous use of tongues in church and shamed them by his own example. "I thank God that I speak in tongues more than all of you. But in the church I would rather speak five intelligible words to instruct others than ten thousand words in a tongue" (1 Corinthians 14:18-19).

In order to keep your pride in check, look to other people whom God has elevated but who are more humble. If God's judgment comes upon notable people because of their pride, we ought to think, *What will become of me?* If "the kings of the earth, the princes, the generals, the rich, the mighty" tremble, will "every slave" go free (see Revelation 6:15)?

Most of all I commend to you the example of the Lord Jesus Christ to remove your pride. This is an example that will indeed shame us, whatever pride we have. Are you puffed up with pride or vain conceit? Christ stripped himself of all his glory. "Christ Jesus . . . made himself nothing, taking the very nature of a servant" (Philippians 2:5, 7). Remember that "a student is not above his teacher, nor a servant above his master" (Matthew 10:24). If we are scorned, do we expect better treatment than our Master suffered? Many times you have seen a master do the work of a servant to shame him. So did Christ. You must ponder Christ's excellency and your own base condition. Thus in this verse, to shame the brutish Gnostics, the apostle Jude tells them that they were setting themselves above the glorious angel.

Note 2. Consider again the archangel disputing **about the body of Moses**. The devil wanted to find the location of Moses' grave, and the archangel was ready to resist him. The point to note is that God has angels and archangels who are always ready to defend a good cause. There are numerous angels and archangels; the court of heaven is filled with them. "Thousands upon thousands attended him; ten thousand times ten thousand stood before him" (Daniel 7:10). Christ said that he could pray for "twelve legions of angels" to help him (Matthew 26:53). A legion consisted of 6,000 foot soldiers and 700 mounted soldiers. Angels are always prepared to carry out God's commands. One angel killed 185,000 people in one night (Isaiah 37:36). "Praise the LORD, you his angels, you mighty ones who do his bidding, who obey his word" (Psalm 103:20). They are more concerned to serve God than to seek their own honor. They carry out their work speedily. They are described as having six wings each (see Isaiah 6:2). They are at the Lord's beck and call, ready to carry out his commands as soon as they hear them.

1. This should remind us of the danger wicked people are in when they oppose a good cause. They are fighting not just against other people but against angels.

2. Angels are more active in human affairs than we are aware of. There are evil angels fighting against the church and good angels resisting these attacks. The fight is not just between people but between angels. "But the prince of the Persian kingdom resisted me twenty-one days. Then Michael, one of the chief princes, came to help me, because I was detained there with the king of Persia" (Daniel 10:13). The protection of the holy angels is invisible but true and real.

3. Here is comfort for God's children when they engage in dangerous but holy business. "Those who are with us are more than those who are with them" (2 Kings 6:16). God the Father's power is on the church's side; and the Son contributes the strength of his mediation. "The LORD said to Satan, 'The LORD rebuke you, Satan! The LORD, who has chosen Jerusalem, rebuke you! Is not this man a burning stick snatched from the fire?'" (Zechariah 3:2). Furthermore, the Spirit comforts us and gives us life, and then holy angels are used as God's instruments. The Lord Jesus and his angels will work on behalf of the church when nobody else dares to. "No one supports me against them except Michael, your prince" (Daniel 10:21). When all human strength fails, Christ through the ministry of angels upholds the affairs of the church. Omnipotence is a great deep. Normally we can more readily understand the work of finite creatures than of the infinite God. Therefore the Lord represents the help of the

church as managed by these powerful instruments. So beware that you do not betray those who are helping you or rob yourself of their protection.

Do not neglect to seek help from the God of angels. "Then he continued, 'Do not be afraid, Daniel. Since the first day that you set your mind to gain understanding and to humble yourself before your God, your words were heard, and I have come in response to them'" (Daniel 10:12). We should not pray *to* them but *for* them as we pray to the Lord.

Do not join in evil actions, for then you link up with Satan and oppose good angels. "The angel of the LORD encamps around those who fear him, and he delivers them" (Psalm 34:7). Trust God, who, if he sees fit to glorify himself through our deliverance rather than our sufferings, can find means enough to save us when men fail.

Note 3. Notice, too, that angels have a concern not only for the souls, but for the bodies, even the dead bodies, of the saints, for Michael disputed with the devil **about the body of Moses**. I will mention several propositions so you can understand the particular care angels have for God's people.

1. It is certain that angels greatly cared for God's people in ancient times. Examples of this are found everywhere in the Word of God. Lot was led out of Sodom by angels; Daniel was taught by angels; Cornelius was answered by an angel; an angel walked with the three children of God in the fiery furnace (see Daniel 3:25); an angel shut the mouths of lions so they would not hurt Daniel in the lions' den (Daniel 6:22); and an angel comforted Paul in a storm at sea (Acts 27:23-24). Hardly any remarkable thing happened to God's people that was not accompanied by the ministry of angels.

2. The ministry of angels, though not visible, has not completely ceased. This ministry comes to all the saints. "Are not all angels ministering spirits sent to serve those who will inherit salvation?" (Hebrews 1:14). All who are called to inherit a blessing are taught by them and protected by them. "They will lift you up in their hands, so that you will not strike your foot against a stone" (Psalm 91:12). The ministry of angels was more apparent in the early church because it was new and needed to be encouraged. But God wants us to live by faith and to expect all our supports to come in a more spiritual way. Though we cannot see the angels, we still experience their succor. Similarly, we cannot see the evil angels, but we do not doubt the damage they do. At the beginning of the gospel age Christ's bodily presence was needed, but now only his spiritual presence is necessary.

3. God's children are the proper object of angels' ministry and care. Wicked people are not under their secret protection. It is true that they may come under their general care, as Hagar and Ishmael did, who are set out in Scripture as types of those who are rejected by the Lord. Yet

Genesis 21:17 states, "God heard the boy crying, and the angel of God called to Hagar from heaven and said to her, 'What is the matter, Hagar? Do not be afraid; God has heard the boy crying as he lies there.'" This might have happened to Ishmael because he was Abraham's son; dogs in the house eat the crumbs.

4. The ministry of the angels is over all of God's children without exception. This applies not only to Moses; the lowest saint is under angelic protection. God's love for his people is not given according to their particular pomp and greatness. "See that you do not look down on one of these little ones. For I tell you that their angels in heaven always see the face of my Father in heaven" (Matthew 18:10). This is especially true of those who are nothing in the eyes of the world. The message of Christ's birth was given by angels to shepherds as they fed their flocks in the fields.

5. As no saints are excepted from receiving the benefit of the angelic ministry, so no angels are excepted from being used in this way. Michael contends with Satan, and the apostle says, "Are not *all* angels ministering spirits?" (Hebrews 1:14). The archangels themselves are ministering spirits. It is rash of the scholastics to exempt an angel from this office. What a wonderful example of God's love is here, that the highest angel should not be exempt from caring for the lowest saint!

6. That every single believer has his proper and allotted angel to attend him from his birth to his death is a matter for conjecture rather than a positive assertion. There are some Scriptures that make this probable but not certain. Sometimes we read of one angel attending many men, and at other times of many angels attending one man. See Genesis 32:1-2; 2 Kings 6:17. It is true that the idea of each Christian having a guardian angel is ancient. Among the ancient fathers quotations from Scripture are used to support this idea. Again, this is probable but not definite. They quote Matthew 18:10, "See that you do not look down on one of these little ones. For I tell you that their angels in heaven always see the face of my Father in heaven." This verse does not say *the* angels, but *their* angels, although the word there may only imply their common interest in the whole host of God. Christ does not say that each of them had his own angel.

For example, one may say that these soldiers have their captains, these prisoners have their keepers, these scholars have their masters; it does not necessarily follow that each one has a particular captain, keeper, or master. Another place that is quoted is Acts 12:15. When the girl said Peter was at the door, the Christians, not believing her, said, "It must be his angel." But this example may be answered thus: the things people say in Scripture are not themselves necessarily Scripture or a part of God's rule. Also, there are many things spoken about by the disciples in their ignorance that are not completely justifiable. Because this is the main Scripture quoted to support the idea that every Christian has his own guardian angel, let me examine it a little more.

This verse is understood in three different ways. Some understand it as meaning it is Peter's angel or messenger, sent by him from prison. In Luke 7:24 John's disciples were called *angelon*, angels or messengers of John. But Rhoda heard Peter's voice, and that was the basis of the sayings. Other people understand this to refer to some angel who had come to announce Peter's death, but that is groundless. Lastly, some, such as Chrysostom, believe that this refers to a particular protecting angel. But since when have angels taken the shape and habit of the people they are looking after? Also, angels do not knock at doors, waiting for the door to be opened. And even if Peter did have a special angel it does not follow that everyone else does. This verse probably means a spirit that had taken Peter's shape.

7. While it remains uncertain if every believer has one angel assigned to attend him, in a general sense we have an assurance of angelic protection. If a whole city is well guarded, it is as good as each citizen having an individual soldier assigned for his protection. Indeed, it gives us more comfort to know that we have many soldiers maintaining our safety and not just one. "For he will command his angels concerning you to guard you in all your ways" (Psalm 91:11). Many angels are commanded to keep us safe. They are in God's presence, beholding his face, ready to carry out God's will. "Praise the LORD, you his angels, you mighty ones who do his bidding, who obey his word" (Psalm 103:20). The angels care for each of us as if they had nobody else to look after.

8. This protection is from our conception until our body and soul are translated into glory. The ministry of the angels does not stop until the final resurrection. They start to care for us as soon as we are conceived, for then they have another distinct charge to look after. "For when God, who set me apart from birth and called me by his grace . . ." (Galatians 1:15). The angels watch over us in infancy and childhood. Jesus Christ was provided for as an infant by an angel. "When they had gone, an angel of the Lord appeared to Joseph in a dream. 'Get up,' he said, 'take the child and his mother and escape to Egypt. Stay there until I tell you, for Herod is going to search for the child to kill him'" (Matthew 2:13). The devil attacks the elect while they are still in their baby clothes. The angels rejoice over our conversion (see Luke 15:7, 10). Nothing gives the angels more pleasure than when they rejoice over our conversion. The devil tries to stop this in every possible way, but the angels rejoice over a "burning stick snatched from the fire" (Zechariah 3:2).

After our conversion the angels watch over us in duty, danger, and temptations. In duties, where Satan is most active to hinder, the angels are most helpful. "Then he showed me Joshua the high priest standing before the angel of the LORD, and Satan standing at his right side to accuse him"

(Zechariah 3:1). The angels are in the assemblies of the faithful (see 1 Corinthians 11:10). Also, in our dangers the angels are present with us. When Peter was in prison, God sent him an angel to bring him out (see Acts 12:1-11). Ruffinus speaks about a young man, a martyr on the rack, who had his face wiped by an angel and was refreshed by him in the midst of his pains. In the dangers that we cannot foresee, the angels are there to rescue us. "They will lift you up in their hands, so that you will not strike your foot against a stone" (Psalm 91:12). Also, the angels help us in our temptations. "Then the devil left him, and angels came and attended him" (Matthew 4:11). The angels came to show how God would deal with his people in similar circumstances.

The angels are present to comfort us as we die. In the midst of his agonies in the Garden of Gethsemane Jesus was refreshed and comforted by an angel. "An angel from heaven appeared to him and strengthened him" (Luke 22:43). The angels are also like this with the faithful in their sicknesses. After death they carry our souls to heaven, as Lazarus was carried to Abraham's side (see Luke 16:22). Even if the body does not have the honor of a grand funeral, the soul is solemnly conveyed by angels and gathered up into the communion of the souls of just people made perfect. It will be the same as when Christ himself ascended into heaven in the company of angels (see Acts 1:9-11). Even after death they guard our bodies in the grave, as the angels guarded Christ's tomb (Matthew 28:2-4). Not only the high priests, but God too set his guards. The angels' last ministry and service to the faithful is to gather up their bodies on the last day. "And he will send his angels with a loud trumpet call, and they will gather his elect from the four winds, from one end of the heavens to the other" (Matthew 24:31).

9. This protection is always undertaken according to God's pleasure. "Praise the LORD, all his heavenly hosts, you his servants who do his will" (Psalm 103:21). The angels do not work for *their* pleasure or for *our* pleasure but for *God's* pleasure. The help of angels is more powerful, but no more absolute, than the help of other means, for it still depends on God's will, as do all other means of defense and outward support. Their work is to attend us and serve us, according to the Lord's direction.

Let us now apply what we have said.

Application 1. First we are given a great deal of information about how the angels help us.

1. The care of God for the elect. God uses his own power for our preservation, as well as the mediation of Christ, the guidance of the Spirit, and the ministry of angels. In Zechariah we are given a sample of God's providence. "Then the man standing among the myrtle trees explained, 'They are the ones the LORD has sent to go throughout the earth'" (Zechariah 1:10). The "man standing among the myrtle trees" is Jesus

Christ, who, to prefigure his incarnation, is represented in this way. He has all the angels at his command and sends them out as his church needs them. Thus does the Lord himself help us, and we may believe him more firmly.

2. The condescension and humility of the angels. They rejoice more in serving than in receiving honors. They are happy to carry out God's will for the lowest of his creatures. An angel clothed in light and glory came to the shepherds. The angels never refuse to wait on those who are despised and rejected if they are directed to do this by Christ.

3. This informs us about how kind the angels are to people, which should put our envy to shame. Their love for mankind is great, and they always want our good and so never decline any office of love and service for us. They rejoiced when the world was created as a dwelling place for us. "On what were its footings set, or who laid its cornerstone—while the morning stars sang together and all the angels shouted for joy?" (Job 38:6-7). The angels also sang when Christ came for our restoration. "Suddenly a great company of the heavenly host appeared with the angel, praising God and saying, 'Glory to God in the highest, and on earth peace to men on whom his favor rests'" (Luke 2:13-14). The angels also rejoice at the calling and conversion of a sinner. "I tell you that in the same way there is more rejoicing in heaven over one sinner who repents than over ninety-nine righteous persons who do not need to repent" (Luke 15:7).

4. This informs us about the dignity of the saints. What a price the Lord and his holy angels set on the humblest Christian! God's own court is their guard. It was a great favor for Mordecai to have a king toward whom to act as courtier and to wait on him for one hour. We have angels who wait on us for our good.

5. This informs us about the obedience of the angels, even in their most humble duties. God says, "Go!" and they go, even if that means they have to serve some lowly creature. We often ignore commands when they involve self-denial. In the Lord's Prayer we have this pattern: "Your will be done on earth as it is in heaven" (Matthew 6:10). No office or work that God calls us to should be looked on as being too low or base for us. The angels, who excel in strength, are willing to condescend to protect us when God commands them.

Application 2. Second, this serves to exhort God's children to behave in certain ways.

1. To wait for the angels' help. If you keep in God's ways in your callings, you will have safety and defense when the Lord sees it is fit for you. Remember, you are seen by God, by other people, and by angels in all your actions, trials, and sufferings; bear up with a confidence that befits Christians. Although you can do little to promote Christ's interests, what cannot God do through his angels?

2. Live as people who expect this help, so as not to tempt God or grieve his angels. We should be careful how we behave in the company of such honorable angels. Angels are pure and holy creatures; pride, lust, and vanity are very offensive to them, and especially impurities and indecencies in God's worship.

Application 3. Third, here is reproof for wicked men, who perform the devil's ministry, act the part of the bad angels rather than the good ones, and despise, slander, oppose, seduce, and tempt God's children. How dare you despise those whom the angels honor! You think of them as being unworthy of your company and countenance, though angels never disdain to serve and attend them. You slander those whom the angels defend and oppose, and persecute those whom the angels protect. You tempt and seduce those whom the angels rejoice to see brought home to God.

Application 4. Get this interest if you want to be under this protection. Get an interest in Christ, and then you will get an interest in the angels. Hereafter the saints will be like the angels in heaven (Luke 20:36), and here on earth, until we have this glory, we will have their defense.

Note 4. **The archangel Michael.** Observe from the style and character of the angel that there is an order among the angels, both good and bad. They have their distinct leaders. We read of Michael, and we read of Beelzebub. There is an order of bad angels in hell, hence the expression, "the devil and his angels" (Matthew 25:41). This seems to indicate a prince among the unclean spirits, and there is an order among the good angels as well. God made all things in order, but to define this order in all its details would be to intrude into things that have not been revealed. The scholastics speak as if they knew all the particulars of the angels' government. But in things that have not been revealed there can be no certainty.

The apostle Paul does speak about several classes of invisible creatures. "For by him all things were created: things in heaven and on earth, visible and invisible, whether thrones or powers or rulers or authorities; all things were created by him and for him" (Colossians 1:16). But who can define exactly their order and functions? There is a distinction, but we do not know what it is. However, it is useful to look at this in a general way. This shows us the necessity for order and subordination. No creatures can subsist without this. Those who are against the office of magistrate are against peace and happiness. The angels and devils are not without their heads and princes. It is the misery of the wicked that they will be cast out with the devil and his angels, and part of our happiness will be to make up one church and assembly with angels and archangels. "Therefore, since we are surrounded by such a great cloud of witnesses, let us throw off everything that hinders and the sin that so easily entangles" (Hebrews 12:1).

Note 5. **When he was disputing with the devil about the body of Moses.** The devil probably wanted Moses' body so he could abuse it in an idolatrous way. The devil loves idolatry. All false worship, either directly or indirectly, tends to honor the devil. That is why idol feasts were called "the table of demons" (1 Corinthians 10:21). It is noteworthy that those sacrifices offered to the true God, though in an unbecoming way, are called the sacrifices of devils. "They must no longer offer any of their sacrifices to the goat idols [demons, NIV margin] to whom they prostitute themselves" (Leviticus 17:7). "Any Israelite who sacrifices a cow, a lamb or a goat in the camp or outside of it instead of bringing it to the entrance to the Tent of Meeting to present it as an offering to the LORD in front of the tabernacle of the LORD—that man shall be considered guilty of bloodshed; he has shed blood and must be cut off from his people" (Leviticus 17:3-4). Although an Israelite might kill a goat or an ox or a lamb to the Lord for a sacrifice, if it was outside the camp and not before the Tent of Meeting, God considered it a sacrifice to devils. We are told that God's people "sacrificed to demons, which are not God—gods they had not known, gods that recently appeared, gods your fathers did not fear" (Deuteronomy 32:17). The devil delights in idols and false worship. The Lord, above everything else, cares about how people worship him, and therefore Satan is always seeking ways to corrupt our worship. There are two things dear to God—his truth and his worship. Satan uses all his strength to corrupt God's truth with error and his worship with superstition.

Application 1. This shows us what great care we should take to be right in worship. It is idolatry not only to worship false gods in the place of the true God, but to worship the true God in a false manner; both false ways of worship gratify the devil. When the devil cannot keep people in complete blindness and paganism, he is happy if he can distract them with unnecessary rites and ceremonies in worship. Therefore let us hate the least kind of idolatry. David said he would not even mention idols. "I will not . . . take up their names on my lips" (Psalm 16:4).

Application 2. We must beware of idolatry. Satan loves it, and that is motive enough for us to avoid it. We should hate as Christ hated and love as Christ loved. "But you have this in your favor: You hate the practices of the Nicolaitans, which I also hate" (Revelation 2:6). We should love what Satan hates and hate what Satan loves. We are inclined toward the sin of idolatry, and so it is listed as one of "the acts of the sinful nature" (Galatians 5:19).

1. Take care that you do not make the true God an idol in your thoughts, by thinking things that are unworthy of his essence. "But to the wicked, God says: . . . 'you thought I was altogether like you'" (Psalm 50:16, 21). It is easy to turn the true God into an idol in your own mind. To remedy this, consider God in his deeds and in Christ. Concerning his works, Cyril observed that we do not read about any idolatry before the

Flood. Aquinas adds a reason for this: the memory of the creation was then fresh in their minds. Look also to God in Christ. We saw in Leviticus 17 that if they did not bring their sacrifice to the Tent of Meeting, it was called a sacrifice of devils. The Tent of Meeting was a type of Christ. You make God an idol when you worship him outside Christ, for the Father must be honored in the Son: ". . . that all may honor the Son just as they honor the Father. He who does not honor the Son does not honor the Father, who sent him" (John 5:23). Therefore, whenever you go to God, take Christ along with you.

2. Take care that you do not set up any idol against God in your affections. When you set up anything above God in your esteem, especially in your trust, it is an idol. Covetousness is twice called idolatry in the New Testament because it takes our affections away from God. "Put to death, therefore, whatever belongs to your earthly nature: sexual immorality, impurity, lust, evil desires and greed, which is idolatry" (Colossians 3:5). "For of this you can be sure: No immoral, impure or greedy person—such a man is an idolater—has any inheritance in the kingdom of Christ and of God" (Ephesians 5:5). I mention this because Satan is as gratified with spiritual idolatry as with bodily idolatry.

Note 6. **About the body of Moses.** Notice that of all kinds of idolatry, the devil abuses the world most with idolatrous respect for the bodies and relics of dead saints. Why? It is partly because this kind of idolatry makes our religious affections a trap for us. For it is most plausible to reverence those who are departed in the Lord. Also, when men become objects of worship and adoration, the Godhead is held in contempt. The devil has found that this is a very successful way to divert people away from worshiping God. Lactantius has shown that the idolizing of famous men led to the rise of all idolatry. And Tertullian, at the end of his *Apology,* also observes that heathen idolatry came in this way: "by a reverence to the images of dead men whose memory was precious among them." In the primitive church, before any idol was brought into the church, Christians made idols among their tombs and among the shrines of the martyrs.

Note 7. **He . . . did not dare to bring.** The archangel did not have the boldness to do anything contrary to God's law or unbecoming his rank and ministry. Every sin is an affront to the law that forbids it. "Why did you despise the word of the LORD by doing what is evil in his eyes?" (2 Samuel 12:9). A sinner, in effect, says, "What do I care for the commandment? I will go on for all that." But the godly man fears the commandment. "He who respects a command is rewarded" (Proverbs 13:13). If any of God's laws stand in his way, he dares not proceed.

We should fear God on account of his power. Do we think we can compete with God who can command legions of angels? We should fear God because of his love and mercy. This should instill a fear or an unwillingness to displease God. "They will come trembling to the LORD and to his blessings in the last days" (Hosea 3:5). There is a holy fear that comes from grace. There is a holy reverent fear, by which we fear to offend our good God, as we think that is the greatest evil in the world. This arises out of our new nature and from thankfulness to God because of his mercy in Jesus Christ. Boldness in sin resembles the devil, but a holy fear resembles Michael. People who neither fear God nor care about men (see Luke 18:4) have outgrown the heart of a man and are next to devils.

Note 8. Note one more thing concerning **he . . . did not dare to bring**. This shows us that angels have a most holy nature, which will not allow them to sin. Though angels are called "holy angels" (see Matthew 25:31, KJV), the devils are called "unclean spirits." When angels appear, they are usually dressed in a way that represents their innocency. At Christ's tomb there were "two angels in white, seated where Jesus' body had been, one at the head and the other at the foot" (John 20:12). Angels are preserved in Jesus Christ as we are and have their strength from him, or else they would have fallen with the other apostate angels.

Application. This serves to humble us. How do we differ from the angels? Their natures engage them in holiness, and ours, being corrupted, engage us in sin. Their nature will not allow them to sin, and our nature will not allow us to do what is good. "So I find this law at work: When I want to do good, evil is right there with me" (Romans 7:21). These holy angels when they compare themselves with God are abased; so should we not be even more abased?

Note 9. **A slanderous accusation**. In the original this is, *krisin blasphemias*, "the judgment or sentence of blasphemy or evil-speaking." The meaning is, unworthy language that would not be found in any serious judgment or process. Railing and reviling must not be used with the worst adversary in the best cause.

1. Such reproaches come from an evil principle, contempt, or passion, all evidence of pride. A person who thinks too highly of himself disdains other people. When he is crossed he becomes angry, like a full stream hitting a dam.

2. Such reproaches are most unsuitable in matters of religion. The God of peace is not served with an angry spirit, and Christ's battles need no worldly weapons. Christianity, of all religions, is the meekest and most humble; the foundation of it is the slain Lamb. Those who are called to inherit a blessing should not curse people. "Do not repay evil with evil or insult with insult, but with blessing, because to this you were called so that you may inherit a blessing" (1 Peter 3:9).

3. These kinds of reproaches go directly against the Word. The Scripture is a great friend to the peace of human societies, for it condemns the slightest offensive word and gesture. "If you do away with the yoke of

oppression, with the pointing finger and malicious talk . . ." (Isaiah 58:9). God wanted the pointing finger, a gesture of indignation, put aside as well as the yoke of oppression. "But I tell you that anyone who is angry with his brother will be subject to judgment. Again, anyone who says to his brother, 'Raca,' is answerable to the Sanhedrin. But anyone who says, 'You fool!' will be in danger of the fire of hell" (Matthew 5:22). The scribes and Pharisees had restricted the sixth commandment to the act of murder. Christ told them that rash anger, with all its expressions, *is* murder.

Note 10. **"The Lord rebuke you!"** Although Michael did not rant and rage, he did refer the matter to God. From this, observe that in religious contests we must oppose evil but not in an unseemly manner. Michael did not let Satan alone, and we must not let errors alone and so allow the devil to have everything his own way. Many, under the guise of meekness, are still and silent in the cause of Christ. Cursed is this peace and meekness, allowing envious people to sow their weeds, never warning anyone. God's messengers have been compared to watchdogs. When the wolf comes, they should bark. If the sleepy world objects to being awakened, we must bear that.

Note 11. **"The Lord rebuke you!"** Note, again, that Michael refers the matter to God, who is the best patron of his causes. In our contests about religion, God must especially be sought for a blessing. Michael joined in the contest but said, **"The Lord rebuke you!"** Times of argument should also be times of prayer. Prejudices will never disappear until God sends out his light and his truth; see Psalm 43:3. If the devil is not prayed down as well as disputed down, little good comes from our contests.

Verse 10

Commentary on Verse 10

Yet these men speak abusively against whatever they do not understand; and what things they do understand by instinct, like unreasoning animals—these are the very things that destroy them.
In this verse Jude shows the difference between the seducers and the archangel Michael. Michael was modest in a good cause, but the seducers were contemptuous and given to railing in matters about which they were completely ignorant. They are accused of two faults in this verse: first, pride, seen in their condemning things without knowledge; and, second, wickedness, seen in their abusing the knowledge they did have.

Yet these men—*outoi*, the seducers spoken about in the context—**speak abusively**, *blasphemousi*; they take liberty to thrust their reproaches **against whatever they do not understand**. What are these things? I take this to mean their ignorance in all spiritual matters. **And what things they do understand by instinct, like unreasoning animals—these are the very things that destroy them.** The sense here is the knowledge they have in common with the beasts. In his reason and upper part of the soul, man resembles an angel, but in his appetite and senses, a beast. What they know by their senses and animal desires they are guided by. But in these things they are worse than animals, corrupting themselves by the excesses of the sensual appetite as they eat and drink and use women in sexual intercourse, as if there were no law.

What things they do understand (*phusikos*) **by instinct**. There is a threefold light: first, sense or instinct; second, reason; and third, grace. If a man is endowed with grace he is said to be spiritual, *pneumatikos*, or furnished with the light of grace. *Phusikos*, **instinct**, signifies being guided by blind motion and natural instinct, without reason, counsel, and choice, just as the beasts are. So it is said here, **what things they do understand by instinct**. That is, what they understand by natural inclination, or the mere judgment or perception of sense, to be good or evil, **these are the very things that destroy them**. They destroy themselves by sinful defilement of themselves and so draw down punishment both on their souls and bodies. "But these men blaspheme in matters they do not understand. They are like brute beasts, creatures of instinct, born only to be caught and destroyed, and like beasts they too will perish" (2 Peter 2:12).

Notes on Verse 10

Note 1. Note that truth is usually ignorantly slandered. Men condemn the ways and things of God because they do not understand them. In the apostle Paul's day teaching about the cross was seen as foolishness by those who knew the least about it. "For the message of the cross is foolishness to those who are perishing" (1 Corinthians 1:18). Later on the Christian religion was condemned because it could not be heard. Tertullian said in his *Apology*, "When they knew it, they could not hate it." It is the devil's cunning to keep us at a distance from truths and therefore burden them with prejudices, that we may be suspicious about them rather than search them. We condemn them out of ignorance. It is our perverseness and pride to speak evil of things that are out of our reach and to disapprove what we have not reached or cannot understand. "He who answers before listening—that is his folly and his shame" (Proverbs 18:13).

Note 2. Observe that people of corrupt mind are usually sensual, and sensual people are usually people of corrupt minds. An unsound heart is often sheltered under unsound doctrine, and worldly delights blunt and weaken the intention of the mind, so that it is very vulnerable to mistakes. Therefore, on the one hand we should work to keep the mind right and sound in the faith. Fish stink first at the head. When the judgment is poisoned, the taint is soon conveyed to the affections. On the other hand, add "to knowledge, self-control" (2 Peter 1:6). Solomon, so famous for wisdom and knowledge, was enticed by ungodly women. Oh, do not let fleshly lusts betray you!

Note 3. Once more observe that where sin reigns, it turns men into **unreasoning animals**. "But man, despite his riches, does not endure; he is like the beasts that perish" (Psalm 49:12). This means that people did not remain in the honor of their creation. Hence they are compared to wolves for their cruelty, dogs for their filthiness, horses and mules for their anger, and a wild donkey's colt for lack of understanding. See Jeremiah 5:8, Ezekiel 23:20, Job 11:12, and Revelation 22:15. If we had the head of a horse or the face of a pig or the hoofs of a mule, we would be thought to be monsters. But to have the heart of a beast is worse. To be like them in the inner person is more terrible in God's sight.

Further, sin does not only make an unreasoning animal out of you but a devil. See John 6:70. The devil said, "What have we to do with you, Jesus, son of David?" And wicked men say, "What is the Almighty? Depart from us; we do not want the knowledge of your ways."

Note 4. I will now show you some ways in which people turn into beasts. When, in indulging in the pleasures of the world, we are neither modest nor keep them within limits, we are behaving like pigs, wallowing in our own filthiness. A wild animal cannot help doing this, but even many wild animals do not do this. When a person lives by his appetite rather than by reason and conscience, nourishing the body but not bothering to refresh the soul, he is behaving like an **unreasoning animal**. This ought to humble many people who have a high opinion of themselves. They have a beast's heart, under the cover of a human shape.

Note 5. Sensuality paves the way for corruption. To check the brutish rage of sensual inclinations, say, "This will feed my corruption and help me perish forever." But "the one who sows to please the Spirit, from the Spirit will reap eternal life" (Galatians 6:8). Then say, "Shall I, for pleasures on this earth, forfeit the pleasures at God's right hand forever? God forbid."

Verse 11

Commentary on Verse 11

Woe to them! They have taken the way of Cain; they have rushed for profit into Balaam's error; they have been destroyed in Korah's rebellion.

Here the apostle comes to enumerate these evil men's sins, and he does it by giving examples so they could apply the sin and punishment to themselves. Three examples are given in this verse: that of Cain, to highlight their malice and cruelty; that of Balaam, to indicate their covetousness and seduction; and that of Korah, to underline their opposition to magistrates and to God's ministry, just as Korah and his accomplices rose up against Moses and Aaron.

Woe to them! This is a denunciation. **They have taken the way of Cain.** Cain's example is given because he was the leader of those who left the true church and the pure service of God. "So Cain went out from the LORD's presence and lived in the land of Nod, east of Eden" (Genesis 4:16). Tertullian says that Cain was the devil's patriarch, the first root of the worldly seed or of the seed of the serpent, in whom persecution started. Cain's way was the way of murder. He killed his brother because he was more righteous and godly than he was (see 1 John 3:12). People who follow his path envy and hate their holy brothers, and this often develops into violence, persecution, and murder. Cain killed Abel, just as the Gnostics were prepared to attack those who did not agree with them and stirred up the Jews to persecute the Christians.

They have rushed for profit into Balaam's error. The story of Balaam starts in Numbers 22; his death is recorded in Numbers 31:8: "They also killed Balaam son of Beor with the sword." Balaam was hired to curse Israel, even though this went against his conscience. In the same way these seducers perverted the truth. Simon Magus, out of whose school the Gnostics came, wanted, as you know, to buy and sell the Holy Spirit (see Acts 8). Jude says that they **rushed for profit** (*exechuthesan*, "were poured out"). This is a metaphor taken from a river overflowing its banks.

They have been destroyed in Korah's rebellion. This last example is added to emphasize their factious practices. Korah's deeds are recorded in Numbers 16. He was overcome by ambition and wanted to join the priesthood. He and his accomplices rebelled against Moses and Aaron but perished in the attempt. In the same way these people who oppose magistrates and the ministry of Christ would perish as certainly as if it had already happened. Although they were not even born in the time of Korah, they are said to perish when Korah perished.

Notes on Verse 11

Note 1. **They have taken the way of Cain.** Wicked people today are just like wicked people from the past. Cain's club, as Bucholcer says, is still carried about in the world, stained with the blood of Abel. "The son born in the ordinary way persecuted the son born by the power of the Spirit. It is the same now" (Galatians 4:29). Today we have the same devil tempting us. Do people today separate themselves from Christian churches? There were the Donatists in former times. Are there now those who deny the Godhead of Christ? There were Arians then. Are there now ranters? There were Gnostics then. And are there now bloody enemies of the truth? Every age produces its Cains. The devil is but playing his old games. While the scene is different, and there are different actors, the plot is the same.

Note 2. Observe again, heretics and libertines usually become persecutors. **They have taken the way of Cain.** Satan, who is a liar, is also a murderer. A false way cannot exist without the tools of blood and cruelty; witness the Circumcellians, the Priscillianists, the Arians, the Donatists, and the tragedies at Munster. I tell you, the great danger of the latter times is from libertines. Many people are fearful about a second deluge of anti-Christian attacks, but this is not as likely as the seditious insurrections of people who cause divisions. What sad havoc they will make among God's people as soon as those bloody-minded wretches gain power! The latter times are perilous times. "But mark this: There will be terrible times in the last days" (2 Timothy 3:1). Why? From what sort of people will the danger arise? Not from the anti-Christian or the Popish party so much as from the libertine party.

Note 3. **They have rushed for profit into Balaam's error.** The devil entices his slaves to a variety of sins, such as the malice of Cain and the covetousness of Balaam.

Note 4. People are usually drawn into error by the bait of gain and worldly profit. "In their greed these teachers will exploit you with stories they have made up. Their condemnation has long been hanging over them, and their destruction has not been sleeping" (2 Peter 2:3). "The love of money is a root of all kinds of evil" (1 Timothy 6:10) and is often the root of heresies or sect-making. Balaam had many good gifts. God is said to have put words into his mouth (see Numbers 23:26). Balaam asked for God's guidance but was loath to follow it, and covetousness eventually took over his heart.

Note 5. **Rushed** (*exechuthesan*). From this word we deduce that people sin wholeheartedly. They are reckless as they break through all the restraints of their conscience. Balaam, despite the checks and disappointments that met him, was urged on by the violent impulse of his own lust and his greedy desire for reward. "But he was rebuked for his wrongdoing by a donkey—a beast without speech—who spoke with a man's voice and restrained the prophet's madness" (2 Peter 2:16). The apostle Paul refers to some people as "having lost all sensitivity"; "they have given themselves over to sensuality so as to indulge in every kind of impurity, with a continual lust for more" (Ephesians 4:19).

Note 6. **They have been destroyed in Korah's rebellion.** Note that ambition breeds faction. Diotrephes loved his own preeminence and so troubled the church. "I wrote to the church, but Diotrephes, who loves to be first, will have nothing to do with us" (3 John 9). All divisions can be traced back to our lusts. People who are not content with their own position and desire to be promoted break rank. It is an excellent thing to be content with your own position in life. Jesus Christ was content with his lowly position. If God has denied you a particular position in the world that you desire, you are either not worthy of it, or it is not a suitable position for you to hold.

Note 7. The idea that everyone should be equal is no new thing in God's church. "Isn't it enough that you have brought us up out of a land flowing with milk and honey to kill us in the desert? And now you also want to lord it over us?" (Numbers 16:13). This is like saying: "All the Lord's people are holy, so why should anyone be set over us?" Let us beware of the parity that some people desire. There must be rule and superiority, or all will come to nothing. God made the world of hills and valleys, and in the church and state there must be governors and governed, teachers and taught. It is Korah's sin to invade offices without a call, and to destroy the order that God has established.

Note 8. Again, observe that schisms and factions in the church bring destruction in the end. The earth swallows up those who make a split in the congregation. Surely people would be more sensitive about this if they just thought about the punishment that we know overtakes those who disturb a well-ordered society.

Note 9. Note that Scripture speaks about things to come as if they were already past: **they have been destroyed.** In the same way Revelation 14:8

says, "Fallen! Fallen is Babylon the Great." What is threatened is as certain as if it had already taken place. This is also true of God's promises. You possess his mercy if you have the promise of mercy. By God's word everything was created and continues to exist. "Let it be" was enough to make a world. Well, then, let us through faith see the ruin of wicked people when they are at the height of their power.

Note 10. Last, observe that wicked people may read about their own destruction in the destruction of others who sinned before them. They break the same law, and God views this in the same way as he did before. The intention of divine providence to take vengeance is as powerful as ever. These people act from the same lusts, which God hates as much as ever. Sin has not grown less dangerous now in the latter days. Surely, then, you would think that men would grow wiser, having so many precedents. Pride may see its downfall in Nebuchadnezzar, sedition in Korah, rebellion in Absalom, violence in Cain, adultery in Jezebel, and the usurping of sacred offices without a call in the leprosy of Uzziah. There is hardly a persistent sin that we are not warned about from examples of people who committed them in the past. They are like signposts along the path we travel, saying in effect, "Take heed; do not enter here. If you do, it will result in your ruin and destruction." We must look to Christ and be godly.

Verse 12

Commentary on Verse 12

These men are blemishes at your love feasts, eating with you without the slightest qualm—shepherds who feed only themselves. They are clouds without rain, blown along by the wind; autumn trees, without fruit and uprooted—twice dead.

In the previous verse the apostle used examples to expose the seducers; in this verse he uses metaphors.

These men are blemishes at your love feasts. The word used for blemishes, *spilades*, means "rocks" and can be translated as "spots." "They are blots and blemishes" (2 Peter 2:13). Jude called them **blemishes** either because they were defiled themselves or because they could infect others by their example.

At your love feasts. These were suppers in the early days of the church. They either showed brotherly unity or refreshed the poor, obeying Christ's command in Luke 14:12-14. But they did not now fulfill the purpose for which they were started, for each person brought his own food and excluded the poor (see 1 Corinthians 11:20-22).

Eating with you. The word means "to feast liberally together." This is added to show how they perverted the nature of the meeting and turned it into a time to luxuriate, though it was meant to be a time when the poor were attended to. In the feasts of the godly there was moderation and temperance, but these people were merrily filling their paunches at the church's expense.

Shepherds who feed only themselves (*poimainontes heautous*), feeding themselves as a shepherd feeds his sheep. This indicates their excess, eating beyond all measure and without respect for the fellowship that should exist between saints. They fed themselves, not other people. They fed their own bodies and not other people's souls. "Son of man, prophesy against the shepherds of Israel; prophesy and say to them: 'This is what the Sovereign LORD says: Woe to the shepherds of Israel who only take care of themselves! Should not shepherds take care of the flock? You eat the curds, clothe yourselves with the wool and slaughter the choice animals, but you do not take care of the flock'" (Ezekiel 34:2-3).

A heap of metaphors now follow that express the ostentation of these people in professing themselves to be far above what they were in reality. They were inept teachers, and yet they gave the impression that they were enlightening people.

They are clouds without rain. These seducers promise rain but do not produce one drop or one positive idea that will help people in their understanding.

Blown along by the wind. The Holy Spirit's comment on this metaphor is found in Proverbs 25:14: "Like clouds and wind without rain is the man who boasts of gifts he does not give." The apostle Peter says that "these men are springs without water and mists driven by a storm" (2 Peter 2:17).

Autumn trees, without fruit and uprooted—twice dead. This is the second metaphor. It reveals the characteristics of evil trees.

1. The first characteristic is that they are **trees, without fruit.** These trees only bear rotten and withered fruit. This applies to these seducers whose lives are not full of good fruits. They claim much, but what fruits do you find? Do you find more holiness, true dying to self, strict obedience, piety toward God, or mercy toward other people? No; in place of this you find brutishness, disobedience to civil powers, neglect of God, abuse of the Gospel, and contempt for their betters.

2. The second characteristic of these trees is that they are **twice dead.** If you apply this to trees, they may be twice dead either in regard to fruit, as a barren thing is said to be dead (see Romans 4:19), or in regard to their state, in that they are rotten and growing worse and worse. **Twice dead** is a Hebraism meaning "very dead," as **twice** stands for much. If you apply this to these seducers, they are **twice dead** both with regard to their natural state, being dead in trespasses and sins, and with regard to their apostasy, or the decay of that life they seemed to have by the grace of the Gospel. "If they have escaped the corruption of the world by knowing our Lord and Savior Jesus Christ and are again entangled in it and overcome, they are worse off at the end than they were at the beginning" (2 Peter 2:20). "It is impossible for those who have once been enlightened, who have tasted the heavenly gift, who have shared in the Holy Spirit, who have tasted the goodness of the word of God and the powers of the coming age, if they fall away, to be brought back to repentance, because to their loss they are crucifying the Son of God all over again and subjecting him to public disgrace" (Hebrews 6:4-6).

3. The third characteristic of these trees is that they are **uprooted** (*ekrizothenta*), plucked up by the roots. When this happens, the trees are past all hope of sprouting again. This is an apt picture of their incurable apos-

tasy. They are deprived of all spiritual communion with Christ and his mystical body. They are incapable of bearing fruit. They are only fit for burning and destruction.

Notes on Verse 12

Note 1. **These men are blemishes.** Observe from this that sensual people are blemishes on a Christian society. They are not only filthy in themselves, but they bring dishonor on the whole church they belong to. "See to it that no one misses the grace of God and that no bitter root grows up to cause trouble and defile many" (Hebrews 12:15). What that bitter root is is clear from the following verse: "See that no one is sexually immoral, or is godless like Esau, who for a single meal sold his inheritance rights as the oldest son" (Hebrews 12:16). When any bitter or immoral root springs up, the whole of society is defiled. So when such persons are discovered, they should be ejected from the church. They do not have God's mark on them but Satan's. Calvin observed that nothing harms the church more than being kind to wicked people. In Salvian's time the pagans accused the Christians thus: "They talk of a holy Christ, and yet are unjust, unclean, covetous; they talk of a meek and patient Christ, and yet are rapacious and violent; they talk of holy apostles and yet engage in impure speech."

Note 2. **At your love feasts.** It is odious filthiness to make religion serve our bellies and to turn charity into luxury. They were accused of a sin that is often practiced by the world. "Such people are not serving our Lord Christ, but their own appetites" (Romans 16:18). They speak about Christ, but "their god is their stomach" (Philippians 3:19). When people aim at nothing but their own ease and pleasure, their stomachs take the place of God.

Note 3. **Eating with you without the slightest qualm—shepherds who feed only themselves.** Our meetings and feasts should focus on Christian fellowship. We should not only digest meat but receive wholesome instruction. Christ, when he sat down to a meal, raised people's thoughts to a superior banquet. "When one of those at the table with him heard this, he said to Jesus, 'Blessed is the man who will eat at the feast in the kingdom of God'" (Luke 14:15). When the body is fed, the soul must not be neglected. The Word of God is the food of souls. It should not be completely banished from our tables. At every meal the devil usually brings in his dish. We should remember God as our Creator, through whose bounty we enjoy what is set before us, so that our spiritual appetite may be refreshed as well as our bodily appetite.

Note 4. **Without the slightest qualm.** This may mean "without the slightest fear of God"; or it may refer to the church, meaning "without the slightest fear of the church"; or it may refer to people, meaning "without the slightest fear of the snare of the creature."

1. If we take this phrase to refer to God, it may apply to his presence, meaning that it is sinful to sit down to eat without giving any thought to God. As the lungs are in constant use, whether we are asleep or awake, so should be some graces. We should never forget God, who remembers us all the time.

2. If we take this phrase to refer to God, it may apply to his judgments. If so, we must remember that riotous living hardens the heart and that people who are given over to a life of luxury grow falsely secure in their thoughts. If you want to avoid such security and hardness of heart, avoid indulging to excess in worldly pleasures. We lose our tenderness by steeping the soul in these delights.

3. If we take the phrase to refer to the church, it means that these people were not stopped from behaving in a riotous way in the middle of a holy meeting. Such sensuality makes people impudent. Their spirituality was gone, and so was their shame. Their bodily spirits were on fire with food and wine, and so they became bold. Solomon said, "Do not join those who drink too much wine or gorge themselves on meat, for drunkards and gluttons become poor, and drowsiness clothes them in rags" (Proverbs 23:20-21). In such cases people feel free to say or do anything that is unseemly. I do not exclude this sense because Peter, in the parallel text, shows that their sins are presumptuous and sensual.

This is especially true of those who follow the corrupt desire of the sinful nature and despise authority. Bold and arrogant, these men are not afraid to slander celestial beings; yet even angels, although they are stronger and more powerful, do not bring slanderous accusations against such beings in the presence of the Lord. But these men blaspheme in matters they do not understand. They are like brute beasts, creatures of instinct, born only to be caught and destroyed, and like beasts they too will perish. They will be paid back with harm for the harm they have done. Their idea of pleasure is to carouse in broad daylight. They are blots and blemishes, reveling in their pleasures while they feast with you. With eyes full of adultery, they never stop sinning; they seduce the unstable; they are experts in greed—an accursed brood. (2 Peter 2:10-14)

4. Some apply this phrase to having no fear of the traps that creatures can be to us. So we should be cautious about indulging in any pleasures and outward comforts. When Job's sons feasted, he offered God a sacrifice in case any of them should sin against God (see Job 1:5). At a feast more guests arrive than are on the guest list; evil spirits are on the lookout to trip

us up. Solomon advised, "Put a knife to your throat if you are given to gluttony" (Proverbs 23:2). Christians, you may think it unnecessary that we speak to you about your eating and drinking, as if all you needed in these situations was your conscience. Beware! You cannot take too much care. The throat is a slippery place, and a sin may occur before you are aware. Christ did not think it was unnecessary to warn his disciples about this: "Be careful, or your hearts will be weighed down with dissipation, drunkenness and the anxieties of life, and that day will close on you unexpectedly like a trap" (Luke 21:34).

Note 5. **They are clouds without rain, blown along by the wind.** The Word of God is like a moist, rainy cloud. "Let my teaching fall like rain and my words descend like dew, like showers on new grass, like abundant rain on tender plants" (Deuteronomy 32:2). We, like parched ground, wait for drops of rain from God's clouds. In a time of drought, with all the grass burned and turned into stubble, we cry to the God of heaven for a little rain. In the same way we should wait on God for his message to come to us through his Word. "I spread out my hands to you; my soul thirsts for you like a parched land" (Psalm 143:6). Oh, for a little refreshing from the presence of the Lord.

Note 6. False teachers are clouds that produce no rain. This is the point of the text. They make a great show without possessing what they claim. "Like clouds and wind without rain is a man who boasts of gifts he does not give" (Proverbs 25:14). We learn from these people that we behave like seducers if we promise more than we can do. There are two things that these seducers never do, which may be explained by two properties of rain—namely, refreshing the earth and making it fruitful. They do not refresh the earth; they never offer any teaching that comforts the conscience in times of distress. In this way they are like barren clouds. They also do not make the earth fruitful. Do you find that you progress in holiness through their ideas? "They promise them freedom, while they themselves are slaves of depravity—for a man is a slave to whatever has mastered him" (2 Peter 2:19). They promise a new way for self-denial, but your bondage to your lusts remains.

Note 7. **Blown along by the wind.** These false teachers are easily driven along by various ideas. They are **blown along** by this opinion and that opinion, just as light clouds are tossed about by the wind. The winds controlling them are their corrupt passions, lusts, and interests. "Then we will no longer be infants, tossed back and forth by the waves, and blown here and there by every wind of teaching and by the cunning and craftiness of men in their deceitful scheming" (Ephesians 4:14). We see many scrupulous people who at first have a conscience about everything but later grow so lax that they have a conscience about nothing.

Note 8. **Blown along by the wind.** According to Peter, "these men are

... mists driven by a storm" (2 Peter 2:17). They give no rain but breed factions, schisms, and turbulent commotions. Light clouds are driven with great force. So then, "I urge you, brothers, to watch out for those who cause divisions and put obstacles in your way that are contrary to the teaching you have learned. Keep away from them" (Romans 16:17). They are not what they appear to be. You will find in the end that you achieve nothing by dancing to their pipe.

Note 9. **Autumn trees, without fruit and uprooted—twice dead.** Observe from this that corrupt doctrine produces corrupt fruits. Principles have an influence on the life and way of living. Our Saviour directs us to scrutinize people: "By their fruit you will recognize them. Do people pick grapes from thorn-bushes, or figs from thistles?" (Matthew 7:16). These false teachers may start with a great show of sound doctrine in order to gain credence, but a discerning eye will discover their deceit, and in due time God will reveal this to the congregation. "But they will not get very far because, as in the case of those men [Jannes and Jambres], their folly will be clear to everyone" (2 Timothy 3:9). This also means that your lives must be lived according to God's laws or you will bring shame on God. You are to "produce fruit in keeping with repentance" (Matthew 3:8).

Note 10. The next evil characteristic of these false teachers is that they are **without fruit**. This implies that they do not bring any honor to God, nor good to others, and are not wise for the benefit of their own souls. To be barren and unfruitful while professing to follow Christ is a sign of great hypocrisy. A vine is good for nothing if it is unfruitful. God compared Israel to a vine because they poured out all their strength, time, and care on their own interests. "Israel was a spreading vine; he brought forth fruit for himself. As his fruit increased, he built more altars; as his land prospered, he adorned his sacred stones" (Hosea 10:1-2). So then, do not be "ineffective and unproductive in your knowledge of our Lord Jesus Christ" (2 Peter 1:8). Grace is an active thing. Where it is, it will reveal itself.

1. There are four important aspects to fruitfulness. First, if you want to be fruitful, you must be planted with the right seed. A wild vine will only produce wild grapes. Trees of righteousness are planted by God. "They will be called oaks of righteousness, a planting of the LORD for the display of his splendor" (Isaiah 61:3). When you are grafted into the noble vine, Jesus Christ, then you will be laden with clusters of grapes, like the vine of Eshcol. "I am the vine; you are the branches. If a man remains in me and I in him, he will bear much fruit; apart from me you can do nothing" (John 15:5).

2. Second, there must be good husbandry and cultivation. "He dug it and cleared it of stones and planted it with the choicest vines. He built a watchtower in it and cut out a winepress as well" (Isaiah 5:2). "Planted in the house of the LORD, they will flourish in the courts of our God. They will still bear fruit in old age, they will stay fresh and green" (Psalm 92:13-

14). Good fruit grows from God's commandments, whereas wild plants grow and bear fruit of their own accord.

3. Third, this fruit must be ripe. It must not only produce blossoms but fruit. There must not only be the flowers and leaves of profession, but the solid deeds of godliness.

4. Fourth, the fruit is for the owner. "This is to my Father's glory, that you bear much fruit, showing yourselves to be my disciples" (John 15:8). ". . . filled with the fruit of righteousness that comes through Jesus Christ—to the glory and praise of God" (Philippians 1:11). Spiritual life begins in God and must always stay rooted in him. God must have all the glory, although you will be comforted. "The benefit you reap leads to holiness, and the result is eternal life" (Romans 6:22). The grave is a winter that takes away your leaves for the present, though the sap and life remain in the roots.

Note 11. **Twice dead.** People who fall away from professing the truth are **twice dead** through the habit of sin and by rebelling against God after professing to give themselves to him. Habitual sin hardens their hearts. "Because of this, God gave them over to shameful lusts. Even their women exchanged natural relations for unnatural ones. In the same way the men also abandoned natural relations with women and were inflamed with lust for one another. Men committed indecent acts with other men, and received in themselves the due penalty for their perversion. Furthermore, since they did not think it worthwhile to retain the knowledge of God, he gave them over to a depraved mind, to do what ought not to be done" (Romans 1:26-28). Those who rebel against God are left to their own devices and are held by the power of the devil because of their dark and foolish hearts.

Note 12. **Uprooted.** Barren and corrupt trees will be utterly uprooted from God's vineyard. This is partly brought about by their own acts. "They went out from us, but they did not really belong to us. For if they had belonged to us, they would have remained with us; but their going showed that none of them belonged to us" (1 John 2:19). They separated themselves from the fellowship of the faithful, to which they never really belonged. They are also uprooted partly as a result of God's action. It is an act of judgment on his part. "They were broken off because of unbelief" (Romans 11:20). They are also uprooted by the church, as open sinners must be ejected by them. "Expel the wicked man from among you" (1 Corinthians 5:13). So then, let us so walk that this heavy judgment is never laid on us. Let us have a real union with Christ, for then we will never be broken off. You can no more sever Christ and a believer than the leaven and the dough. So walk with caution. It is a dreadful thing to be thrown out of the true church.

Verse 13

Commentary on Verse 13

They are wild waves of the sea, foaming up their shame; wandering stars, for whom blackest darkness has been reserved forever.
Here are two more comparisons.

They are wild waves of the sea. There are numerous ways of interpreting this. Two things should guide us—the scope and the force of the words. The scope of the apostle in all these metaphors is to show that these seducers were less than what they pretended to be. They were clouds—just dry, barren clouds; trees, but those that either bore no fruit or bore rotten fruit; waves that seemed to mount up to heaven and to promise a great deal, as if they would swallow the earth, but on being dashed against a rock, all their raging and swelling turned into a little foam and froth. Thus Calvin applied this to the libertines, who scorn and disdain common forms of speech and talk about illumination, so that their hearers seem to be transported to the heavens; but, alas, they suddenly fall into dreadful errors. The whole metaphor alludes to what is said about wicked people in general. "The wicked are like the tossing sea, which cannot rest, whose waves cast up mire and mud" (Isaiah 57:20). Here you have restless activity. They are tossed to and fro. "Concerning Damascus: 'Hamath and Arpad are dismayed, for they have heard bad news. They are disheartened, troubled like the restless sea'" (Jeremiah 49:23). These people cannot rest from evil. "With eyes full of adultery, they never stop sinning" (2 Peter 2:14). This clause describes how turbulent they were. They filled every place with their trouble and strife.

Foaming up their shame. This raging sea throws up dirt and scum. This phrase, alluding to the foam that the waves leave on the rocks, reveals these seducers' abominable opinions and practices.

Now we come to the metaphor **wandering stars.** This phrase may apply to the stars that we call planets as they wander. But this phrase may refer to shooting stars, which appear with exceptional brightness but then fade away. The latter depicts the characteristic of these seducers, who pretend to have a great deal of knowledge, and are therefore called Gnostics, and seem to give out a great amount of light, but are soon extinguished and cannot be seen. It is notable that the apostle uses a wide variety of elements with which to compare these false teachers. From the air, clouds without rain; from the earth, barren, rotten trees; from the sea, wild waves; and from the heavens, wandering stars, which are fiery by nature.

The last clause in this verse is, **for whom blackest darkness has been reserved forever**. Having described them with different metaphors, Jude now speaks about their punishment. Some suppose that he continues the last metaphor, as bright meteors after a while vanish into a perpetual night and darkness and are never seen or heard of again. So these people vanish and are swallowed up by the horrors of eternal darkness.

Notes on Verse 13

Note 1. **They are wild waves of the sea.** From this observe that spiritual boasters will certainly come short of their great promises. They only produce noise, like empty vessels make. In the latter times we will be troubled with people who boast. "But mark this: There will be terrible times in the last days. People will be lovers of themselves, lovers of money, boastful" (2 Timothy 3:1-2). These men will pretend to show you new ways, even a shortcut to heaven, as well as rare discoveries about Christ and the Gospel. But, alas, they leave you worse servants of sin than you were before.

Note 2. These **waves** indicate how inconsistent they are. Reuben is described as being unstable, "turbulent as the waters" (Genesis 49:4). Water is moved along by the winds. "Then we will no longer be infants, tossed back and forth by the waves, and blown here and there by every wind of teaching and by the cunning and craftiness of men in their deceitful scheming" (Ephesians 4:14). Note from this that seducers are unsettled and uncertain in their opinions. They are "ignorant and unstable" (2 Peter 3:16). You may ask why they are like this. It is because they are not rooted and grounded and are led by sudden interests rather than by sound judgment. They are unstable because they are unlearned.

Note 3. **Waves of the sea.** Wicked men usually have restless spirits that lead them into evil ways. They are influenced by Satan, who is a restless spirit himself. There is a close link between their sinful activity and Satan's persistent malice. "Your enemy the devil prowls around like a roaring lion looking for someone to devour" (1 Peter 5:8). Blind zeal leads men on with an incessant rage to poison others with their error and to draw them into their sect. We have even more reason to be diligent than our enemies. Are they going to be busier perverting the truth than we are in propagating it? "For they cannot sleep till they do evil; they are robbed of slumber till they make someone fall" (Proverbs 4:16).

Note 4. **Wandering stars.** The guides of the Lord's people should be stars, carrying God's light, but not **wandering stars**. These seducers pretended to be great lights of the church, which is the office of ministers, but in reality they were **wandering stars** that seduced people and led them into error.

1. First, I will outline what God's stars in the church should be.

a. As regards teaching, they should be the light of the world (see Matthew 5:14). They should bring honor to Christ, who is "the true light that gives light to every man" (John 1:9). They are the light in a subordinate sense. They are stars, but they are not the sun. Christ is the original and the fountain of all light, and we are used as a means to convey that light to others. Thus John the Baptist was called "a lamp that burned and gave light" (John 5:35).

b. They should be stars with regard to the luster of their conversations. It is said of all Christians that they should "shine like stars in the universe" (Philippians 2:15). They are the bright part of the world, just as the stars are the shining part of heaven. As a star directed the wise men to Christ, so they must shine to bring light to others through their example.

2. Second, they must not be shooting stars. This was the accusation made about the seducers. A false teacher is like a shooting star because it is a counterfeit star. In the same way the devil is only "an angel of light" (2 Corinthians 11:14) in appearance. Hypocrites devote themselves to pretending to be other than they are.

So then, for a guide to heaven, choose a star, but not a shooting star. New light is easily admired, but you should be skeptical about it. We have a tendency to run after new things rather than excellent things. True stars not only enlighten you and fill you with good ideas but inflame you and stir you into action.

Note 5. **For whom blackest darkness has been reserved forever.** There are three things to note about this warning: first, the dreadfulness of the punishment; second, the certainty of the punishment; and, third, the appropriateness of the punishment.

1. The dreadfulness of the punishment has two aspects to it: first, its nature and, second, its duration.

a. The nature of this dreadful punishment comes in the words **blackest darkness**. This is a Hebraism for exceeding great darkness, called "outer darkness" in the Gospels. It is the furthest point away from God, the fountain of life and glory, and so expresses that extreme misery, horror, and torment that constitute hell. Hell is a dark and dismal region where men are deprived of the light of God's presence and are tormented with the presence of the devil.

b. The duration of this punishment is expressed in the word **forever**. The torment prepared for the wicked is everlasting (see Mark 9:44). The hellishness of hell is that as the torments cannot be measured, so they are without end. On earth men could have had life but refused it, and now that they have death, they cannot die—that is, cease to exist. They will be tormented forever (see Revelation 20:10, 15).

2. The certainty of this dreadful punishment is expressed by the word **reserved**. Hell's torment is sure, prepared, and kept for the wicked. "Depart from me, you who are cursed, into the eternal fire prepared for the devil and his angels" (Matthew 25:41). Heaven is prepared for the saints, and they are prepared for heaven. Worldly men may lord it over everyone for a time and shine with great pomp, but for them the **blackest darkness has been reserved forever**.

3. Observe the appropriateness of this judgment on sin. Jude says it is **darkness**, not fire. Clouds (verse 12) that darken the truth are rightly punished with **blackest darkness**. Those who wanted to quench the light are thrown into eternal darkness. Those who declined to enjoy God's presence are banished from his presence, and to those who loved darkness more than light the **blackest darkness has been reserved forever**.

Verse 14

Commentary on Verse 14

Enoch, the seventh from Adam, prophesied about these men: "See, the Lord is coming with thousands upon thousands of his holy ones . . ."
The apostle now uses another argument to imply the destruction of those seducers—the prophecy of Enoch. Whether this prophecy was written or not, the same Spirit who spoke in Enoch also inspired our apostle. If he received it by tradition, it is here made authentic and put into the canon. Most probably it was a prophecy that was handed down from father to son. Jude says, **Enoch . . . prophesied.** He does not say this prophecy was written down, as if he were quoting a passage of Scripture. So why should he prefer to use Enoch's prophecy rather than a passage from the authentic books of Scripture? I answer: this was done through God's providence, to preserve this for the church.

Enoch, the seventh from Adam. That is, inclusive, putting Adam as the first. Why is this detail mentioned? I answer: to distinguish this Enoch from the other Enoch, the son of Cain, who was the third generation after Adam (see Genesis 4:17). This Enoch was the *seventh* generation after Adam.

Prophesied. It is clear from this that Enoch was a prophet, which may also be gathered from Genesis 5:22, where it is said he "walked with God." This phrase refers to people who served God in some special ministry. It is applied to Enoch, who was a prophet, and to Noah (see Genesis 6:9), who was "a preacher of righteousness" (see 2 Peter 2:5).

The Lord is coming—that is, the Lord Jesus, who was appointed to be the Judge of the world. This is given special emphasis by the word **see**: **See, the Lord is coming**, as if to say, "Note this—he is in front of your eyes."

With thousands upon thousands of his holy ones. This may be translated "his holy myriads" or "ten thousands." The original word signified the highest possible number. This means the Lord will come with huge multitudes of angels and saints; as another apostle says, "when our Lord Jesus comes with all his holy ones" (1 Thessalonians 3:13).

Notes on Verse 14

Note 1. **Enoch . . . prophesied about these men**. Observe that what is spoken about in general terms in Scripture concerns us as much as if it had been written to us personally. Enoch prophesied **about these**. So although the word is spoken in general terms, we take home with us our share of it, just as men take out of the common river water for their own fields.

Note 2. Note something here about prophecy or preaching. Such a calling is an ancient one, for **Enoch, the seventh from Adam, prophesied**. Some people are still set apart for this work. Enoch was a prophet, and Noah was a preacher of righteousness. It is sad that 6,000 years after this we should be uprooting an ancient ordinance that has stood from the beginning of the world until now. In Christ's time apostles were used to unveil the figures of the law and to deliver the Gospel more clearly. Once the canon was settled and delivered to make us wise about salvation, some were set apart to be pastors and teachers to explain and apply the Scripture. "It was he who gave some to be apostles, some to be prophets, some to be evangelists, and some to be pastors and teachers" (Ephesians 4:11).

Note 3. Note that the doctrine of the day of judgment is an ancient one. Enoch prophesied about it. Even the sentence of death pronounced in paradise implied it, and the Lord's messengers have always spoken about its terror. Many passages from Moses' writings are concerned with this, such as Deuteronomy 32. David speaks clearly about the day of judgment too. "Consider this, you who forget God, or I will tear you to pieces, with none to rescue" (Psalm 50:22). In a similar way Solomon says, "Follow the ways of your heart and whatever your eyes see, but know that for all these things God will bring you to judgment" (Ecclesiastes 11:9). It is unnecessary to give you further examples about this from Daniel, Job, Malachi, Christ, Paul, Peter, and John.

The ancient judgments of flooding the world and burning Sodom were types and forerunners of judgment day. So we need to welcome this teaching with open arms. Can a person believe in God's impending judgment and wallow in sin? Our actions are the best expression of our thoughts. The apostle Peter says that in the last days there will be people who scoff and mock. There may be atheists in the church, but there are none in hell. We are prepared to deny and doubt what makes the devils tremble. If the Spirit, Scripture, conscience, and reason will not teach us, there is no other way of learning but by feeling and experience.

Note 4. **Enoch . . . prophesied**. Enoch, the man who walked with God, prophesied and saw the day of judgment, even though it was so far off.

From this we learn that people who have the closest communion with God discern his mind best. If a person walks humbly and closely with

God, he is near not only to the root of life but to the fountain of light. "The LORD confides in those who fear him; he makes his covenant known to them" (Psalm 25:14). Pure souls are most quickly enlightened. People who are not darkened with lusts and selfish interests discern most of the Lord's counsel.

Note 5. **See.** Enoch speaks about this day of the Lord as if it were already in front of his eyes. We should always keep the day of the Lord in our thoughts. It is the work of faith to keep things that are absent and are far away from us in our hearts. "Now faith is being sure of what we hope for and certain of what we do not see" (Hebrews 11:1). Six thousand years ago Enoch said, **See, the Lord is coming.** It is not for us to fix the seasons that the Father has put in his own hands, although we are often tempted to do that. For this reason the apostle Paul rebukes those who confidently say the Lord's coming is here. "Concerning the coming of our Lord Jesus Christ and our being gathered to him, we ask you, brothers, not to become easily unsettled or alarmed by some prophecy, report or letter supposed to have come from us, saying that the day of the Lord has already come" (2 Thessalonians 2:1-2).

Note 6. **With thousands upon thousands of his holy ones.** When Christ comes to judge, his saints will judge the world with him. This will be done so the world will know what God will do with those who honor him. So we should walk like those who will be associated with Christ in judging the world. Walk with Christ now, and you will come with him then. You will follow the Lamb wherever he goes. He will say to you in effect, "You have been with me in all my sufferings and sorrows; now you will be with me in my glory" (see Matthew 19:28-29). Also, you are to judge the world now, as you condemn people with your lives, and you know that you will also condemn them later on. Noah "condemned the world" (Hebrews 11:7). A serious Christian is a living rebuke to those who do not follow Christ.

Note 7. **With thousands upon thousands of his holy ones.** At Christ's appearance his train will be made up of multitudes of saints and holy angels. When they appear together in that great rendezvous, they will be those "numbering thousands upon thousands, and ten thousand times ten thousand" (Revelation 5:11; see also Revelation 7:9). This is a comfort as we see how few people now are upright with God. In heaven we will have company enough. God's family, when it comes together, is very numerous, or rather innumerable. As the wicked will be exposed to the fellowship of devils and to people like themselves, so will we be called to "the assembly of the righteous" (Psalm 1:5) and to be in that glorious train that comes with Christ.

Verse 15

Commentary on Verse 15

". . . to judge everyone, and to convict all the ungodly of all the
ungodly acts they have done in the ungodly way, and of all the harsh
words ungodly sinners have spoken against him."

Having described the Judge, with his attendants, Jude now describes his
work, which is to convince and execute judgment on **all the ungodly**. The
reasons for this? Because of their **ungodly acts** and their **harsh words**
against Christ.

To judge everyone. Note: **Everyone**—that is, upon all who are spoken
about here, all the ungodly. Judgment is not executed *upon* the saints but
for them. **And to convict.** This implies such damning evidence that it is
impossible that it should be otherwise on the day of judgment. Wicked
men are speechless and self-condemned. "When the king came in to see the
guests, he noticed a man there who was not wearing wedding clothes.
'Friend,' he asked, 'how did you get in here without wedding clothes?'
The man was speechless" (Matthew 22:11-12).

All the ungodly—that is, among the wicked. The severity of the
process is especially against the ungodly. **Of all the ungodly acts.** In
Greek this is, "the deeds of their ungodliness." Ungodliness here is not
taken in the sense of denying God his due honor and worship but means
any opposition against his servants or against worship or against truth.

They have done in the ungodly way. This speaks of the malice and
spite they used in their opposition and reproaches.

And of all the harsh words. Harsh can apply to things as well as to
spoken words, but it is what we say that is meant here, as is clear from the
next clause. Wicked practices and an evil tongue are rarely severed. **Harsh
words** means any proud, taunting, or abusive language. "They pour out
arrogant words; all the evildoers are full of boasting" (Psalm 94:4).

Ungodly sinners. For the emphasis used here, remember Psalm 1:1:
"Blessed is the man who does not walk in the counsel of the wicked or
stand in the way of sinners or sit in the seat of mockers." **Have spoken
against him**—that is, against Christ—against his person, as well as against

his messengers, for what is spoken against any of these is spoken against Christ himself.

This verse is wide-ranging and full of important teaching, but because the doctrine of the day of judgment has been already touched on, and ungodliness was spoken about in verse 4, the notes that follow will be brief.

Notes on Verse 15

Note 1. Christ's second coming is for judgment. **The Lord is coming with thousands upon thousands of his holy ones to judge everyone.** It was said of his first coming, "For God did not send his Son into the world to condemn the world, but to save the world through him" (John 3:17). He came not as a judge but as a redeemer, offering and procuring grace and life. When we frustrate the purpose of his coming as a redeemer, we make way for his coming as judge. Then he who had originally come *to* us will come *against* us.

Note 2. When Christ comes to judge, one great part of his work will be to convince sinners. I think that conviction, trial, and sentence will all be open and public. I cannot say for certain that every particular sin will be exposed to the whole world; yet enough will be shown for the sentence to be seen as being a just one. Such things as men's unfaithfulness to their callings, their opposition to God and godliness, their opposition to God's followers, and their neglect of grace will be exposed.

1. This conviction implies two things. First, the opening of the conscience. The books will be opened (see Revelation 20:12)—the book of conscience and the book of God's remembrance. The consciences of people will then have a perfect view of all their past deeds, for he will **convict all the ungodly of all the ungodly acts they have done in the ungodly way, and of all the harsh words ungodly sinners have spoken against him.** Their words and works are not forgotten but follow them into the next world, are seen by their consciences, and challenge them, saying, "Sinner, these are the things you have done and spoken. We will not leave you but now bring you to judgment." "But they do not realize that I remember all their evil deeds. Their sins engulf them; they are always before me" (Hosea 7:2). The statement "You may be sure that your sin will find you out" (Numbers 32:23) will come true.

2. There is a public manifestation of all these sins, or of most of them, before the world. The apostle says, "He will bring to light what is hidden in darkness and will expose the motives of men's hearts" on that day (1 Corinthians 4:5). These sins will not only be remembered by the sinner

himself but will be exposed to the censure of others, as the context says. So it is God's purpose to shame them before all the world.

Note 3. When Christ has convinced, he will condemn, and when he has condemned, he will execute. At the present, conviction often leads to conversion, but on the day of judgment it will only bring confusion. At the present God kills so that he may make people alive, but on the day of judgment sinners will be sent to everlasting hell. So let us examine, judge, and execute not ourselves, but our sins. Voluntary acts prevent compulsory acts from taking place.

Note 4. **Of all the ungodly acts**. Notice that the process on the last day is mainly taken up with the ungodly. These are specifically mentioned in the text. "The wrath of God is being revealed from heaven against all the godlessness and wickedness of men who suppress the truth by their wickedness" (Romans 1:18). Ungodliness is the chief culprit, for the first part of the law states what our duty to God is. The dignity of every command is governed by this.

If you want to have a comfortable time on the day of judgment, you must not only be just and strict, but godly, for godliness is different from holiness. "You ought to live holy and godly lives" (2 Peter 3:11). Holiness implies a conformity to God's law, but godliness is total respect for God's glory. A Christian's whole life should be directed to this end. "For through the law I died to the law so that I might live for God" (Galatians 2:19).

Note 5. Ungodly people are judged because they commit sin with an ungodly mind or sin with a sinning mind. **. . . convict all the ungodly of all the ungodly acts they have done.** A child of God may fall into wickedness, but he does not commit it wickedly, with full consent. People are not condemned for their weaknesses but for their iniquities. As a child of God cannot act with such freedom, purity, and perfection in the ways of God as he wishes to, so in the ways of sin he cannot do what he would, nor does he carry them out with the same kind of heart that wicked people do, because such deeds are contrary to the new nature. "For the sinful nature desires what is contrary to the Spirit, and the Spirit what is contrary to the sinful nature" (Galatians 5:17). Wicked men follow the devil's work with all their might. "Both hands are skilled in doing evil" (Micah 7:3). A godly person does not so much commit sin but suffers through sinning. He does not pour his whole heart into his sin. His soul is constantly restraining him from doing evil. Usually the sins of the godly are either sins of ignorance or occur when they are taken unawares. If they do sin deliberately, there is not so much spite and rage as there is found in the sins of the wicked.

Note 6. **All the harsh words ungodly sinners have spoken**. Regarding **all the harsh words,** note that not only the deeds of ungodly people but their **words** will be judged. Words do not perish with the breath with which they are uttered. They remain on the record, and we must give an account of them on the last day. "But I tell you that men will have to give account on the day of judgment for every careless word they have spoken" (Matthew 12:36). "Speak and act as those who are going to be judged by the law that gives freedom" (James 2:12). People are careful about their actions, but their words are rash and inconsiderate; people who do not dare to act in an evil way are prepared to speak in an evil way. If Christ only called us to account for our actions and not our words, that would be a different matter. But he will call us to account for our words.

Note 7. Of all the words that have been spoken, it is men's **harsh words** that will be exposed on the day of judgment. What are these **harsh words**? They are words full of anger, as Solomon said: "Put away perversity from your mouth; keep corrupt talk far from your lips" (Proverbs 4:24). They are words full of contempt and pride. "For they persecute those you wound and talk about the pain of those you hurt" (Psalm 69:26). Such people triumph over others' failings and pour salt and vinegar into new wounds. Do not be quick to speak harshly about God's children. "Why then were you not afraid to speak against my servant Moses?" (Numbers 12:8).

Note 8. The next thing to note is that of all harsh words spoken, the worst ones are those that directly attack the honor and glory of Christ. **All the harsh words ungodly sinners have spoken against him. Harsh words** spoken against Christ must be blasphemies spoken about one of his two natures. The Ebionites denied that Christ was God, and the Valentinians likewise said that Christ was only a man in appearance. These harsh words spoken against Christ also include grumbling at God's providence. "'You have said harsh things against me,' says the LORD" (Malachi 3:13). When we accuse providence, as if the Lord were blind, careless, and unjust, we are using **harsh words**. Another example of the use of **harsh words** is when people scoff at God's Word. Oh, Christians, such **harsh words** will cost us dearly, here or hereafter.

Verse 16

Commentary on Verse 16

These men are grumblers and faultfinders; they follow their own evil desires; they boast about themselves and flatter others for their own advantage.

Here the apostle applies his words and shows that these false teachers were just as Enoch had described them and thus liable to the threatened judgment. They are accused of being **grumblers**, *gongustai*, signifying the kind of muttering that people use when they are angry and discontent. The other word is **faultfinders**, *memphimoiroi*, meaning complaining about their lot—that is, about what God has given them. The one implies their discontented thoughts, the other their querulous expressions.

Their next characteristic is that **they follow their own evil desires**. This is rightly linked to what has gone before, for evil desires make people demanding and hard to please. The people described here exactly fit the libertines, who make their evil desires their rule and law. They walk after these evil desires, implying that they give themselves over to such a course and oppose all fear of God and care of his laws.

The third clause in this application of Enoch's prophecy is that they **boast about themselves**. In Enoch's prophecy not only unholy deeds were noted but **harsh words**. These Gnostics were guilty in both these areas. What men are accused of here concerns their words. These words relate to the unsavory gibberish they used to present their own opinions. Peter calls them, "empty, boastful words" (2 Peter 2:18).

The fourth clause in this verse is, **and flatter others for their own advantage**. Junius applied this to those who set up angels and unknown people in the church to oppose Christ. But I think this should apply to false teachers who flattered others to further their own ends. In this way they tried to win over such people to join them. They would have used such a method in order to gain some worldly advantage from the rich and powerful.

Notes on Verse 16

Note 1. **These men are grumblers.** I will show, first, what grumbling is and, second, demonstrate that it is a great sin.

1. What is grumbling? It is the scum of discontent or the bold complaints that flow from a polluted mind. In the text you see that men first mutter and then complain. The heart boils with impatience, and then the froth is thrown out in passionate words and complaints. Humble complaints are not murmuring, or else there would be no room for prayer. But bold expostulations are grumbling when they complain *of* God rather than *to* God. Thoughts are audible with God, but it is worse when thoughts are not controlled and break out openly in words that bring dishonor on God. If the fire is alight in our hearts, it is some kind of victory if we smother it and prevent its sparks from flying everywhere.

There are several kinds of grumbling—either against other people or against God, although they are really all against God, as they are against God about other people.

a. There is grumbling against other people, either against our equals or our superiors.

First, grumbling against our equals. We complain that they have the same privileges as we have. "When they received it [a denarius], they began to grumble against the landowner. 'These men who were hired last worked only one hour,' they said, 'and you have made them equal to us who have borne the burden of the work and the heat of the day'" (Matthew 20:11-12). When Beza was faced with some people who reproached him for the sins he had committed in his unregenerate days, he said, "Surely these men are angry because God has shown me mercy." There is an envious nature in man. We want to shine alone.

Second, there is grumbling against superiors, especially against magistrates and ministers. Some men have a yokeless, libertine spirit and will acknowledge no law except their own lusts. As well as grumbling against the office, people grumble against people who are in elevated positions, as if they would teach God how to run the world, whom to lift up and whom to cast down. God will not allow this evil to go unpunished. "Moses also said, 'You will know that it was the LORD when he gives you meat to eat in the evening and all the bread you want in the morning, because he has heard your grumbling against him. Who are we? You are not grumbling against us, but against the LORD" (Exodus 16:8). The *calling* is God's ordinance, the *people* are designed by God's providence, and the *work* concerns God's glory. Therefore God is greatly interested in the quarrel.

b. There is a grumbling that is immediately against God himself. Since the Fall man is always grumbling against his Maker, either against his decrees or his laws or his providence.

First, people grumble against God's decrees. Proud man cannot endure to hear of God's absolute sovereignty. We will do what we like, but we will not allow God to do his will. We can see no reason why God should pass by one person and choose another. Although we can see no reason for this, it is enough that it is God's pleasure (see Matthew 11:26). It is good to turn disputes into wonder and reverence. "But who are you, O man, to talk back to God? 'Shall what is formed say to him who formed it, "Why did you make me like this?"'" (Romans 9:20).

Second, people grumble against God's laws. A proud creature cannot bear to hear about restraints. We love other things in God, but not his legislative power. "The sinful man is hostile to God. It does not submit to God's law, nor can it do so" (Romans 8:7). The worldly mind will never bow but complains about God as if he were harsh and severe, as if he had forbidden us from satisfying those desires he has planted in us. The Israelites grumbled in this way. The land was a good land, but there were giants and sons of Anak. "And they spread among the Israelites a bad report about the land they had explored. They said, 'The land we explored devours those living in it. All the people we saw there are of great size'" (Numbers 13:32). The promised heaven is a good heaven, but the way to it is rough and impassable. Our duties will be difficult, and our lusts will have to be thwarted. The aim of worldly nature is to find an easy and smooth path to eternal happiness. "Then they despised the pleasant land; they did not believe his promise. They grumbled in their tents and did not obey the LORD" (Psalm 106:24-25). Heaven, pictured by the land of Canaan, is not thought to be worth the pains and difficulty of getting there.

Third, people grumble against God's providence. This generally occurs when the wicked prosper, and this temptation has shaken the tallest cedars in Lebanon. It befell David, though he was later ashamed of it and counted it brutish ignorance. "I was senseless and ignorant; I was a brute beast before you" (Psalm 73:22). "You are always righteous, O LORD, when I bring a case before you. Yet I would speak with you about your justice: Why does the way of the wicked prosper? Why do all the faithless live at ease? You have planted them, and they have taken root; they grow and bear fruit. You are always on their lips but far from their hearts. Yet you know me, O LORD; you see me and test my thoughts about you. Drag them off like sheep to be butchered! Set them apart for the day of slaughter!" (Jeremiah 12:1-3).

2. Second, let me show you the heinousness of the sin of grumbling by, first, its causes and, second, by the injustice of it.

a. The causes of grumbling are many.

First, pride and self-love. When people are conceited, they become angry that others are preferred before them. The best thing to say is, "I am not worthy." God's blessings are few to those who are high in their own estimation.

Second, impatience causes grumbling. We cannot endure the least inconvenience. Touchy natures want to be at ease, tumbling and wallowing in all kinds of pleasure. Therefore, as soon as we are inconvenienced we are full of grumbling, "Why has this evil happened to me?" or "Why should I wait on the Lord any longer?"

b. I now come to consider how unjust it is to grumble. It harms God, others, and ourselves.

First, grumbling is injurious to God. Grumbling is a sin that in our estimation pulls God off his throne. It dares to judge God. But David prayed, "Enter not into judgment with your servant, O LORD." Grumbling either denies God's providence or taxes it in men's minds. It is dreadful to see how grumbling denies all God's attributes. It limits his sovereignty. We will not let him do with his own as it pleases him. The great contest between God and us is, Whose will will stand, his or ours? Grumbling limits his power and slights it. When God does not satisfy us, we think he cannot. "When he struck the rock, water gushed out, and streams flowed abundantly. But can he also give us food? Can he supply meat for his people?" (Psalm 78:20).

Second, grumbling harms other people. It leads to violent acts. The people who grumbled in Numbers 17:10 are called "rebellious." "The LORD said to Moses, 'Put back Aaron's staff in the front of the Testimony, to be kept as a sign to the rebellious. This will put an end to their grumbling against me, so that they will not die.'" People who are not content with their own rank and station grumble and are upset at all around them. Absalom complained, "Oh, that I were a judge!" Later he headed an open rebellion. Small complaints end in great storms.

Third, grumbling damages ourselves. Man is a foolish creature. What does he expect to gain from grumbling about God? Of all sins, grumbling is the most unreasonable, but very pernicious. What do we derive from it except disquiet and judgment? It makes us unsettled. A grumbling spirit is a greater evil than any affliction. Like an infected bowl, it spreads its infection to everything that is placed near it. Miriam was afflicted with leprosy for grumbling, and Dathan and Abiram were swallowed up alive. "And do not grumble, as some of them did—and were killed by the destroying angel" (1 Corinthians 10:10).

We will now apply this teaching. Beware of grumbling. It is a greater sin than the world realizes. Let me give you a few remedies against grumbling.

Application 1. When your heart is taken by storm, look back. There were inconveniences in the desert, but there was a terrible slavery in Egypt. A good memory is a great help to thankfulness. When I am at my wits' end, I think about the times that are past, when private meetings were unlawful, and in public one could only sigh, not speak; when it was a crime to hear the Word preached. One great defect the people of God are troubled with is a bad memory.

Application 2. There is nothing new under the sun (see Ecclesiastes 1:9). We say, "Is there any sorrow like my sorrow?" Or, "Things were never as bad as they are now." If you say this, you are not looking at the matter correctly. The world is still the world. Men have always had the same principles, the same corruptions, the same temptations. There were Donatists then as well as Separatists now, Pelagians then as well as Arminians now, Arians then as well as Socinians now. Much so-called new learning is but old darkness revived. New lights are neither new nor lights.

Application 3. The worse the times are, the more we need to exercise grace. We have more opportunities to show God's love than before. Man is never content. Sometimes we forget God's love when we meet with no opposition, and yet we complain when the ways of God are opposed.

Application 4. Complaining does not excuse us from carrying out our duties. Grumbling reveals a lack of faith. Is not Christ King? Does he not reign? Grumbling indicates that a person does not care to obey God. A gracious heart always looks for faults in himself, instead of grumbling. If times are bad, say, "What have I done to make them better?" If you do not say this, you are the one who has made them worse.

Note 2. **They follow their own evil desires.** The point here is that it is evidence of ungodliness when people indulge their own lusts. The apostle, applying the prophecy of Enoch against ungodly people, brings as part of the charge that they **follow their own evil desires.** I will inquire, first, what **evil desires** are; second, what it means to **follow** their own evil desires. Third, I will show this an indication of ungodliness.

1. First, I ask, what are **evil desires?** This phrase signifies our original proneness to all that is evil. "But each one is tempted when, by his own evil desire, he is dragged away and enticed" (James 1:14). Our evil desires are sometimes lusts of the flesh and sometimes lusts of the world. Lusts of the world are stirred by worldly objects. "It [God's grace] teaches us to say 'No' to ungodliness and worldly passions, and to live self-controlled, upright and godly lives in this present age" (Titus 2:12).

2. Second, what does it imply to walk after our own evil desires? Elsewhere it is said to mean, "enslaved by all kinds of passions and pleasures" (Titus 3:3) and "gratifying the cravings of our sinful nature and following its desires and thoughts" (Ephesians 2:3). It means being willing to submit oneself to being mastered by these evil desires. A child of God may be overcome by his lusts, but he does not walk after them or serve them. He may be hit by a sword, but he does not give up the combat and is still resisting, striving, praying, and calling on the help of the Spirit. If we take

pleasure in indulging in our own evil desires, we are allowing them to dominate us. In that case we are far from thwarting those desires. We may even provide opportunities so we can indulge in them. "Do not think how to gratify the desires of the sinful nature" (Romans 13:14). We either allow evil desires to nourish our hearts or we crucify them.

3. Third, following our own evil desires indicates a state of ungodliness. The apostle Paul describes the natural state as being "enslaved" (Titus 3:3) by evil desires and "gratifying" them (Ephesians 2:3). The negative work of regeneration is described as putting off "your old self, which is being corrupted by its deceitful desires" (see Ephesians 4:22). Those who walk after their own evil desires cherish what Christ came to destroy. Those who walk after their own evil desires have not taken the rule of the new creation upon them. Those who walk after their own evil desires have never felt the power of grace on them. See Titus 2:11-12.

Application 1. The more you walk after your lusts, the more you will want to keep on indulging your evil desires. They are not quenched when they are satisfied but are increased, like a fire receiving new fuel. "Not given to much wine" (Titus 1:7) means "not enslaved to wine" in the Greek. In this sense we are "not mastered . . . by anything" (1 Corinthians 6:12).

Application 2. What can we achieve from sin except a little pleasure? "At one time we too were foolish, disobedient, deceived and enslaved by all kinds of passions and pleasures. We lived in malice and envy, being hated and hating one another" (Titus 3:3). Such pleasure is the great sorceress who enchants the whole world, the root of all sin. Such people are "lovers of pleasure rather than lovers of God" (2 Timothy 3:4). For a man to enslave himself forever, and that for only a little pleasure, which is base itself and lost as soon as enjoyed, is monstrous and absurd. The pleasure is but short and vanishing, but the pain is forever. Will you for something empty break away from God and forfeit your immortal souls? Oh, let it not be.

Application 3. Let all this persuade you to deny your evil desires rather than feed and cherish them, to renounce them and not to walk after them. There are three stages of this denial. First, these evil desires must be prevented and kept from rising. It is not enough to abstain from the acts of sin—we must abstain from the evil desires. The root must be killed off. Second, evil desires must be suppressed and kept from growing. It is a great sin to quench the Spirit's prompting, and it is a great neglect not to take notice of the first thoughts of sin. The little sticks burn first and then set the great logs on fire. Third, do not indulge your evil desires in your behavior, even if they have gained a foothold in your heart. "Then, after desire has conceived, it gives birth to sin; and sin, when it is full-grown, gives birth to death" (James 1:15). It is not good to harbor sin in your thoughts, to plot and muse about sin; but it is even worse to practice it, for every act strengthens the inclination to sin again. "Woe to those who plan iniquity, to those who plot evil on their beds! At morning's light they carry it out because it is in their power to do it. They covet fields and seize them, and houses, and take them. They defraud a man of his home, a fellowmen of his inheritance" (Micah 2:1-2).

Three duties apply to these three stages of dealing with our evil desires. First, there is mortification, if we wish to prevent them; second, there is watchfulness, if we wish to suppress them; and, third, there is resolution, if we do not want to put them into practice.

Note 3. **They boast about themselves.** The pride and vanity of seducers is usually seen in their use of affected speech. The affected language of the Gnostics and Valentinians may be seen in the writings of Irenaeus. Do not be taken in by novel and conceited expressions, nor troubled with "the opposing ideas of what is falsely called knowledge" (1 Timothy 6:20). It is the devil's scheme, first, to capture people's attention, as birds by a light at night, and then drive them into the net. If you want to remain in wholesome doctrine, keep to a form of wholesome words. A holy use of words becomes saints, but an affected phraseology is one of Satan's lures, and a means to corrupt many.

Note 4. **They . . . flatter others for their own advantage.** Nobody is so fawning as the proud when they seek their own advantage. Ambrose noted this about a spirit of ambition: Men with proud spirits bow low for their own ends. Absalom courted the people to jostle his father off the throne (see 2 Samuel 15:2-5). Tacitus observed of Otho that he adored the people, kissed the lowest, and basely dispensed his courtesy to the vilest, all to further his designs on the empire. Certainly a proud spirit is no great spirit, no more than a swollen arm can be said to be a large or strong arm.

Note 5. To flatter men in order to further your own proud ambitions is sinful. We may admire the gifts of God in others in order to praise the Giver, but we must avoid being guilty of man-worship. "So then, no more boasting about men!" (1 Corinthians 3:21).

Note 6. Seducers are prone to worm their way into fellowship with great people and men of power and interest. Once they have gained their ear and their confidence, they use them to oppose the truth. They do not have truth on their side, so they are reduced to using craft. Similarly, the ivy, which cannot support itself, entwines itself around the mighty oak until it sucks out its life. God's messengers herald their message more openly and in a straightforward way. "Now this is our boast: Our conscience testifies that we have conducted ourselves in the world, and especially in our relations with you, in the holiness and sincerity that are from God. We have done so not according to worldly wisdom but according to God's grace" (2 Corinthians 1:12).

Verse 17

Commentary on Verse 17

But, dear friends, remember what the apostles of our Lord Jesus Christ foretold.

Having described these seducers, Jude exhorts his readers to beware of them. He shows that not only Enoch, who it might be thought spoke only about the wicked people of his day, but the apostles, who specifically spoke about their own time, predicted that scoffers and sons of Belial would arise in the church.

There is nothing difficult in this verse, but there is one doubt to be discussed. Does not this verse provide an argument against the authority of this letter? Jude speaks of **the apostles** and what they **foretold** as if he were inferior to them. I answer, no. First, Peter mentions the letters of Paul in his own letter, and this does not weaken his own authority. "Bear in mind that our Lord's patience means salvation, just as our dear brother Paul also wrote you with the wisdom that God gave him. He writes the same way in all his letters, speaking in them of these matters. His letters contain some things that are hard to understand, which ignorant and unstable people distort, as they do the other Scriptures, to their own destruction" (2 Peter 3:15-16).

Second, in the parallel passage in Peter, the apostle cites other writings but does not weaken his own apostolic authority. "I want you to recall the words spoken in the past by the holy prophets and the command given by our Lord and Savior through your apostles. First of all, you must understand that in the last days scoffers will come, scoffing and following their own evil desires" (2 Peter 3:2-3).

Notes on Verse 17

Note 1. **Dear friends.** This name is used to denote affection. It is used by Peter as well. "Dear friends, this is now my second letter to you. I have written both of them as reminders to stimulate you to wholesome thinking" (2 Peter 3:1). When we speak against errors, we should do it out of love and a tender heart, seeking the good of people's souls. In all discussions we need to watch our own hearts.

Note 2. We may fight earnestly against error when corrupt people are held in high esteem. But it should be in love that we express ourselves to others, with warmth and affection. It should be noted that John, the disciple of love, was most earnest against deceivers. "Many deceivers, who do not acknowledge Jesus Christ as coming in the flesh, have gone out into the world. Any such person is the deceiver and the antichrist. Watch out that you do not lose what you have worked for, but that you may be rewarded fully. Anyone who runs ahead and does not continue in the teaching of Christ does not have God; whoever continues in the teaching has both the Father and the Son. If anyone comes to you and does not bring this teaching, do not take him into your house or welcome him" (2 John 7-10).

Note 3. **Remember.** Timely recalling of truths is a great help and relief for the soul. "After he was raised from the dead, his disciples recalled what he had said" (John 2:22). When events take place, it is good to remember prophecies. They confirm the soul and support it against present distress and temptation. Both sins and discomforts arise mainly from forgetfulness and a lack of remembrance. "You have forgotten that word of encouragement" (Hebrews 12:5). When the Spirit is ready with the remedy, as the flesh is with the temptations, remembrance is a mighty support. Lay up a good stock of knowledge, so that you may always have fresh truths at hand. They will help you in prayer. "Take the helmet of salvation and the sword of the Spirit, which is the word of God. And pray in the Spirit on all occasions with all kinds of prayers and requests. With this in mind, be alert and always keep on praying for all the saints" (Ephesians 6:17-18). Remembering God's Word will help you resist the temptation to sin. "I have hidden your word in my heart that I might not sin against you" (Psalm 119:11). This is also a remedy against error. "But the Counselor, the Holy Spirit, whom the Father will send in my name, will teach you all things and will remind you of everything I have said to you" (John 14:26).

Note 4. **The apostles of our Lord Jesus Christ foretold.** It is not wrong to make use of the writings of other people. Compare Isaiah 15—16 with Jeremiah 48. In particular compare Isaiah 16:8-11 with Jeremiah 32—36, and you will see how they agree almost word for word. The gifts and labors of others are for our use, not to feed laziness, but to exercise industry.

Note 5. **Remember what the apostles . . . foretold.** Jude, an apostle, quotes apostles. Daniel, a prophet, read from the prophecies of Jeremiah (see Daniel 9:2). Peter was conversant with the letters of Paul (see 2 Peter 3:15-16). Ministers, and those who abound in knowledge, may be stirred up by the admonitions and exhortations of others.

Verse 18

Commentary on Verse 18

They said to you, "In the last times there will be scoffers who will follow their own ungodly desires."

In the last times. The days when the Gospel was first preached are called "the last times" in two ways. First, "the last times" is applied to the approaching judgments. "Dear children, this is the last hour; and as you have heard that the antichrist is coming, even now many antichrists have come. This is how we know it is the last hour" (1 John 2:18). God's time for having mercy was running out. So James tells worldly readers, "Your gold and silver are corroded. Their corrosion will testify against you and eat your flesh like fire. You have hoarded wealth in the last days" (James 5:3). When God was pulling down and uprooting, they were scraping together and hoarding up wealth, and so became a greater prey to the destroyer. Second, "the last times" applies to the last dispensation, which has already begun and which God will continue without alteration until the end of the world. "But in these last days he has spoken to us by his Son" (Hebrews 1:2).

Scoffers. When people slight what they themselves and others hold in high esteem, they usually do so by scoffing and scorning. What did they scoff at? I think in general they attacked the lordship of Christ and in particular the glorious exercise of it on the day of judgment. "They will say, 'Where is this "coming" he promised?'" (2 Peter 3:4). This links up with the stated prophecy of Enoch: **See, the Lord is coming with thousands upon thousands of his holy ones to judge everyone, and to convict all the ungodly of all the ungodly acts they have done in the ungodly way, and of all the harsh words ungodly sinners have spoken against him** (verses 14-15).

The scoffers are said to **follow their own ungodly desires** (see also verse 16). **Follow** implies a settled state. Their evil desires are called **ungodly** to indicate the profane nature of their spirits and to distinguish from the desires of the new nature.

Notes on Verse 18

Note 1. What is said to the church in general we must understand applies to us in particular. Paul tells Timothy, and Peter tells "God's elect, strangers in the world," and Jude says the apostles told his readers. "The word of encouragement that addresses you . . ." (Hebrews 12:5). This is said as if the Hebrews were the people to whom the quoted proverbs were directly written. The Scriptures speak to every age, every church, every person, no less than to those to whom they were first directed. This shows us how we should be affected in reading the Word. We should read it as a letter written by the hand of God from heaven to us by name. If an angel were to bring us a letter from heaven, we would be sure to take notice of it. The Bible *is* a message sent from heaven to acquaint us with the mind of God. If we believe its divine authority, why do we pay so little attention to it?

Note 2. We should not be troubled about what is foretold. We are more prepared to combat evils when we know they will come. This also assures us that the Lord has a hand and a counsel in all our troubles, for he has told us about them before they take place.

Note 3. The Scriptures speak a great deal about the evil of the latter times. There is greater knowledge, yet there is more sin and error. Knowledge that is not sanctified puffs people up and makes them curious as they hanker after novelties.

Note 4. Mockers and scoffers are usually the worst of sinners. In the first psalm there are three degrees of sinners mentioned, and the worst rank are those who sit in the seat of mockers. "Blessed is the man who does not walk in the counsel of the wicked or stand in the way of sinners or sit in the seat of mockers" (Psalm 1:1). The Septuagint translates "mockers" as "pestilences," the pests of mankind. Scorning comes from the habit of sinning and prepares the way for freedom in sinning. When the conscience is seared, and people have lost not only the restraints of grace but of natural modesty, they fall to scoffing. Once they become mockers, nothing can reclaim them. "Do not rebuke a mocker or he will hate you; rebuke a wise man and he will love you" (Proverbs 9:8).

Note 5. Observe that people who throw out the awe of the Lord's coming are sure to give themselves over to animal lusts. Those mockers who said, "Where is the promise of his coming?" are here said to **follow their own ungodly desires**. They deny the coming of Christ to avoid the fear of his judgment.

Verse 19

Commentary on Verse 19

These are the men who divide you, who follow mere natural instincts and do not have the Spirit.

Here the apostle informs his readers who these scoffers are, of whom the apostles of the Lord had spoken. He describes them in three ways. First, **these are the men who divide you**; second, these are the men **who follow mere natural instincts**; and, third, these are the men who **do not have the Spirit**.

1. **These are the men who divide you**. One old English translation reads, "These are the makers of sects." The word translated **divide**, *apodiorizontes*, signifies those who uproot the bounds that God has set. The apostle means that these people, without any warrant from God, cut themselves off from the church.

2. **Who follow mere natural instincts**. These people have a reasoning soul that, since it is corrupt, cares only about the things of the flesh. The word for **natural instincts** in the Greek is *psuxikoi*, which means sensual or animal or soul-man. It is used on two other occasions in Scripture. "The man without the Spirit" (1 Corinthians 2:14), *psuxikos*, is contrasted with the spiritual man, *pneumatikos*. This word, "unspiritual" or "the natural man," appears also in James 3:15, "Such 'wisdom' does not come down from heaven but is earthy, unspiritual [*psuxike*], of the devil." Left to himself, man can only bear fruits that are carnal. When people are destitute of sanctifying grace, their natural instincts take over. So these seducers were sensual, given over to animal desires and practices.

3. **And do not have the Spirit**. This is added not only to show that they were destitute of true grace and regeneration, but to rebuke their vain pretenses. The Gnostics and other disreputable seducers of that time arrogated to themselves a singularity and peculiarity of the Spirit, as if all other people were carnal and only they had the Spirit. In reality, the opposite was true. They had given themselves over to evil practices and demonstrated that they did **not have the Spirit**.

Notes on Verse 19

Note 1. To separate or divide oneself from the fellowship of God's church is sinful, a work of the flesh. "The acts of the sinful nature are obvious: . . . dissensions" (Galatians 5:19-20). The option of separation lies in the dark, but obligations to loving unity are clear and open (see Ephesians 4:4-6). It is sad that many people have no conscience about causing a schism.

Note 2. It brings no honor to Christ when his body is crumbled into small pieces. Christ prayed, "that all of them may be one, Father, as you are in me and I am in you" (John 17:21). This implies that our divisions and breaking into sects puts the Gospel in a bad light in the eyes of the world. Apostasy began in forsaking assembling together (see Hebrews 10:23-25 and 1 John 2:19).

Note 3. There are only three lawful grounds for separation. First, intolerable persecution. When we are thrown out, Christ tells us to flee to another city. Second, blatant heresy. We cannot give a Christian greeting to people who teach gross heresy, in case we share in their evil deeds (see 2 John 10-11). Third, we may separate from a fellowship if they take part in gross idolatry.

Note 4. Sensual people **do not have the Spirit**. These two oppose each other. "For the sinful nature desires what is contrary to the Spirit, and the Spirit what is contrary to the sinful nature" (Galatians 5:17). People who cherish the one naturally banish the other. The Spirit is a free spirit, and sensual people are slaves. The Spirit is a pure spirit, and they are unclean.

1. Sensual people have little enlightenment from the Spirit. Their palate is more active than their understanding. "Do not get drunk on wine, which leads to debauchery. Instead, be filled with the Spirit" (Ephesians 5:18). In marshy countries we do not expect clear air. People who are given over to pleasures can taste food and drink but not biblical doctrines.

2. Sensual people have little of the life of the Spirit in them. The more they waste away days given over to pleasure, the more they grow sapless and dead and lose all tenderness of conscience and liveliness of affection. They quench the vigor of nature but quench the Spirit even more. Indulging natural instincts results in the loss of "all sensitivity" (Ephesians 4:19).

3. Sensual people have little comfort from the Spirit, which comes from meditating on the deeds of God. "May my meditation be pleasing to him, as I rejoice in the LORD" (Psalm 104:34). Comfort from the Spirit comes from tasting his love. ". . . now that you have tasted that the Lord is good" (1 Peter 2:3). Comfort from the Spirit comes from contemplating our great hope. "So we fix our eyes not on what is seen, but on what is unseen. For what is seen is temporary, but what is unseen is eternal" (2 Corinthians

4:18). When the soul is swamped by worldly pleasures, it is not able to think about God and his deeds or enjoy inner consolation.

Application. So, then, we should take care not to be sensual, for a sensual person never has a great measure of the Holy Spirit's gifts or graces. It is easy for the devil to enter the pigs, but the Holy Spirit will not live there. We have to choose between pleasures or the Spirit. It will be sad for you if you are "lovers of pleasure rather than lovers of God" (2 Timothy 3:4).

Verse 20

Commentary on Verse 20

But you, dear friends, build yourselves up in your most holy faith and pray in the Holy Spirit.

The apostle now exhorts his readers, just as he has all along mixed exhortation with his descriptions of the seducers. The object of the exhortation is to make them use the means of grace in order to persevere in the Christian faith. **Build yourselves up,** *epoikodomountes,* signifies continuing to build a structure that is in the process of being erected, which aptly applies to their need to grow spiritually. **Yourselves** is sometimes translated to mean that they should build one another up, which is the apostle's intention. First they have to look to their own salvation and then care for one another. "Therefore encourage one another and build each other up, just as in fact you are doing" (1 Thessalonians 5:11). This might be written to oppose those who wanted to separate themselves from the fellowship.

In your most holy faith. Here **faith** may stand for the *grace* of faith or the *doctrine* of faith. I favor the latter, that true and pure religion they had learned from the apostles, the foundation that had already been laid. This faith is called **most holy** to contrast it with the profane mysteries of the Gnostics and Valentinians. It is the holy rule that makes us holy. "Sanctify them by the truth; your word is truth" (John 17:17).

Pray in the Holy Spirit. This phrase, *en pneumati hagio,* may be rendered, "*in, with,* or *by* the Holy Spirit." That is, by his inspiration, with the gifts and graces received from him. Elsewhere it is said that the Holy Spirit prays in us (see Romans 8:26); but here we pray in the Holy Spirit. He prays in us so we can pray in him.

Notes on Verse 20

Note 1. It is not enough to be grounded in the faith, for we must daily grow more and more in the faith. After the foundation has been laid, the builder must add to it brick by brick. People who are content with little faith have no faith; but graces that may be imperfect are always growing (see Luke 17:5). It is the holy ambition of Christians to be more like God every day. If they ever think they have learned enough, they are not holy enough. As I stated before, on this earth we are in a state of progress, not of rest and perfection. The corn grows in the field, but it does not grow in the barn. See Ephesians 4:12-13 and Philippians 3:13.

Note 2. Faith is the appropriate foundation of holiness and good deeds. Deeds without faith are but a building without a foundation, and faith without deeds is a foundation without a building. Good fruit indicates a good tree.

Note 3. The faith of Christians is a **most holy** faith. No teaching has such pure precepts, such high examples, such elevated motives, such blessed rewards. All of these are meant to promote holiness. The precepts of the law require this, and the example of the saints shows this is possible. A moral lecture may affect the outer man, as Xenocrates' moral lecture made Polemo leave his sensual way of life. But regeneration is only found in the school of Christ.

Note 4. **Build yourselves up**. This building up refers to growth and perseverance.

Note 5. We pray in the right way when we **pray in the Holy Spirit**.

1. God acknowledges nothing in prayer except what comes from his Spirit. "And he who searches our hearts knows the mind of the Spirit, because the Spirit intercedes for the saints in accordance with God's will" (Romans 8:27). God prepares our hearts and then grants our prayer requests. Surely God's ear will be open if our hearts are open. When God himself moves us to work in prayer, we need not doubt that he will hear us. Fire from heaven consuming the sacrifice was the solemn token of acceptance of that sacrifice. Fire from heaven is still a token from heaven, a holy ardor brought to us by the Spirit.

2. Prayer is a work that is too hard for us. Left to ourselves we can babble on, but we cannot pray without the Holy Spirit. We can put words into prayer, but without the Spirit they are cold and spiritless. If we realized what prayer was, we would see how much we need the help of the Holy Spirit. Prayer is hard work. See Romans 15:30 and Colossians 4:12. Prayer is striving with God himself. This was seen in Jacob's wrestling in Genesis 32. The Lord wrestled both *in* and *against* Jacob. God wrestles against us with his left hand and strengthens us with his right hand, so that God's power prevails over himself. This is all said to show how much we need divine power when we strive with God.

Note 6. What does it mean to **pray in the Holy Spirit**? My short answer is that the Spirit helps us in prayer through his gifts and graces.

1. The ordinary gift of the Spirit is that special dexterity that enables

people to put their meaning into apt words. "My tongue is the pen of a skillful writer" (Psalm 45:1). In the same way, discerning of spirits is turned into sagacity and prudence, the gifts of tongues are turned into a special facility to speak, and gifts of healing are transformed into skills in medicine. While we are to strive after the best gifts, we must remain content with whatever gifts we have been given. Gifts are for the benefit of the body. Usually gifts are given to people according to their God-given constitution and natural receptivity. Not everyone can expect to be an excellent public speaker. We see that the different personalities and skills of the writers of Scripture were not obliterated. Isaiah wrote in a majestic style. In the New Testament, Paul argues his case, and Peter writes in a soft and appealing way.

2. There is the gracious assistance of the Holy Spirit in prayer. We should take great care about how we approach God in prayer. The correct way is to go to God with affection, confidence, and reverence. The Spirit helps us with all three of these aspects of prayer.

a. With affection. It is the Holy Spirit who enables us to groan. "The Spirit helps us in our weakness. We do not know what we ought to pray, but the Spirit himself intercedes for us with groans that words cannot express" (Romans 8:26). Words are only the outside of prayer. Sighs and groans are the language that God understands, and these are the prayers that the Holy Spirit makes for us and in us.

b. With confidence. We do this when we come in a childlike way and call God Father. "You received the spirit of sonship. And by him we cry, '*Abba*, Father'" (Romans 8:15). Usually we do not keep in mind this part of the Spirit's help in prayer. We love to look for his gifts but not to this childlike confidence, that we may be able to call God Father without blasphemy and reproach. It is easy to mouth words, but to have a sense of our adoption in our hearts is a difficult thing. Sometimes the Spirit witnesses to this more explicitly. It is as if as we start praying he says, "Cheer up, your sins are pardoned, God is your God."

c. With reverence. If we are to be serious and full of awe as we pray, we must see God in the light of his own Spirit. We need light from God when we come to speak of or to God. A sense of the Lord's greatness, and those fresh and awe-full thoughts that we have about his majesty as we pray, are stirred up in us by the Holy Spirit. He unites and gathers our hearts together so that we may not be distracted by wandering thoughts. "Teach me your way, O LORD, and I will walk in your truth; give me an undivided heart, that I may fear your name" (Psalm 86:11).

Application 1. So then, when you start to pray, look to the Holy Spirit who has been appointed by the Father and purchased through the Son to help you in this sweet service. "The Spirit helps us in our weakness" (Romans 8:26). The Spirit bears part of the burden.

Application 2. We see how much we sin if we pray with our own spirit instead of with the Holy Spirit. Alas, there will only be babbling when the heart does not go along with the lips.

Application 3. This informs us about the privilege of the saints. God is their Father and is willing to hear their prayers. Christ is their advocate, willing to present their requests in court. And the Spirit draws up their requests for them. "For through him [Christ] we both have access to the Father by one Spirit" (Ephesians 2:18).

Verse 21

Commentary on Verse 21

Keep yourselves in God's love as you wait for the mercy of our Lord Jesus Christ to bring you to eternal life.

The apostle continues to speak about the means of perseverance. He mentions here two graces—love and hope.

Keep yourselves. That is, use the means of grace.

In God's love. This may be taken for the love that God bears to us, or else for the love with which we love God. God is the object of this love. God is the author of this love. God commands or brings it to birth, increases it, and completes it in the soul. I take the love of God in this second sense here—namely, for the grace worked in us. The great work committed to us is to keep it, increase it, and discover it in all its many different aspects.

Wait for is the formal act of hope. You hope for **the mercy**. All the good that we will receive at Christ's coming is called **mercy**, for God's dealing with the elect on the last day will be on the terms of grace. **Mercy** is called **the mercy of our Lord Jesus Christ** because it is bought by Christ and dispensed by him. "For you granted him authority over all people that he might give eternal life to all those you have given him" (John 17:2). At his coming he will introduce his people into their happy state. "Now this is eternal life: that they may know you, the only true God" (John 17:3).

To bring you to eternal life. Our happiness in heaven is sometimes called **eternal life** and at other times everlasting glory.

Notes on Verse 21

Note 1. In perseverance, human effort and divine grace work together. "Work out your own salvation with fear and trembling, for it is God who works in you to will and to act according to his good purpose"

(Philippians 2:12-13). The main part of the work is God's work. "He who began a good work in you will carry it on to completion" (Philippians 1:6). "Let us fix our eyes on Jesus, the author and perfecter of our faith, who for the joy set before him endured the cross" (Hebrews 12:2). Our spiritual growth comes from God. "And the God of all grace, who called you to his eternal glory in Christ, after you have suffered a little while, will himself restore you and make you strong, firm and steadfast" (1 Peter 5:10). But all this divine help has to link in with our human effort. A child in the womb is nourished by the mother, lives through the life of the mother, and feeds through the food of the mother. But once a child is born, he lives a separate life of his own, although he still remains under the mother's care and protection. It is the same with us after we have received grace. We have power to do what is necessary for the preservation of the spiritual life. So then, let us not neglect the means of grace. You must not take your ease and think that God must do everything. He does do everything, but in us and through us. Idle wishes will do us no good as long as our hands refuse to work.

Note 2. We who have grace must continually work at keeping ahold of it, for we are prone to rebellion. "This is what the LORD says about this people: 'They greatly love to wander'" (Jeremiah 14:10). Even though God has helped them, "they are a people whose hearts go astray" (Psalm 95:10). It must be noted that in Scripture we read about decay of faith, love, and obedience, the three main graces. Some "bring judgment on themselves, because they have broken their first pledge" (1 Timothy 5:12). To others God says, "Yet I hold this against you: You have forsaken your first love" (Revelation 2:4). David committed scandalous sins in the latter part of his life.

Note 3. This next point is more particular. Of all the graces, love needs especially to be fostered. Why?

1. Because of all the graces, love is most likely to decay. "Because of the increase of wickedness, the love of most will grow cold" (Matthew 24:12). "You have forsaken your first love" (Revelation 2:4). A flame soon goes out. The graces that act most powerfully need the most looking after. We lose our affections more quickly than anything else.

2. Love is an indispensable grace. It is the source and goal of all of our duties to God and other people.

First, to God. Love is the first affection corrupted and renewed. It is love that makes us angry and love that makes us hate. "Let those who love the LORD hate evil" (Psalm 97:10). Love makes us grieve. "Jesus wept. Then the Jews said, 'See how he loved him!'" (John 11:35-36). More than this, it is love that makes us hope and desire and delight in people and things. It is also gracious love that makes us mourn over sin. "Therefore, I tell you, her many sins have been forgiven—for she loved much. But he who has been forgiven little loves little" (Luke 7:47). Love makes us hate evil things and delight in God and his laws (see 2 Corinthians 5:14; 1 John 5:3). "The only thing that counts is faith expressing itself through love" (Galatians 5:6). If we want to resist sin and keep God's commands, we can never let go of love.

Second, to other people. Love is a grace that makes us work hard for the good of others. So we read about "your labor prompted by love" (1 Thessalonians 1:3). Love is *gluten animarum*, the glue of souls, the cement and solder of the church. "And over all these virtues put on love, which binds them all together in perfect unity" (Colossians 3:14). Lack of love for the saints is the cause of apostasy, for the less we love them, the more we associate with the wicked, and then zeal burns low.

3. The decline of love is seen when acts of love are interrupted. Since you value your souls, you must beware of this great evil happening to you.

a. Be rooted and grounded in love. "I pray that you, being rooted and established in love, may have the power, together with all the saints, to grasp how wide and long and high and deep is the love of Christ" (Ephesians 3:17-18). Do not be content with flashes of good moods and melting hearts as you listen to a sermon. You must have solid grace and deep experiences of God. Sudden affections will come to nothing (Matthew 13:4-5). A tree that has taken root is in little danger of withering.

b. Increase and grow in love. "And in fact, you do love all the brothers throughout Macedonia. Yet we urge you, brothers, to do so more and more" (1 Thessalonians 4:10). Nothing brings on decay as quickly as being content with what we have received. Every day you should love sin less, the self less, the world less, but Christ more and more.

c. Take special note of the first decline in love, for this will cause a further lack of love. Evil is best stopped in the beginning. If we take heed when we first begin to grow careless, we would never totally decline. A heavy object, rolling downhill, gathers more and more momentum as it travels and goes faster and faster. Note your first breaking away from God and return to your previous spiritual fervor. It is easier to crush the egg than to kill the serpent.

d. Plead with your heart. The highest degree of our love does not match up to Christ's dignity, nor to the duty we owe him. He is to be loved with all our soul, all our heart, and all our might. It is a disgrace to give him anything less than this. Surely he who has loved us so completely expects to be greatly loved.

e. If you do lose your first love, take this advice from the Holy Spirit: "Remember the height from which you have fallen! Repent and do the things you did at first. If you do not repent, I will come to you and remove your lampstand from its place" (Revelation 2:5). This verse requires you to do three things: first, to consider; second, to be humble, and, third, to reform your ways.

First, consideration: "Remember the height from which you have fallen!" Think about your situation. In your examination, compare yourself with God's law. Recall what a difference there is between how you are now and how you used to be. "How I long for the months gone by, for the days when God watched over me, when his lamp shone upon my head and by his light I walked through darkness!" (Job 29:2-3). Here are some of the thoughts we should have about ourselves: "I used to spend some time every day with God. I remember when I delighted in thinking about God. Now I have no heart to pray or meditate."

Second, humiliation. This is intimated by the word *repent* (Revelation 2:5). It is not enough to know that you have fallen. Many people know they have fallen from grace but do not judge themselves for this in God's presence. Bewail this before God; pray for pardon. That is the idea behind the word *repent*.

Third, reformation: "Do the things you did at first" (Revelation 2:5). We must not spend our days in idle complaints. Many people know they should repent but do not; some may in some sense repent, but they do not change. You must not rest until you recover your previous spiritual state. Christ called Peter to witness to him three times because of his triple denial (see John 21:15-17).

Note 4. The next note comes from linking two thoughts together— **God's love** and **wait for the mercy of our Lord Jesus Christ to bring you to eternal life.** From this we observe that the love of God will encourage us to look for Christ's second coming. Two reasons are given for this.

1. Love allays fear. "There is no fear in love. But perfect love drives out fear, because fear has to do with punishment. The man who fears is not made perfect in love" (1 John 4:18). Of whom should a Christian be ashamed on that day? Of the devil? He is held in chains of darkness and judged by the saints with Christ. Is the Christian afraid of Christ? Are the ransomed afraid of their Redeemer, or the beloved of their Saviour? He will then come as Judge, but he will come to plead their cause, to take revenge on their enemies, and to reward their services. If he is then your Judge, he who has always been your advocate on earth, he will not then condemn you. He has even prayed for you.

2. Love heightens desire. "As you look forward to the day of God and speed its coming" (2 Peter 3:12). Those who love God look for his coming. "We eagerly await a Savior from there [heaven], the Lord Jesus Christ" (Philippians 3:20). We ". . . have longed for his appearing" (2 Timothy 4:8). The children of God want to see him of whom they have heard so much, so often and whose sweetness they have tasted. They know him by hearsay and spiritual experience, but they long to see him in person.

Application 1. This shows us what the difference is between a child of God and a wicked person. The wicked wish this day would never come. The thought of Christ's coming is a burden and torment to them. They have the spirit of the devil in them. See Matthew 8:29.

Application 2. Here are some ways to help those who love God to look earnestly for the coming of Christ.

1. Consider our relationship to him. He is our Master, and we are his servants; and good servants wait for their master's coming (see Matthew 24:45-46). Here we have our meals, but there we will have our wages. Christ will not come empty-handed. When he comes, he will bring a reward with him. Christ is also our husband, and we are his wife. The bride says, "Come" (see Revelation 22:17). At present we are but engaged to Christ; then will be the day of the solemn marriage. The Judge is the wicked man's enemy but our redeemer.

2. Consider the privileges we will then enjoy.

a. The day of Christ's coming will be a day of manifestation. All is now hidden. Christ is hidden, the saints are hidden, their life is hidden. "For you died, and your life is now hidden with Christ in God" (Colossians 3:3). Their glory is also hidden. "Dear friends, now we are children of God, and what we will be has not yet been made known. But we know that when he appears, we shall be like him, for we shall see him as he is" (1 John 3:2).

b. The day of Christ's coming will be a day of completion. Christ comes to bring an end to everything he has begun. He came first to redeem our souls from sin, but at his second coming he will redeem our bodies from corruption. We will then have complete regeneration (see Matthew 19:28). When heaven is new, earth is new, our bodies are new, our souls are new—that is a regeneration indeed. It is the same with adoption. We are God's children now, and yet we are still servants, looking for adoption. "We wait eagerly for our adoption as sons" (Romans 8:23). It is the same with justification. Our pardon will be proclaimed from the housetops, in front of the whole world. It is the same with redemption. "When these things begin to take place, stand up and lift up your heads, because your redemption is drawing near" (Luke 21:28). The body is now a captive though the soul is set free; the body is held under death until that day.

c. The day of Christ's coming will be a day for the congregation to gather together. The saints are now scattered and live in different countries, but then all will meet each other.

Note 5. The next point is from the clause, **the mercy.** The ground of our waiting and looking for eternal life is God's mercy, not any deeds or merits of ours; we cannot claim it as a debt. Sin and death are like work and wages, but eternal life is a gift. "For the wages of sin is death, but the gift of God is eternal life in Christ Jesus our Lord" (Romans 6:23).

1. God's mercy encourages us to wait with hope, despite infirmities and afflictions. What a good Master we serve! He has provided comforts not only in our misery, but in spite of our unworthiness. He gives glory as a reward, but also mercy.

2. We should ascribe everything to mercy, from the beginning to the end of our salvation. We were taken into a state of grace at first out of sheer mercy. "Even though I was once a blasphemer and a persecutor and a violent man, I was shown mercy because I acted in ignorance and unbelief" (1 Timothy 1:13). "He saved us, not because of righteous things we had done, but because of his mercy" (Titus 3:5). He does not just say, "not because of things we had done," but "not because of *righteous* things [*en dikaiosune*] we had done." So we were not saved even for our best works, or by deeds of righteousness that we did. It will be the same when we are taken into a state of glory; it will still be mercy. We can merit no more after grace than before we received grace. "May the Lord grant that he will find mercy from the Lord on that day! You know very well in how many ways he helped me in Ephesus" (2 Timothy 1:18).

Note 6. This mercy is called **the mercy of our Lord Jesus Christ**.

1. This tells us of the fullness of this blessedness. An infinite merit bought it; an infinite mercy bestowed it. Surely the building will be answerable to the foundation. It is no small thing that we may expect from infinite mercy an infinite merit.

2. This mercy tells us about the certainty of this blessedness. He died for you before you were born. He called you when you were unworthy. He warned you about dangers that you never even feared. Instead of giving you wrath as you deserved, he gave you mercy that you did not deserve. He who remembers you at every turn will not be harsh with you at the last.

Note 7. The last note is regarding the clause **to eternal life**. The great benefit we receive from Christ is **eternal life**.

1. There is **life**. All that you work for is life. What you prize above everything else is life. A person will do anything to save his life.

2. It is an excellent life. One of its rewards is rightly called "the crown of life" (Revelation 2:10).

3. It is a happy life, not subjected to the necessities of food and drink. Then we will have spiritual bodies (see 1 Corinthians 15:44). It is a life of which we will never tire.

4. It is **eternal** life. This present life is but a flower that soon withers, a mist that soon blows away. But eternal life is forever and ever. As eternity increases the torment of the wicked, so the blessedness of the godly will increase. So then, let this make you **keep yourselves in God's love** until this happy state comes about.

Verse 22

Commentary on Verse 22

Be merciful to those who doubt.

Here is the second part of the exhortation, explaining the duty of Jude's readers toward others, teaching them how to behave toward those who have gone astray.

The word for **merciful** comes from another word that means bowels, and so it signifies not only the gentleness of censure but inner affection, or as I like to translate it, "compassion."

Notes on Verse 22

Note 1. Reproofs must be given with compassion and holy grief. Our words must have mercy in them. This is to be like God. "For he does not willingly bring affliction or grief to the children of men" (Lamentations 3:33). There are tears in his eyes when he has a rod in his hand. This is to be like Christ. "As he approached Jerusalem and saw the city, he wept over it" (Luke 19:41). The Jews were his enemies, and this was the day of his solemn triumph, and yet he wept.

Note 2. **Those who doubt.** Ministers need to be wise and know how to apply which teaching to each person and situation. Deep learning, much godliness, and great prudence make an accomplished minister. This shows us how much care we must take in knowing the state of the flock, that we may know how to apply God's truth to them.

Verse 23

Commentary on Verse 23

Snatch others from the fire and save them; to others show mercy, mixed with fear—hating even the clothing stained by corrupted flesh.
This is the other part of the duty that Jude's readers owed to others.

Save. That is, do your best to be instruments of their salvation (see 1 Timothy 4:16).

With fear. That is, by some more severe action—either making the admonition more fierce, or denouncing them, or by the reverent use of church censures. "Hand this man over to Satan, so that the sinful nature may be destroyed and his spirit saved on the day of the Lord" (1 Corinthians 5:5).

Snatch . . . from the fire. This is an allusion to a person being snatched from a fire that would otherwise have burned him. We do not just reach out a hand but grab him and pull him out of the fire with great force.

Hating even the clothing stained by corrupted flesh. This is a figure of speech. Some apply it to avoiding the appearance of evil. There is a story of Valentinian in Theodoret, who accompanied Julian the Apostate to the temple of fortune. Those who were in charge of the house sprinkled their holy water on the emperor. One drop fell on his clothes. He beat the officer, saying that he was polluted, not purged, and tore off the piece of his garment on which the drop of water had fallen. The historian commented that he "hated the garment stained by the flesh." However, I think the expression alludes to the old law about legal uncleanness. See Leviticus 15:4, 17. I think it means they are to avoid the company of evil people, which showed how much the church detested wickedness.

Notes on Verse 23

Note 1. There is a time when we have to be severe.

Mixed with fear. There is a time for the trumpet as well as for the flute. Who were these **others** who must be dealt with so roughly?

1. The seducers themselves. They must be exposed in their true colors, although the seducers must be shown compassion.

2. **Others** also applies to hardened people who had grown perverse and stubborn. When the iron is blunt, we have to use more strength. Softer strains would only harden these people more.

Note 2. Observe that this severity must arise from zeal, a desire for God's glory and their salvation. **Save them ... with fear,** says the apostle. "For even if I boast somewhat freely about the authority the Lord gave us for building you up rather than pulling you down . . ." (2 Corinthians 10:8). God wants us to use both gentle and violent means for the same general purpose. "Rebuke them sharply" (Titus 1:13).

Note 3. Again observe that **fear** is a way to reclaim obstinate sinners. It is sweet to use arguments of love, but sometimes we must set the terrors of the Lord before people. "Since, then, we know what it is to fear the Lord, we try to persuade men" (2 Corinthians 5:11). Paul, a chosen vessel, made use of threats. Sluggish creatures need the goad.

God's wrath is the proper object of fear and must be seen like this by the converted and the unconverted. As for as the unconverted, it is quite wrong that they should not consider what a dreadful thing it is to lie under the wrath and displeasure of God. "Who knows the power of your anger? For your wrath is as great as the fear that is due to you" (Psalm 90:11). There is but a step between them and hell, and yet they take no notice of it. If you tell them about their danger, they scorn it. As far as the converted are concerned, they are to fear God's wrath as well. "Do not be afraid of those who kill the body but cannot kill the soul. Rather, be afraid of the one who can destroy both soul and body in hell" (Matthew 10:28). These words not only contain a description of the person who should be feared, but the reason why he ought to be feared. Fear him "who can destroy both soul and body in hell." This is saying that we should fear him *because* he is able to destroy both soul and body in hell. It comes by way of antithesis. Do not fear those who kill the body—that is, *because* they are able to kill the body. See also Hebrews 12:28-29.

Note 4. **Snatch others from the fire**. A poor, guilty sinner is like a drunk who has fallen into the fire. He is like this in three ways.

1. He thinks he is safe. A drunk is ready to be burned, for he is past feeling. In the same way, those who are on the brink of hell are unaware of the danger they are in. They have "lost all sensitivity" (Ephesians 4:19).

2. He is in danger. Sinners are often compared with "a burning stick snatched from the fire" (Zechariah 3:2; see also Amos 4:11). They are already under the wrath of God, just as a believer already has eternal life while he is here in this world. Sinners are in the suburbs of hell, and the fire is already lit.

3. He is impotent to help himself. A drunk lies where he falls. Unless

some friendly hand helps him up, he will perish. This is exactly the situation with sinners. They are happy with their condition, and if they are not soundly awakened from their slumber, they will rest where they are and die in their sins. So then, pluck them from the fire. Warn them to "flee from the coming wrath" (see Matthew 3:7). Minister, are you alert to the danger souls are in? Christian, are you alive to the danger of your worldly neighbor?

Note 5. The next point concerns the last clause, **hating even the clothing stained by corrupted flesh**. Some sinners are so unclean that we cannot help being contaminated if we mix with them. See 1 Corinthians 5:9-11; 2 Thessalonians 3:14-15. We need to do this for our own preservation and to ensure that Christ's name is not dishonored.

Verse 24

Commentary on Verse 24

To him who is able to keep you from falling and to present you before his glorious presence without fault and with great joy—
The apostle, having persuaded them to carry out their duty, now commends them to God's grace. It was usual for the apostles to end their letters with a prayer, to show that all spiritual fruit comes from God, without whose blessing exhortations or endeavors would be nothing.

To him who is able to keep you. This may either refer to God or to Christ as mediator.

From falling. That is, from total apostasy. God is certainly able to keep us completely from sin, referring to his absolute power. But Jude speaks here of the power that is used through promise. Christ, who is the guardian of believers, has received a charge about them and will preserve them from total destruction.

And to present you . . . without fault. This clause shows more clearly that this verse is speaking about Christ. For it is his office to keep the church until she is presented to the Father, and at length he will present believers **without fault**. "And to present her to himself as a radiant church, without stain or wrinkle or any other blemish, but holy and blameless" (Ephesians 5:27).

Before his glorious presence. That is, at his glorious appearance, when he will come to judge the world. "When Christ, who is your life, appears, then you also will appear with him in glory" (Colossians 3:4). **With great joy** means that Christ will rejoice to see us, and we to see him.

Notes on Verse 24

Note 1. Without the Lord's grace, nothing would stop us from falling. The apostle requires the faithful to do their duty but prays that they will have grace from God. He had said previously, **"keep yourselves in God's love** (verse 21), and now he says, **To him who is able to keep you from falling**. We do not fall because God does not let our hand slip from his. Our necessities and difficulties are so great that nothing less than divine power can support us. "Who through faith are shielded by God's power" (1 Peter 1:5). God's power works to encourage hope, not to check diligent service. Use all the means available to you, but look for God's blessing. We cannot stand a moment if God does not uphold us. We are like a staff in the hand of a man; take away the hand, and the staff falls to the ground. Or rather, we are like a little infant in a nursemaid's hand (see Hosea 11:3). As mentioned earlier, one of the fathers said: The flesh says, "*Ego deficiam*, I shall fail"; the world says, "*Ego decipiam*, I will deceive them"; the devil says, "*Ego eripiam*, I will take them away"; but God says, "*Ego custodiam*, I will keep them, never fail them, nor forsake them." That is where our safety lies. Unless God keeps us, we will be tossed to and fro like feathers with the wind of temptation.

Note 2. Note that it is a great relief to faith to remember that God is able to keep us. So we find this urged in Scripture. See John 10:28-29 and 1 Peter 1:5. "And he will stand, for the Lord is able to make him stand" (Romans 14:4). The two pillars in the temple were called "Boaz" and "Jachin," "strength" and "he will establish." The power of God and the mercy of God are the two pillars on which our confidence stands.

Note 3. Jesus Christ will one day make a solemn presentation of his people to God. The apostle says here that he will **present you before his glorious presence**. There are three presentations mentioned in Scripture.

1. One presentation is made by believers themselves. "Therefore, I urge you, brothers, in view of God's mercy, to offer your bodies as living sacrifices, holy and pleasing to God—this is your spiritual worship" (Romans 12:1). "Offer yourselves to God" (Romans 6:13). When we consent to set ourselves apart for God's use, we are said to yield or present ourselves to God.

2. Another presentation is made through Christ's messengers. They have a charge, and when they have done their work, they present us to God. "I promised you to one husband, to Christ, so that I might present you as a pure virgin to him" (2 Corinthians 11:2). It is sweet when ministers can say, "Here are the fruits of my labors, the pledges of my faithfulness."

3. The third presentation is applied to Christ himself.

a. Christ is said to present us to himself—"to present her to himself as a radiant church" (Ephesians 5:27) In that passage our interest in Christ and his interest in us is represented by marriage. In the world we are engaged to Christ, but then we will be presented to him and actually brought to him.

b. Christ is also said to present us to God. Christ's faithful followers have acknowledged him in the world, and Christ will acknowledge them before God. There is no saint whom Christ will not acknowledge. "Whoever acknowledges me before men, I will also acknowledge him before my Father in heaven" (Matthew 10:32).

Note 4. Observe that when Christ presents the elect, he will present them **without fault**—that is, in respect to justification and sanctification. This was the intention before the creation of the world. "For he chose us in him before the creation of the world to be holy and blameless in his sight" (Ephesians 1:4). At present we are humbled with many infirmities and sins, but then we will be presented "holy in his sight, without blemish and free from accusation" (Colossians 1:22). The work is undertaken by Christ, and he will continue it until it is completed. Now the wedding clothes are being made, but then we will put them on.

1. The work must be begun here. The foundation is laid as soon as we are converted to God. "But you were washed, you were sanctified, you were justified in the name of the Lord Jesus Christ and by the Spirit of our God" (1 Corinthians 6:11).

2. This work increases daily. "May God himself, the God of peace, sanctify you through and through. May your whole spirit, soul and body be kept blameless at the coming of our Lord Jesus Christ. The one who calls you is faithful and he will do it" (1 Thessalonians 5:23-24). We are not faultless; but Christ will not rest until we *are* faultless. He is sanctifying us more and more, so that we may be blameless at his coming. He will pursue this work until it is completed.

3. On the last day everything will be completed. "But now he has reconciled you by Christ's physical body through death to present you holy in his sight, without blemish and free from accusation" (Colossians 1:22). So then, let us wait on God and press on to perfection with this hope, for we will be faultless. Christ would never have given us a down payment if he did not intend to give us the whole gift. "Christ . . . set his seal of ownership on us, and put his Spirit in our hearts as a deposit, guaranteeing what is to come" (2 Corinthians 1:21-22).

Note 5. The next clause is, **before his glorious presence**. From this, note that Christ's presence on the day of judgment will be exceedingly glorious, for he will appear not only as the Son of Man, but as the Son of God. "For the Son of Man is going to come in his Father's glory with his angels, and then he will reward each person according to what he has done" (Matthew 16:27). He will then appear not only as the Saviour but as the Judge of the world.

Note 6. The last phrase is, **with great joy**. From this note that the day of Christ for the godly is a joyful day. When others howl, you will triumph. When other people are dejected and ask "the mountains and the rocks, 'Fall on us and hide us from the face of him who sits on the throne

219

and from the wrath of the Lamb!'" (Revelation 6:15-16), you will "lift up your heads, because your redemption is drawing near" (Luke 21:28).

Before Christ came in the body, the patriarchs caught sight of him through the eagle eye of faith and rejoiced at the thought of his coming. "Your father Abraham rejoiced at the thought of seeing my day; he saw it and was glad" (John 8:56). Oh, surely our hearts should be able to say, "There, even there, is our great Lord!"

Verse 25

Commentary on Verse 25

To the only God our Savior be glory, majesty, power and authority, through Jesus Christ our Lord, before all ages, now and forevermore! Amen.

The apostle in this verse continues with the doxology that he had previously begun. Here you may note:

1. The description of the person to whom the praise is given. He is described:

a. By his excellency—**the only God.**

b. By our interest and the benefit we receive through him—**our Saviour.**

2. The ascription of praise—**be glory**, etc. Here is:

a. What is ascribed—**glory, majesty, power and authority.**

b. The duration, how long he would have this ascribed—**now and forevermore.**

What is ascribed is **glory, majesty, power and authority**. Let us look at these words. **Glory** is excellency discovered with praise and approbation and indicates the high honor and esteem that is due to Christ. **Majesty** implies the greatness and excellency that makes one honored and preferred above everyone else. Therefore this word is used of kings and queens. Nobody deserves this title more than Christ, who is the King of kings and Lord of lords. The third term is **power**, which signifies that all-sufficiency in God whereby he is able to do all things according to the good pleasure of his will. The last word is **authority**, which implies the sovereignty of Christ over all things, especially over the people he has bought with his blood.

The last thing in this inscription is **Amen**. This signifies the hearty consent to God's promise and a steady belief that it will continue unto all generations. This word often occurs at the end of prayers and doxologies in Scripture. See Revelation 5:13-14; Romans 16:27; Philippians 4:20. It is sometimes repeated for emphasis (see Psalm 41:13; 72:19; 89:52). It seems from Jude's epistle and elsewhere that it was the custom of people in public assemblies to say this word aloud together at the conclusion of the prayers. "If you are praising God with your spirit, how can one who finds himself among those who do not understand say 'Amen' to your thanksgiving, since he does not know what you are saying?" (1 Corinthians 14:16). Jerome tells us that the amen was sometimes so heartily called out by the church that it sounded like a crack of thunder.

Notes on Verse 25

Note 1. **To the only God our Savior.** Christ is **Savior.** Those who have had any benefit from Christ will be very much involved with his praise. So then, consider the Lord's excellencies more, and observe his benefits, and let them work in your heart until you are filled with a deep sense of his love and find such a compulsion in your spirit that you cannot but break out and praise him.

Note 2. **. . . be glory, majesty, power and authority.** A gracious heart has such a sense of God's worth and perfection that it would have everything that is honorable and glorious ascribed to him. Therefore there are a variety of words used here. When we have done our utmost, we still come short of being able to give the praise Christ deserves, for God's name is "exalted above all blessing and praise" (Nehemiah 9:5). Yet it is good to do as much as we can. Love for God will not be satisfied with a little praise. Love enlarges the heart toward God. It is a sign of a dead heart to be sparing in praises for God

Note 3. **Now and forevermore.** The saints have such a great desire for God's glory that they want him to be glorified forever, without ever stopping. They desire that God not only be praised in this age, but in the next one as well. When they are dead and gone, the Lord remains, and they do not want him to remain without honor.

Note 4. There should be an **Amen** to our praises as well as to our prayers, so that we may express our zeal and affection, for God's glory as well as for our own benefit. Our hallelujahs should sound out as loudly as our supplications, and we should as heartily consent to God's praises as to our own requests.

Note 5. Lastly, in desiring the glory of God for all ages, we should express both faith and love—faith in determining that it *will be,* and love in desiring that it *may be* so—with all our hearts. Both are implied in the word **Amen.** This will be the case no matter what changes take place in the world. God will be glorious! The scene is often changed and furnished with new actors, but still God has those who praise him, and he will throughout all eternity. So then, let your faith subscribe and put on its seal,

To the glory of God in Christ. And let earnest love interpose, "Lord, let it be so; yes, Lord, let it be so." Heartily desire it with the whole strength of your soul. The world will continue no longer when God will have no more glory in it. You may be sure you pray according to God's will when you pray, "Lord, whatever becomes of us and our affairs, may your name be glorified. Amen, Lord, let it be so."

> *Praise be to his glorious name forever; may the whole earth be filled with his glory. Amen and Amen. (Psalm 72:19)*